WILD SPIRIT

FREEDOM, LOVE, AND ADVENTURE IN AFRICA ON A MOTORCYCLE

Helen Lloyd

Take On Creative

First published in 2023
by Take On Creative.

Cover design, maps and photographs
by Helen Lloyd

ISBN 978-0-9576606-6-3

www.takeoncreative.com

Contents

"Two caterpillars in West Africa were wandering through the tall grass looking for their favourite leaves when a beautiful butterfly fluttered overhead. One caterpillar was intrigued and in awe of the beautiful flying creature, while the other said that not for all the money in the world would he ever fly into the air like that. It was far too frightening. He felt that he belonged on the ground, safe and secure, with plenty of food, and that was where he was going to stay. The first caterpillar felt something stir in his heart when he saw the butterfly. He had an inner conviction that crawling on the ground was not his true nature. One day he would be up there, too, soaring with the birds and the butterflies.

After some time of crawling and eating and yearning, the caterpillar changed into a beautiful butterfly with strong wings and many bright colours, as he had dreamed all his life. But the other one stayed as he was, a caterpillar, crawling and eating leaves for the rest of his life because he never dared to dream or to know the meaning of his inner nature; he clung to what was familiar, what felt safe. He had no inkling of his true self. Only those who know their own true selves can soar like butterflies."

West African folktale
Spirit of the Butterflies (Maraleen Manos-Jones)

The Author

Helen Lloyd grew up in Norfolk, England. She studied engineering and has worked in industry. Travelling has been a part of her life since she was sixteen. She has cycled 50,000 kilometres through 58 countries on four continents as well as making journeys by river, on foot and horseback. Between journeys, she often lives in her camper van in the UK. Her most recent adventures have been by motorcycle.

Route Map

0   500 1,000   2,000 Kilometers

01.

Western Cape
South Africa

My heartbeat quickened and my toes twitched involuntarily in my bike boots as the plane banked. Orange-red desert and dotted bush spread out below filling the window view. I paused mid-breath – captivated. A long-forgotten feeling brewed in my chest, overwhelming me like storm clouds consuming the sky. *Soon, I will be down there.* Excitement and anticipation surged through my veins. I could hardly wait to be reunited with this landscape to which I had once felt so intimately connected.

I gripped the armrests and tensed my shoulders, then wriggled into another position and tried to relax. I glanced over to my partner Kieran sitting next to me, but he was engrossed in his iPad, his mind some place else.

Turning back, I pressed my fingers to the window and breathed deeply. I could almost feel the fine orange dirt on my fingertips and smell the unforgettable subtle earthy aroma that permeates the atmosphere and gets in your hair and under your skin. A smile crept across my face, the corners of my lips creasing into an unstoppable grin as these feelings evoked memories from a time when I'd lived only for each day and had felt truly alive, of the place where I'd been happiest.

Gradually I relaxed as the plane straightened and the horizon came into view, where dreams of a peace and contentment I had once known were waiting.

Africa.

———

Several years ago I'd cycled across the continent and had known then, long before I reached Cape Town, that one day – I couldn't say exactly when – I would return. It was the closest thing to a certainty that existed in my life.

There were so many places I still yearned to see. I wanted to explore Kaokoland in northwestern Namibia, travel in Angola, buy a horse and ride through Lesotho or the Drakensberg, and take a barge down the Congo River. I hoped to visit Zimbabwe, Mozambique and Rwanda one day too. Budget, the seasons, logistical problems, red tape and regional instability had been the main hindrances in the past. Some still existed; whether I'd be able to overcome them and any other unexpected issues remained to be seen.

About to embark on another trans-continental journey, this time on a motorbike from south to north via the east coast, my dream route would take in all of these places and more. Scouring the map, I envisaged initially exploring the Garden Route, the coastal region between Cape Town and Port Elizabeth to the east. A popular tourist route, it would be a good introduction for Kieran, who had never been to sub-Saharan Africa. From there we could make our way to Lesotho. There was no point planning further ahead, knowing from experience that Africa would have other ideas. Kieran didn't care where we went; it was all new to him.

I also desperately wanted to visit the Cederberg Wilderness Area. Several South Africans I had met as I neared the Western Cape on my cycle ride across the continent had extolled its trails and stunning landscape. At the time, like climbers suffering summit fever on Everest, I could not be swayed from the lure of Cape Town, a few days' ride away. After almost two years on the road, my aching legs had needed rest, not pedalling more gravel tracks and hiking rough trails.

Now, no matter how I traced my finger over the map, I couldn't conceive a route that would take in the Cederberg unless we looped north first. *Well, why not?*

So we collected our Yamaha XT225 Serow motorbikes from the importer's warehouse in Cape Town, went sight-seeing and hiked up Table Mountain on New Year's Eve, then set off north following the coast along the same route I had cycled.

Daytime temperatures were searing; the thermometer hovered around the mid-forties. I was glad we had decided to wear cool fitted mesh tops with protective armour rather than traditional heavy touring bike jackets. I wore a vest underneath the armour for maximum ventilation; by the end of the day, my arms were spotted red.

Despite the sunburn, I relished the heat, energised by the fierce sun. It was a welcome change from the dreary British weather. Kieran disagreed, visibly melting in the scorching rays. A week earlier, he had been enjoying the fresh snowfall at home.

We headed inland on quiet gravel roads after Lambert's Bay. At a derelict building, Kieran stumbled off the bike, crumpled in a heap in the shade of the wall and gulped his tepid water supply.

I waited impatiently. Finally I was back in Africa and we'd found unpaved roads and I wanted to ride all day long through featureless terrain under the fierce sun until it set and then get up and ride some more. I was in my element and in love with life.

———

By the time we rode into Clanwilliam, the town on the edge of the Cederberg, it was late afternoon. We headed to a campsite. Descending from the guarded entrance to the camping area overlooking the dam, I realised I had stayed here before. With memories of drunken revellers, I feared a sleepless night on the jaded municipal site. I wanted to ride on into the Wilderness Area, but Kieran was done for the day and needed shade and rest. He bribed me to stay with promises of beer. The Cederberg, so tantalisingly close, would have to wait until tomorrow.

The campsite was busy, mostly weekenders and local day-trippers. Families came for picnics where the kids could play safely and groups of friends listened to music on car stereos at full volume. I hoped most would leave once the sun set.

We pitched the tent. Then it dawned on me, 'It's Sunday!' I exclaimed, 'Nooooo!' The liquor shops would be shut, the alcohol aisles in the supermarkets cordoned off.

'Aye, well,' Kieran shrugged. He didn't want a beer and was, instead, content to rehydrate with water.

On the motorbike, we were unable to keep anything cold in this climate. The best we could do was wrap our water bottles with old socks soaked in water and let the air flow cool the drinks. Rather than unpalatable hot water, it was merely a distasteful tepid.

If I were to get a thirst-quenching beer, I would have to be proactive.

'There must be somewhere to get cold beers on a Sunday,' I whined. 'See, the locals know.' Several groups had ice cold beers, the bottles dripping condensation as they took them from their coolboxes.

The security guard confirmed there were no shops selling beer at this hour on a Sunday and apologised. I told him what a tough day we'd had and how much we loved his country and how it could only be bettered by the miraculous appearance of a cold beer on such a hot day.

'Maybe the man selling water by the toilets can help,' he commented.

'Toilets?' I asked, unsure whether I had heard correctly.

'Yes, he sells more than just water,' he smiled.

It sounded like a dodgy drug dealer. I wondered if I could get arrested for trying to buy beer on a Sunday.

The prospect of reward outweighed the risk.

Behind the toilet block I found a man with a couple of large cooler boxes. He opened the lid; I peered inside. Water, Coca Cola, Fanta, Sprite ...

'Beer?' I asked.

'Sold out. Very popular drink today,' he noted. 'I am sorry.'

I bought the cold water instead.

Kieran's eyes lit up like fireworks when I handed it over, and he rolled the bottle against his reddened forehead.

While I contemplated asking one of the families if they would sell me beer a man approached.

'Excuse me madam. You want beer, ja?'

'Yes!' I replied excitedly. 'Do you have some?'

'No, but I know where to buy. You give me money; I bring.'

It sounded like a scam. I looked to Kieran. He remained silent. I handed over some rand, not expecting change. He'd make a tidy profit on four small beers, assuming he didn't just walk away with the cash.

I'd never been stolen from or conned in Africa. I had, however, been helped by numerous strangers and witnessed countless acts of generosity. There was no reason to believe that today would be any different. Besides, I didn't want suspicion and lack of trust to define my actions and set a precedent for how I viewed people on this journey, suspecting every apparent good deed hid an ulterior motive. I also think trust begets trust and prefer to believe that most people in this world are good given the chance.

'I come back very soon.'

We'll see.

As I was beginning to suspect that I had been willingly robbed, a stranger placed a plastic bag beside me. The clink of glass brought a broad grin to my face. In the back of an old black car, the man from behind the toilets waved out the window. I waved back, and he gave a big thumbs up.

In the bag were six, freezing to the touch, large bottles of Castle lager. I baulked at the prospect of drinking four pints each before the beer got too warm.

After savouring the first refreshingly cool gulp, even Kieran rose to the challenge. At least we would sleep through any noise from our partying neighbours.

———

The three months since my first foray into 'off-road' trail-riding seemed a lifetime ago. Lack of confidence and not feeling in total control of the bike were minor details I would have to ignore if we were going to explore more remote regions.

I wobbled nervously along the first tracks through the Cederberg. Gradually, weaving between giant boulders, I began to connect with the bike. I wasn't going to veer off the trail at every turn. Occasionally I lost traction in the loose gravel and, when the back wheel slipped, my heart skipped a beat. I loved riding past towering orange rock formations, throwing up dust clouds into the dry, forty-degree air, and searching out rock pools to bathe in and vineyards to visit.

In the evening we sipped red wine under old oak trees on a quiet campground and were serenaded to sleep by croaking frogs from the river that was inaccessible through the long grass.

Long before Europeans arrived, the Cederberg was inhabited by San people, hunter-gatherers whose territory spread as far as Angola and Zimbabwe. Their artwork, thousands of years old, is still visible; elephants and men painted red on shaded slabs of orange rock. Where the wind has worn away large recesses and caves in the boulder formations, 'modern' graffiti, names and dates over a hundred years old are carved into the walls. It's no wonder people through the millennia have sought out these cool, dark caves. We emerged from them into the blistering heat, blinded by the dazzling daylight.

On a couple of days we went hiking, our routes selected based on their descriptive trail names: the Maltese Cross and Wolfberg Cracks. I'd have hiked more but Kieran couldn't tolerate the daytime temperatures, so we escaped the insufferable heat and headed south through the Winelands back to Cape Town.

Riding around the Cape Peninsula, we saw the African penguin colonies at Boulders Beach and further around the coast at Betty's Bay. The little black and white birds waddled along the sandy shoreline, bathed on giant rocks, floated lazily on their backs and splashed in the crystal clear water. An idyllic, easy life is appealing on occasions, but rough trails, remote regions and a challenge was what I wanted.

Earlier that day, when I'd started my motorbike, I had winced at a crunching sound coming from the engine. I'd ignored it, but now it happened again, a teeth-clenching grinding. I quickly depressed the starter button and tried again. It started smoothly. *Maybe it's nothing.*

The windswept dunes around False Bay offered scant protection from the wild blasts that gusted across the road. I was uneasy riding; something seemed wrong with the bike, a vague feeling, barely detectable like the faint limp of an old injury that is only visible to those who know about it. I slowed down, raised my visor and lowered my head, listening closely for unusual sounds. Attuned to the bike after thousands of kilometres across Europe, I thought I could sometimes hear a subtle tap disrupting the regular hum of the engine. *Am I being paranoid?*

The knocking noise got worse.

We hadn't even reached Cape Agulhas, which being the southernmost point in Africa seemed like the start point of our trip across the continent. It didn't bode well.

Crawling into the next town, we found a repair shop. Fearing the problem was the starter clutch, we instructed the mechanic to remove the left side casing, then the rotor. Sure enough, the three bolts in the starter clutch gear had sheared again. At least they hadn't caused the engine to seize, which is what had happened months before in Europe. Perhaps we hadn't replaced them correctly.

This time, I would let a professional carry out the work; we had a long ride ahead. I called ahead to the Yamaha dealer in Port Elizabeth, who ordered replacement parts and agreed to carry out the repair. I was glad I'd made the decision to get a bike with a kickstart, which doesn't use the starter clutch mechanism to start the engine. In the meantime, we removed the offending pieces of machinery, closed up the left side casing and continued our ride.

I realised now that the motorbike was going to be a more significant part of this trip than I had imagined. It was not only a means of transport from one place to the next like my bicycle had been. The Serow – named after the Japanese mountain goat – was less an inanimate object and more like a creature with its own personality, intricacies and complications that would need care and attention if it were to be a faithful travelling companion.

02.

Baviaanskloof
South Africa

After two weeks showing Kieran the highlights of the Western Cape I'd previously visited by bicycle, I was eager to explore new areas.

A flyer advertising 4x4 excursions into the Baviaanskloof piqued my interest. *Where's that? And how hard can the trails be?*

I asked a friend who ran motorcycle tours in South Africa. 'It's a tough mother,' he replied. 'It's where the enduro riders go to prove how big their nuts are! I wouldn't do it on my own.'

I wasn't travelling alone; I also didn't have any nuts that needed sizing up. Now, though, my curiosity was insatiable. Even if I couldn't ride the tracks, I wanted to see what the fuss was about, wanted to see what bikers meant by technical off-road riding.

Leaving the cool sea breeze behind, we rode inland, stopping at the legendary Ronnie's Sex Shop on Route 62. A regular bar, its unique selling point is the collection of bras and underwear draped throughout from ceiling to floor. It's also the only place to stop and get a cold drink for miles around.

Beyond, we continued into the Little Karoo, the semi-desert region nestled between the verdant coast and Great Karoo, a vast area that stretches north to the edges of the Kalahari. Ascending the Swartberg Pass, a winding road, the rocky landscape was sparsely covered in hardy dry grasses and stunted scrub, beautiful and barren. We continued through the mountains where the fynbos bloomed, pink and red and orange flowering plants brightening the otherwise dull land. At a turning off the main trail, a sign stated, 'Dangerous Road for next 48 km. Use at own risk.' *Excellent!*

And so we rode into 'Die Hel', an apt name for a place at the end of a very long, very hot, very rough dead end trail that descended

13

through arid, scorched earth, the terrain recently ravaged by wild fires that plague the Western Cape in the dry season. The trail went on and on over undulating terrain until the final steep descent of switchbacks. I hugged the inside track, more confident than in the Cederberg but still not feeling in complete control on the rough. After several hours riding there and back out and beginning to think that it wasn't so dangerous, the front wheel slipped in some sand and I dropped the bike, trapping my leg at an awkward angle. I needed to rest; tiredness was the biggest danger, not the trail.

Stopped for a break, we were disturbed by a four-striped mouse with distinctive, dark go-faster lines along its back. Initially interested in the pungent aroma from my boots that I'd removed, it scurried in and out of them like a deranged rodent. It paused, balanced on the top of the boot and eyed up our picnic, then raced over, heedless of our presence, took a sniff and grabbed the plastic packet of sliced cheese, three times its body size. Its tiny jaw lost grip repeatedly, but the mouse never gave up, eventually dragging the packet into the scrub, where it scoffed my sandwich filling without fear of reprisal. I was enamoured with this fearless creature, impressed by its hard work and dogged persistence. *Can I be more like that mouse?*

We spent our first day in the Baviaanskloof walking in the cool shade up a narrow gorge, criss-crossing the crystal-clear stream, clambering over boulders, and watching little frogs — brown and red and pink and green ones — leaping from rocks and vanishing into dark pools of water. I leapt at a blueish-green snake that slithered off through the long grass when I disturbed it. We saw another large snake when we returned to the bikes.

There are two types of wildlife in Africa: the harmless variety and the kind that can kill you. It's wonderful to see it all, but on a motorbike or on foot, I always hope I see the dangerous ones from a safe distance.

Along the main trail running the length of the Baviaanskloof, several places offer accommodation and camping, which make excellent bases to explore the region. We spent one night in a luxury (for us) private cave at Makkedaat. The surrounding natural, sandstone rock overhangs had been enclosed with timber and furnished with simple rustic furniture to create unique accommodation. With firewood, wine, *boerewors* (South African sausage) and freshly baked bread bought from the farm, we were well supplied. We had time for a refreshing shower before the wood we'd lit had burnt down, ready to braai. Sitting on the veranda eating barbecued sausages and sipping wine, I leaned back and looked up at the clear night sky with the stars shining brilliantly. We both agreed that it doesn't get better than this.

The Baviaanskloof, meaning 'baboon gorge' in Dutch, lived up to its name. We encountered several troops of baboons, dozens in each family grouping, sitting about on the trail. Young males played and chased one another, older baboons were on lookout, watching for any threats, and babies clung to their mothers, hanging from their underbellies as they crossed the trail. On our approach, they'd run down the road, then bound and leap into the thick bush, vanishing in front of our eyes. Only the slight rustle of leaves gave any clue as to where they'd gone. The tortoises were much easier to track.

I'd had a close encounter with a Cape Cobra on the first day riding out of Cape Town. It had slithered out of the bush and across the trail right in front of me. I had braked sharply and swerved on the dirt trail to avoid it, narrowly missing its tail. The sandy-coloured snake had swung its head about, reared up and hissed. If I'd known it was highly venomous at the time, my heart would have beaten even faster. I probably wouldn't have stopped to point it out to Kieran either.

More recently, he was the magnet for wildlife.

A long, slim black snake crossed the trail exactly when Kieran was riding through. From behind, I saw the snake emerge unscathed and flee into the bush, and I laughed as Kieran frantically looked left and right while riding with his feet raised to the handlebars, knees near his neck, fearing it was caught in the wheel and could lash out and bite at any moment.

Unbelievably, within two hours, he'd managed to hit another snake, a small, short and well-camouflaged one, which did not fair so well. Neither did the scampering dassie, a rock hyrax.

'You murderer,' I called out, jokingly. 'Dassie-killer!'

'Oh don't say that,' he pleaded. Of course, he felt bad.

But the wildlife would get its revenge.

Having splashed our way across several shallow streams, we arrived at Doringkloof campsite, a base for riding 4x4 trails across the farm and beyond. We made a short ride to some nearby rock paintings along low level sandy tracks, trying to avoid the branches of acacias with inch-long thorns that would easily rip our clothing and tear skin, never mind puncture the heavy duty tyres.

The highlight was the eighty-kilometre trail to Kareedouw.

Rising over the Kouga Mountains with far-reaching views, I quickly despaired as I repeatedly dropped the bike. It was as though I'd forgotten how to ride. I guess I never really knew for these kind of technical, rocky tracks. I was tense and picking the bike up whenever it fell made me more tired. The engine got hotter and hotter and harder to start. I'd stamp and stamp on the kickstart and collapse over the handlebars exhausted when nothing happened. Gathering energy, I'd try again and eventually, just as I wanted to give up, the bike would fire up, so I'd ride on … until the next bend when down I'd go again. After a couple of hours of slow progress, Kieran suggested we take a proper break. He offered helpful tips – more reminders than new advice – about controlling the bike. He was a good teacher.

I'd been riding as though I was on my mountain bike, the mode of transport I was more familiar with. I had been using only the hand levers: feathering the clutch to prevent stalling and using the front brake. Changing into lower gears and using the rear foot brake on the steep downhills made all the difference. *I can ride!*

16

Now it was fun bumping down the dried out gullies and bouncing over rocks, twisting and turning and dodging the thorny bushes. After five hours riding, we emerged from the hills into town, scoffed pancakes at The Sweaty Dutchman cafe, then rode back in half the time.

Speeding along the dusty farm tracks as the sun set, we stopped only when kudu ran across our path and to pass through the gates that separated the farm from the wilderness areas.

'Fancy a cuppa?' I suggested back at camp. A mug of tea with buttermilk rusks, a South African essential, for dunking is perfect after a hard day on the trails.

I unzipped the tent and looked inside the porch. 'Hey, what did you do with the stove?' I asked.

'It should be in there,' Kieran replied.

'I can't see it.'

I could see something brown smeared on the fly sheet though. I peered closer.

Is that ...? It looked disconcertingly like shit. *Surely not ...*

'What the hell!' Kieran called out, interrupting my thoughts. 'Some of the stove's out here by the braai.'

I jumped up from the tent and, looking over to Kieran spotted another piece of the stove in the grass. Like forensic investigators, we followed the trail of destruction, gathering up bits of the stove and the pans that had been scattered across the campground. The last piece we found floating in the lake underneath the jetty.

The culprits were long gone; we knew who they were.

Vervet monkeys.

'I'll fix the stove and make tea,' I quickly offered – I'm thoughtful like that – then added, 'Perhaps you could clean the tent ...'

––––

After a brief stop in Port Elizabeth to get the replacement parts and starter clutch refitted to my Serow, we headed inland towards

Hogsback, high in the Eastern Cape's Amathole mountains. Supposedly the inspiration behind J.R.R. Tolkien's Middle Earth, who used to visit the area in his childhood, I assumed the claim to be the exaggerated rhetoric of tour company's cashing in on vague links to the famous author.

I wanted to visit because I'd read about a six-day hiking trail through the indigenous Afro-montane forests there, which sounded beautiful and challenging. Kieran needed little convincing; it would be much cooler.

Rudely awoken pre-dawn by Kieran's alarm clock, we were ready and at the trailhead with the full morning in front of us. The trail wound up through the forest, and by lunchtime we had reached the first hut amongst the trees, high on the hillside. We gathered wood for the fire, chatted and wandered to a viewpoint with Hogsback in the distance to watch the sun set.

The following morning we were up early and stoked the fire for a brew before breakfast a few kilometres on at another viewpoint. Thick clouds blanketed the valley but they would soon disperse as the searing sun warmed the refreshing mountain air. The trail continued through thick forest, dark and cool beneath the canopy of ancient trees, with hanging vines and unfurled ferns, fungi sprouting amongst moss-covered roots, wild orchids and crystal clear streams. Fine gossamer threads of spiders webs criss-crossed the trail, a clear sign that we were the first to pass that day, week or even month. Then the forest thinned and the trail passed through monotypic plantations before continuing over rocky hills and open grassland with distant views.

On the third day, we passed three hunters with rifles and dogs running ahead. Suddenly I was aware of how vulnerable we were on this isolated route. Since we were staying at huts on the way, any villager who had seen the 4x4 with a tour logo emblazoned on the side en route to the trailhead would have known exactly where we'd be staying each night.

On most of my travels, I have no fixed itinerary and little idea of where I will sleep each night, and when I do wild camp, I do so stealthily. If no one knows where I am, they can't cause me a problem. If only we had our tent, but we hadn't brought it with us because we didn't think we would need it.

I'd read warnings about hikers who camped in caves along the Drakensberg escarpment being robbed of their mobile phones during the night. The people we had organised the hike with had even warned us of a recent robbery on the trail, saying a hiker's phone had been stolen. We dismissed their concerns; we had little worth stealing. Besides, if I heeded everyone's warnings in life, I'd never leave home.

Smouldering embers of an extinguished fire suggested someone had recently been at the hut, situated in a clearing in a valley bowl. We spotted a silhouetted figure emerge from the trees, then disappear over the horizon. Whereas we'd slept out on the hut veranda under the stars the night before, that night we slept uneasily inside with the door locked shut, our backs against the wall and our bags close to hand.

I tried not to let my healthy fear of a real risk consume my thoughts, but it overshadowed the feeling of freedom and simplicity that hiking in nature without another (visible) soul for miles offers. I wondered where exactly on the trail the last tourists had been robbed. The opportunities for ambush were unbounded.

The map we'd been provided with was unsuitable for navigation, so when the trail became less obvious through thick forest and heavy undergrowth, the yellow painted markers infrequent or non-existent, we were forced to backtrack at dead-ends and impassable waterfalls. On the final stretch, we resorted to a long detour on wide logging tracks.

Back at the hostel, I discovered online that a group of four hikers whilst staying at one of the huts had been robbed at gunpoint, the

19

woman raped. I was furious. How could the organiser and promoter of this hiking trail have let us go without divulging the full truth?

I wasn't going to let this stop me from looking for other hikes though. Walking was an activity both Kieran and I had similar experience in and enjoyed with equal enthusiasm. Travelling slowly on foot was the perfect antidote to racing through countries on the motorbike. Next time we'd wild camp.

Online searches for other good hiking areas in southern Africa returned plenty of results for the Drakensberg to the northeast. A 125-mile hiking route running the length of the escarpment captured my interest.

First, though, we had to get across the mountainous kingdom of Lesotho.

03.

The Mountain Kingdom
Lesotho

Buying a horse to ride in Lesotho was to remain locked in my dreams.

Kieran had never ridden before. When I'd mentioned a journey on horseback while still at home, he had eagerly booked a lesson at the local riding school while I was working. He showed me the video of him bouncing atop a stocky cob, loose reins flapping, ending with an inelegant exit from the saddle. Not wanting to destroy his confidence, I mentioned that riding with a Western-style saddle was easier than perched atop the English sort.

I knew that looking after a horse on the trails was tiring without taking a novice on board. I was less concerned about Kieran's riding ability than lack of interest in looking after the horses. He was happy to come along for the ride but never offered to help with the planning and never asked about the practical aspects of equine care.

Stressed by the preparations, complicated by the needs of the inexperienced, I realised that this was one journey I'd prefer to make alone. I didn't want to hurt Kieran's feelings or expectations, so I reeled off feeble excuses for not buying us horses. As a compromise, I suggested that we go on a guided trip instead. I had been on organised rides before and, knowing the freedom and excitement of riding my own horse, found them restrictive. For me, riding is easy; responsibility is the reward. I was happy that Kieran was excited though.

A guided horse-ride would still be a great way to see this landlocked country of few real roads, where people traditionally travelled on horseback and still do. Or, it turns out, they ride bareback on donkeys with no bridle or halter either. With only a short stick in one hand, they tap their donkey's neck on the opposite side to which they want to turn, and as the donkey runs, the rider bobbles about on top, gripping tightly with their thighs and doing untold damage to their future prospects of having children.

After a leisurely breakfast at the lodge we were staying at, having already packed our gear for a six-day ride into the waterproof panniers provided, we wandered over to the thatched hut where the saddles were stored. A slim young man wearing a riding hat walked over leading four horses, necks long, heads low. My heart sank seeing the outline of their hip bones and ribs.

Although very lean, certainly underweight, the horses did appear well-looked after in other respects: clean, groomed, and sound with feet in good condition. Taut muscles rippled, and the two chestnuts' coats glistened in the sun. Seemingly overworked and underfed, I battled silently over whether to say something, refuse to ride or insist on other horses. Would I be imposing my western ideals in a world I didn't understand? After all, I'd only been in the country two days and knew nothing about life or the native Basuto ponies. I decided to keep quiet and see how they were once underway.

The chestnut in best condition was a gelding with beautiful flaxen mane and tail, slightly bigger than the others. Looking strongest and most docile, I was glad the guide handed the reins to Kieran.

I had my hopes set on the other chestnut with the white stripe running the length of its face. Once saddled, his head lifted and ears pricked. He had a spark in his eye not dulled by the monotony of mindless, routine nose-to-tail trail rides. There was something in his long face and kind eye that reminded me of the best pony I'd had as a kid, a 13.2-hand chestnut I'd ridden everywhere. I'd loved galloping across stubble fields in the summer and competing in cross-country competitions. He was fast and strong, too strong at first as I was only just big enough and didn't yet know him, but he was good-natured and willing and within a year we had a bond of trust that made us unstoppable.

'Have you ridden before?' Mokhasi, our guide, asked.

I smiled and nodded. 'Yeah, I can ride'.

'OK, do you want to try this one?' he asked, handing me the chestnut's reins. I let the horse smell my hand, then ran the other down his neck and shoulder. 'If he's too much, we can always swap.'

Not a chance. I checked the girth was tight, put my left foot in the stirrup and swung my other leg over before the guide could change his mind.

Mokhasi loaded up the bay as the pack animal; the little grey would be his ride. Once on flat open ground beyond the lodge gates, he suggested we stretch their legs, a chance for him to check if we were secure enough in the saddle. He seemed satisfied. Kieran was all grins after coaxing his horse into a canter. From thereon we walked at a decent pace.

After an hour of passing through villages, we came to a steep descent. The narrow zig-zag path seemed like it ought to be impassable, but giving the horses free rein and leaning back in the saddles for balance, they carefully placed their hooves between the rocks, picking their way step-by-step all the way down, not once tripping or stumbling. At the stream they lowered their heads to drink. Kieran, still gripping the pommel with both hands, was on a high, surprised to have remained in the saddle.

I was most impressed with the horses. They were smart, agile and sure-footed, and didn't need more than a gentle squeeze of the calf and touch of the heel to quicken their pace. We rode for a couple of hours, stopped for a long lunch, then rode for a couple more along footpaths over rolling hills. It felt good to be moving slowly through a landscape untouched by modernity or machinery. We stopped for the night at a small collection of huts on the rounded hillside. It had seemed a short day, but at least the horses weren't being overworked. We dismounted, took off their saddles and bridles, gave them a nosebag of grain and brushed the sweat from their saddle and girth

23

areas, then let them loose to graze freely. The following days followed a similar laid-back rhythm.

The country had been suffering a severe, prolonged drought, which explained why the animals were so thin, the low-nutrient land over-grazed. Only nine per cent of the land is suitable for cultivation, eight out of ten regions were suffering a food deficit. People were selling assets to buy food or skipping meals.

Adults as well as children stood with an arm outstretched, the other hand patting their stomach. I saw several 4x4s with the World Food Programme logo on. Over 700,000 people were in need of food assistance that year. In my experience begging is always more prevalent where aid agencies operate. Regardless, there was no denying that some people were hungry.

Eventually, the rains did arrive, but it was too little too late to repair the damage from the drought; although, it doesn't feel that way when caught in a torrential downpour.

On the last evening, we camped in a village with beautiful views along the valley against a backdrop of mountains. It had been sunny all day, but now clouds were closing in. They weren't white cotton-wool clouds but dark brooding, oppressive ones that swallow up the sunlight and shroud the world in a heavy blanket. As evening drew near, the light dimmed through a thick haze that turned orange with the clouds a deep purple. The air was disturbingly calm. I stood and watched in awe, stunned by the beauty of it, but as the storm approached, I tensed up, nervous and excited.

Then the wind hit, blasting through the village like a freight train. Instantly, the peace was shattered. Rain was imminent. I stopped photographing, and we hurriedly gathered together the stove and unwashed pans and pegged down the tent.

As the first bullets of hail hit, we dived head first into the tent like rabbits fleeing down a hole. When the wind lashed out with renewed fury, I grabbed the flailing tent flap and grappled until it was zipped firmly shut. We shoved our bags in the corners to help hold down the tent and lay on our backs with legs raised, feet propping up the end wall that was taking the brunt of the assault and risked collapse from the gusts. Rain battered the tent with such force it penetrated the fly sheet and entered through the mesh inner as a fine spray. I draped my towel over us.

Ten minutes later, as abruptly as the storm had arrived, the rain and hail and wind ceased. In the ensuing eerie silence, I contemplated the wisdom of my choice of a cheap tent. I recalled the storms I'd laid awake through during the rainy season in West Africa. I'd had a quality, expensive tent then and still I'd spent nights curled up on my Thermarest, an island in a rising lake fed by streams running down the tent poles into the four corners of my tent.

The next morning we returned to the lodge with bruised backsides from the bum-numbing wooden frame saddles. I looked at my Serow with renewed fondness, the lightly padded seat a comfy armchair by comparison.

Lesotho is not only a horse-rider's heaven but a biker's paradise. The Chinese may be rapidly laying asphalt roads between the few main towns, but there is still a plethora of rocky trails to ride in search of an adventure.

We slowly loaded our bikes under depressing grey skies. I considered putting on my waterproof trousers. I hadn't needed them in two months. Thunder crackled in the distance. Rain was coming. *Perhaps we should delay until the inevitable downpour has passed.*

An almighty explosion overhead tore apart the sky and a blinding flash ripped through the air.

The lightning bolt struck the Serow.

I jumped back and my heart skipped a beat. Momentarily, we were both stunned. The hairs on our arms stood to terrified attention. In the ensuing seconds we made a hasty retreat inside.

Might as well put on those waterproofs.

Afternoon and evening storms were a regular feature during the next month of travel. Lesotho and the Drakensberg region of South

25

Africa have some of the highest rates of lightning strikes anywhere in the world. Everyone I spoke to knew of someone who had been struck by lightning, with varying degrees of injury from mild shock to fatal. I hoped I wouldn't become a story or statistic.

From the comfort, safety and shelter of a lodge, the lightning was a show to behold, as good as any fireworks display I've seen. It's another matter when you are camping on a high, exposed plateau where the tallest objects are the motorbikes and the tent that you're sheltering in is only marginally shorter. Although, having camped through numerous storms during West Africa's rainy season, the possibility of being struck by lightning, or what would happen if the tent were hit, no longer scared me, fear replaced with a calm acceptance and fatalistic attitude that what will be will be.

From Semonkong, we rode southeast towards Qacha's Nek. When time came to camp, we pulled off the track and pitched the tent, hidden from the road by a dip in the ground. Beyond, the vertiginous escarpment dropped away to reveal the unending plains of South Africa. The view was temporary. The clouds closed in, hiding us in the thick mist. We had sufficient time to cook and eat dinner in earnest before the rain began.

We sought refuge in the tent, waiting as the storm marched closer until directly overhead. I lay flat on my back, listening to the thunder rolling and crashing. The tent lit up in a series of flashes before plunging us into darkness. It rained and thundered deep into the night, although the intensity gradually waned until the noise no longer shot right to my core but rumbled and groaned pathetically like an injured animal.

The following day, we rode down to Sehlabathebe, which would have been a safer place to spend the night had we realised. Then we headed back up into the mountains. What are small streams in the dry season had transformed into raging torrents. As the rain continued, each crossing became more concerning. What if the next river were impassable? What if we became trapped, unable to go forward or back? With several days' worth of food, we could afford to wait for water levels to drop if necessary.

We waded in to determine the water depth and check for the best route, our boots quickly becoming waterlogged, jeans drenched. I didn't care; I loved it. Focussing on overcoming a problem or surmounting some obstacle, I forget about everything else. Living in the moment is when I feel most alive and thoughts and fears fade away.

Clear of the rivers, steep rocky tracks challenged my skills to the limit. I'd tap down into first gear, point the bike up the hill and open the throttle.

Don't stop, just keep going ...

I repeated this mantra in my mind as the bike hopped from rock to rock, the front wheel jumping about wildly. It took all my strength to keep a hold of the handlebars and stop them wrestling free. I'd put a foot out here or there when the rear end fishtailed. I swore a lot when the bike fell onto its side. The muscles in my arms burned with the exertion.

Kieran always came to help me pick up the bike, joking about my bike's laziness and asking if I understood the concept that riding a motorbike required keeping it vertical. And I joked that I was only doing him a favour because it seemed like he needed more exercise.

'I thought you enjoyed showing off your masculine strength,' I quipped. 'The reason I brought you along is to pick up my bike when I drop it.'

'I thought it was for making tea,' he replied with a smile.

'Oh that too. And as remover of spiders and killer of mosquitoes!'

As the terrain got rockier, it became harder for Kieran to stop near me, so that by the time he arrived, I'd already picked up the bike. Each time I managed to ride a little further before the bike ended on its side. Energised by reaching the top of the next rise, I wanted to ride on and on. This was the feeling I lived for.

Then came the moment when I made it up a particularly tricky, rocky ascent in one go – upright the entire way. Excited and jubilant, I turned to Kieran only to see his bike crash to the floor. I ran back to help, leaping from rock to rock, still bursting with energy. Finally, I had a chance to return the favour.

'Taking tips from me?' I said with a cheeky grin, 'Not exactly the skill I'd have chosen to emulate.'

He glared at me, unimpressed.

'The clutch slipped,' he said defensively between heavy breaths. 'I don't think we should go on. It's too risky with a slipping clutch.'

'OK,' I said. 'Let's find a place to camp and decide what to do tomorrow.' Caught up in my own whirlwind, I had failed to appreciate how tired he was. It was nearing the end of the day and the black clouds were building anyway.

The cheeriness in my voice belied bewilderment. The clutch seemed a convenient excuse to avoid acknowledging fallibility or admitting defeat. It was unfortunate that it had happened at a time when I was going from strength to strength.

Villages and homes spread along the hillside, so I didn't expect much peace if we tried camping. Surrounded by schoolchildren, one enterprising young girl stepped forward and indicated that we could stay with her family if we gave her money. Several other kids suggested we ask at the school instead.

I followed one girl in uniform on foot across a stream, up towards a spacious high wire-fenced compound. Inside, the school, a rectangular concrete building with glass windows and tin roof, was the only modern structure among several simple rondavels.

The lady I spoke to was the headteacher, short with round face, dark bags under her eyes and lopsided lips. She said camping would be no problem, as though it were any everyday occurrence having foreigners stay at the school, and invited us to sleep in the staff room where it would be dry and secure.

28

There were desks inset from three sides with chairs behind, space for six teachers. A3 papers pinned to the walls listed key teaching words in English, and the teachers' policy was handwritten with large irregularly sized letters on ruled lines as wonky as the teacher's smile. Two printed posters warned of the dangers of human trafficking, advising of the risks of taking lifts from trucks and being kidnapped in the street.

In a poor country, the allure of jobs and money is great; people are vulnerable to exploitation. With so many children asking for sweets and rubbing their bellies to signify hunger, luring them into a truck to transport them across the border would not be hard.

Later, the night watchman made a tour of the school buildings, entered the staff room and nodded to us. He pulled out a chair and sat with legs stretched out in front, arms folded, wrapped in a traditional blanket and pulled his hat down low. As we cooked dinner on the concrete step outside, the heavens opened. The rain pelted down creating muddy pools across the yard. I was glad to be safe from the storm.

My dreams that night were interrupted by the gentle patter of rain and rhythmic snoring of our guard. When I peered out of the windows early in the morning, several children were already outside, standing aimlessly in the drizzle and thick mist. All were wrapped in their heavy Basotho blankets with big woolly hats and wellies to accessorize. We had regularly passed boys herding sheep wearing the same outfit like a modern-day national dress.

By the time we were ready to leave, the sun had emerged. We backtracked the way we'd come, the trails traversing the grassy hillsides now a muddy mess. The thick black earth got churned up and stuck to the tyres and cemented itself between the rear wheel and swing arm. Progress was slow.

One chisel-faced man in cowboy hat and smart black blanket edged with bright red stitching smiled in amusement as he overtook us with his dog running alongside. He commented that in this terrain, the horse is superior. I agreed. There is a reason that horses remain the primary mode of transport and integral part of Basotho life in these rural regions. It didn't stop him asking if he could swap his horse for my bike.

———

Throughout South Africa, I had always done the shopping while Kieran waited outside with the motorbikes and gear. Initially we took it in turns, but I quickly despaired of waiting outside. Kieran always asked what to buy, unwilling to make a decision, then he took forever in the shop trying to find exactly the items I'd suggested because I couldn't know what the shop would have for sale. Rather than finding a substitute, he'd leave it off the list, which meant we wouldn't have sufficient food and I'd have to go in anyway to complete the shop. It was cheaper and more efficient for me to do the shopping in the first place. What irritated me most was that he never paid attention to the price of items, getting food regardless of the price. The satisfaction of picking up a bargain overrode my guilt at always taking control.

I'd already bought most of the supplies needed for our upcoming hike along the Drakensberg escarpment, but Lesotho's shops had limited variety. I'd figured we could leave a food stash at the Sani Pass Hotel, which we'd soon be passing on the bikes and was also on the hiking route. It would save us carrying the last three days' supplies the whole way.

'Do you want to get the rest of the snack food?' I suggested at the next shop.

Kieran headed into the store, wallet in hand, and some time later returned, smiling, carrying a large cellophane wrapped package under his arm.

'We only needed snacks for the hike, not an entire year's ride through Africa!' I exclaimed.

'It was the smallest pack they had,' he replied, proudly showing me the contents in outstretched arms.

30

Packets and packets of salted peanuts and raisins.

'You're meant to open the cellophane and take individual bags, not the whole bloody pack!' I exclaimed. 'How are we meant to carry all that?'

'Look, they've got Simba the lion on them,' he grinned.

I raised my eyebrows. Trail mix is not my favourite snack.

'Do you want to take them back?' he asked.

'No I don't! Do you?'

'It's OK, we'll find space.'

The bags got shoved into every crevice of our roll bags, rucksacks and tank bags.

'That's the last time I let you loose in the shops,' I joked and we both laughed. I meant it.

Months later, sick of the sight of trail mix, I dug into my last pack that had been lingering like a bad smell in the bottom of my tank bag. 'Finally finished!' I rejoiced.

Kieran laughed, quickly dug into his pannier and palmed me off with another handful. 'Plenty more where those came from,' he grinned.

Almost at the eastern edge of Lesotho, we rode over a plateau to the Sani Pass. Before pitching our tent for a fitful, freezing night at over 2,800 metres, we had obligatory beers in the Sani Mountain Lodge bar. The contentious claim of Africa's highest pub undoubtedly draws in punters like us but ignores Ethiopia's Simien Mountain Lodge and Bar situated a heady 400 metres higher.

The Sani Pass is renowned amongst overland adventure travellers for the rough ride up. Since heavy rains had washed away sections, the trail had been repaired and smoothed, hardly the challenging terrain we'd expected or feared. I took great pleasure in watching the strained, nervous concentration of riders on big powerful motorbikes slowly wind their way up as we sped down on our relatively light, nimble machines.

Despite my growing confidence in trail riding, I had to ride carefully to prevent the Serow's rear shock from bottoming out on big bumps. Over time, the rebound had become more sluggish. Now the shock creaked and groaned when I sat on the seat and never returned to its full height when I stood up. Kieran was incredulous when I casually mentioned it.

'How can you ride like that?' he asked, bemused.

'It's still better than my touring bicycle, which doesn't have any suspension at all,' I replied.

We took the bike to a repair shop, who sent off the rear shock to be serviced. I didn't need the bike anyway; we'd be exploring on foot for a while.

04.

Drakensberg & Battlefields
South Africa

I had imagined a very different journey through Africa, back when I thought I'd be going solo, before Kieran entered my life. My travelling would be less about the journey, more a way of life. I would head in whichever direction took my fancy – see and experience those places I'd missed before and have the adventures I'd envisaged and hopefully many more as yet undreamed of – and when I felt no urge to move on, I'd find a place to settle down and write about all I'd seen and experienced.

During those stationary times, my mind would remain free to wander. I wanted to develop my creative writing skills and attempt literary fiction. If I could pick up paid writing assignments for magazines, I might be able to sustain my travels indefinitely. Then if I woke one morning with the desire to move, to meet new people and to see and experience and live a little more, I would pack my bag, start-up the Serow and explore some more. There's no need to chase your dreams when you're living them.

It wasn't to be a fast-paced adrenalin-filled tick-the-bucket-list adventure, but a mellow and calm live-for-today existence. If tomorrow never came, it would not matter; I had lived life to the full, had everything I needed and wanted nothing. After two decades of trial and error, trying to conform to other people's rules, then breaking away from them in frustration, I had glimpsed inner peace and contentment when living my own unconventional life. By caring less what other people thought and listening to myself for advice, I was sure I had discovered what was best for me. Some people never find such serenity. I never realised that once found, it could be so easily lost.

———

At a backpackers hostel on a farm outside Underberg, I suddenly lost all momentum. The desire to walk the Drakensberg escarpment still burned, but the logistics of getting to the start seemed overwhelming. Alone, I would have stood by the side of the road and stuck out my thumb, but Kieran was disinclined. I wished he would help with the planning, but my hints went unnoticed.

I said I was tired and couldn't be bothered about the walk, but I only meant about the preparation. I'd hoped he would rise to the challenge and inject energy into the endeavour. All he said was, OK, we can just rest and relax here.

Relax?! Riled, more like.

Instead, I suggested we get a lift to the bottom of the Sani Pass with an overlander who was travelling that way, walk up, collect the food we'd stashed at the hotel, and then hike the final three days of the original route. Kieran agreed.

As we set off up the Sani Pass, I felt re-energised. After aimlessly pottering for days, we had direction. I marched with purpose: to the top. I marched as I often did on the uphills, attacking them with gusto and determination, spirited on with each sweaty step. At first we talked, but a silence descended as our heart rates began to race.

Kieran faltered in the searing sun and gradually fell further behind, which was normal whenever we hiked uphill. I thought nothing of it, stopping as usual only occasionally for him to catch up.

'Alright!' I beamed each time he reached me. We'd take slugs from the water bottle, then continue. But after each momentary pause, Kieran fell further behind, looking markedly uneasy. And each time he caught up, his answers became shorter until he responded monosyllabically. I could feel the pressured atmosphere, taut and strained and ready to explode. I had tried to ignore it, not wanting to ruin my mood, but I couldn't.

'Alright?' I asked, this time with concern.

'No I'm not! Why are you racing off? It's not a race,' he retorted, red-faced and angry.

'I'm not,' I replied, confused. I had been so happy, my burning calves enlivening me, senses heightened, savouring the fresh mountain air and drinking in the vibrant colours of the landscape under the fierce African sun.

'You always do this.'

'Exactly,' I replied, 'It's never been a problem before.'

Where was this anger coming from? Perhaps it always had been a problem, one he'd hidden from me.

From then on, I slowed down. Although walking only a footstep apart, the distance between us widened, filled with uncomfortable silences that overshadowed the escarpment, darkening the days even when the clouds hadn't rolled in.

When we spoke, we were more like polite strangers than strong partners. Gradually, the tension eased as we made our way back down into South Africa. Navigating the idiosyncrasies of a remote border post helped to bridge the void between us through a shared experience.

Back at the hostel, I reflected on how the hike had been marred by our personal issues and couldn't help recalling the times on this journey my dreams were being curtailed because I wasn't travelling alone. In choosing to be in a relationship, I had sacrificed my freedom and independence to do what I wanted whenever and however I wanted. The need to compromise seemingly at every turn was beginning to get to me.

In the past, I had occasionally suggested having an adventure alone or time to enjoy the solitude of my own company, even just for a week or a day, but he interpreted it as a personal rebuke and that I didn't want to be with him. I would explain how important my independence was to me. It was precisely because I wanted 'us' to work and be together that I insisted he must also allow me my own space at times. Could he not see the tighter the invisible noose, the stronger my urge to pull away?

Six months earlier on a Romanian hillside, this discussion had erupted into an argument. He saw no point in the relationship if we did things apart. If I wanted, I could go off and do my own thing, he said, but if I did, he would go the other way and I would not see him again. I was so angry that he would give up on us so easily, walk away as if our relationship meant nothing. Still, I conceded with the proviso that one day he would have to allow me my freedom.

Over time I had given up raising the issue or suggesting space to do my own thing because I dreaded the inevitable confrontation and reliving of the same argument. I started to blame Kieran for forcing me to repeatedly compromise, and I hated myself for this negativity towards him.

With no one else to talk to, I internalised my thoughts, magnifying the issues disproportionately until they masked the good times we had together.

Something needed to change, so I focused on the things that we enjoyed equally.

During the following days we went for leisurely, low-key day walks in the Drakensberg, ambling along paths through the long grasses of the lower slopes, leaping across streams, scrambling over tricky terrain and clambering up metal ladders bolted to steep rock faces. The dramatic landscapes couldn't fail to raise our spirits, and we found common ground in discussing books and any wildlife, mostly insects and birds, we spotted.

When a black snake with pale markings crossed the path between my legs mid-stride, reared up and slithered off into the long grass, we recalled previous close encounters with other snakes, laughing nervously and joking about which of us they were most attracted to. We later found out that this one was a rinkhals – a ring-necked spitting cobra. The bright green boomslang that had taken up temporary residence in the bush by our tent on the farm, staring at us through its huge black eyes; the sandy-coloured cape cobra I narrowly avoided in the early days of the trip; and the rinkhals are some of the deadliest snakes in South Africa.

At the farm hostel there were other people to engage with and moments when I could have space. As an early riser, I'd take myself off to make tea and read before anyone else got up.

Besides motorbikes, Kieran's main interest was mixed martial arts, which he had taken up again as a way to keep fit. I was eager to learn, and he was happy to teach me some basic moves. It became an activity we both enjoyed but could practise on our own in the cool of morning or under the shade of the trees. We fell into a routine and gradually our stresses dissipated.

East of the Drakensberg, the Kwazulu-Natal landscape is scattered with memorials, museums and graves – reminders of countless battles fought during centuries of war. Having served in the army, Kieran had a strong affinity for anyone who had fought for their country. I'm interested in the history of all the countries I visit. Looking at the past often helps to understand the present. In the evenings I'd been reading aloud books on the Boer and Zulu Wars for us both to learn.

First we visited Spion Kop, a hilltop site of a battle between British forces and the Boers in 1900 during the early stages of the Second Boer War.

Then we rode to Isandlwana, the site of the first major battle of the Anglo-Zulu War in 1879. The Zulus decisively defeated the outnumbered and overwhelmed British colonial troops. Piles of painted white rocks around the site represent the graves of many who fell.

From there we moved on to Rorke's Drift, like a contingent of Zulus had after the battle at Isandlwana. The skirmishes here have been immortalised in the film *Zulu*. The small garrison of British troops succeeded in repelling a series of Zulu attacks throughout the day leaving hundreds dead; there was no mercy for the wounded after the earlier massacre.

Although the tactics of battle differed, they all shared a common end of victors and defeated, though it's hard to see how there are ever any winners amongst so much death and violence.

The rains were upon us now. Under leaden skies we rode slowly. With visor up and cold wind biting at my cheeks, I watched nervously as lightning struck the electricity cables. With every flash and crackle, I felt vulnerable and defenceless. Gradually the rain eased, but as we entered the town of Dundee it returned with renewed vigour.

'You must be loving this weather!' I remarked to Kieran at the junction.

He grinned back at me. Now he was in his element.

———

The clock on our ninety days allowed in South Africa was ticking as we rode on through the rain towards the Blyde River Canyon where the Three Rondavels were masked by clouds and the fine mist rising like steam from a bubbling cauldron at the u-bend in the river. It was time to start heading west towards the dry climate of the Kalahari.

We stopped to visit the Hoedspruit Endangered Wildlife Centre, which focuses on cheetah rehabilitation but also had a pack of African wild dogs, both animals I've never seen in the wild. I was fascinated, and we were late leaving. The campsite in town had shut down. Unsure where we'd find a place to pitch since the roads were largely fenced, we went to the supermarket for supplies as we needed food anyway.

Hastily packing the food into our roll bags, racing against the setting sun, three people returning to their car parked next to us took interest in our bikes. We exchanged greetings and explained we were from the UK.

The tall man exclaimed, 'You're Helen!'

'Err … yes?' I replied, not questioning whether I was but how the hell he might know. My face screwed into a contorted mass of wrinkles as I delved into the depths of my memory for that elusive moment when we had presumably met before. It is always disconcerting when someone recognises you but you haven't the faintest clue who they might be.

'I'm Dave. We met at the Horizons Unlimited event last summer.'

We did? I stood awkwardly whilst Dave elaborated. 'I bought your book and you signed it for me.'

Oh God, this is awkward. Desperate to change the topic, I interrupted his monologue. I asked the two other people, 'We haven't met before, have we?'

They laughed. 'No, I'm Andy and this is Mel. We're all friends.'

They marvelled at the chances of meeting in the opposite hemisphere a year apart, and I commented that in overland travel circles, the world is a small place; although, I would have been less surprised if we had met at a game lodge or on some dusty trail.

'Yes, what are you doing at Hoedspruit's Pick 'n' Pay?' Andy asked.

We explained, suddenly remembering that we ought to get moving. Our car park friends didn't know of a nearby campsite, but Kieran had found a waypoint for one on the GPS unit, which was a thirty-minute ride away. Dave offered to guide us. He said we were also welcome to sleep on the sofas at his place, but that he was going to Mel and Andy's for dinner first.

'You're more than welcome to join us,' Andy said.

'And if you don't think it's too strange to stay with strangers, then you could just spend the night at ours. We have a spare bed.'

Just like that, we went from homeless to happily ensconced in a welcoming home with great food and beer, laughing and joking over absurd and astounding tales because whether you're travelling or living in Africa, everyday is always an adventure.

Occasionally I meet like-minded people on my travels. We get on immediately and know we'll remain friends for life, content that when we one day meet again, we will embrace and laugh as though nothing has changed. Andy and Mel are those kind of friends.

The next morning, they invited us to stay another night. Andy took Kieran to his workshop. A leather craftsman who had apprenticed with a master in Italy, Andy now hand-made custom products to order alongside various designs of bags and belts and other accessories from naturally dyed crocodile, ostrich and cattle hide.

I sat with Mel on the veranda overlooking a pond with terrapins that swam over and begged for dog biscuits to be thrown to them. She told me about her life working with animals in conservation, from protecting rhino and elephants in South Africa's parks to running horse safaris in the Serengeti. Mel is one of those rare people whose heart is full of kindness for all living things. She could not kill a venomous snake or poisonous spider no more than say a harsh word about the cruellest of people.

Having someone else, never mind Mel who exudes a quiet calmness from her tough interior, to listen to was fascinating. We could have easily stayed longer, but when we had only two days remaining on our visa, we said our goodbyes and made a dash through forested hills, across open country with scattered rocky outcrops, naboom trees and aloes, and through the bushveld to the border.

With time apart from Kieran, I had felt myself relax, but as we rode west, deeper into Botswana and further along the Trans-Kalahari Corridor, the tension between us resurfaced. Seemingly inconsequential annoying habits that once I would have ignored now gnawed at me. I had long ago accepted that I would always be ready first in the morning and after every stop, but now I sat impatiently on my bike wishing I could set off and ride towards the distant horizon, unhindered and free.

———

I glanced down at the hand guard protecting the clutch lever and saw a white wing flapping in the wind. Another one was trapped in the front fork dust cover. I touched the brake and swerved a fraction to the right, hoping to avoid another butterfly. I flinched as we collided, my heart skipping a beat as another delicate winged body fell to rest as a tragic, beautiful blot on the tarmac. Butterfly murder by motorbike is as easy as snuffing out the flame of a candle with the pinch of a finger and thumb. I inhaled sharply with each near miss and winced, like a tribute to each extinguished life, and scoffed at myself for being so sensitive to something so small. It's not the death of a living creature that bothers me so much as the senseless waste.

Kieran bulldozed obliviously through the endless butterfly parade leaving a trail of destruction in his wake. It wound me up, and I got angry with myself for letting it get to me. Irritation bubbled through to my fingers, so I opened the throttle, overtook and rode in front. Now, when a butterfly approached, not caught up in turbulence from Kieran's bike, I eased off slightly, allowing it to pass unscathed.

The white butterflies with dark-edged wings fluttered across the road from left to right, dancing in the gentle, warming breeze of mid-morning. All day, every day, one passed here, another there, a slow and endless procession.

Their long journey was in the opposite direction to us. These caper white butterflies originated in the Karoo and Kalahari. They were departing the harsh desert-like environment that I was going in search of. They were going east towards the Indian Ocean where they would die; whereas I was riding west towards the wilderness because that's where I feel most alive.

Their flight path appeared erratic, yet their final destination is precise. Though, if I mapped my eventual 40,000-kilometre route from Cape Town to the Mediterranean port of Alexandria, my journey across Africa would undoubtedly seem unpredictable at any given moment in time too.

I enjoy the calming, meditative effect of long, quiet tarmac roads as much as the thrill and challenge of rough winding trails. With the open road and unimpeded view, I was soon distracted by the thousands of thoughts and ideas flitting through my mind. They flickered and sparkled irresistibly like specks of dust illuminated by a beam of light. I reached out to catch one, letting it develop and live on for more than a fleeting moment.

How green the landscape looks! It was not the dry and dusty shades of rust and brown I'd expected the Kalahari Desert to be. The recent rains had transformed the land, the verges lush with long grass and bursting with bright yellow of the devil's thorn in flower. Cattle and donkeys and sometimes a herd of horses grazed the green verges, oblivious to the occasional traffic. Indeed, red triangle signs warned us of cattle and deer, not elephants, lions or giraffes as were typical elsewhere in the sparsely populated areas of Botswana and Namibia.

Oh, I wish I were cycling. It was the first time I'd thought this since I got my motorbike two years earlier. Until now there'd not been a single road or trail that I'd have rather been pedalling. After all, the motorbike offers all the fun without the hard graft. But the speed of motorcycle travel was too fast now, despite riding slowly to minimise the stress on Kieran's bike engine that was oozing a litre of oil every thousand kilometres like an unstoppable arterial bleed.

We'd already used up the reserve oil we were carrying and struggled to find more. Botswana is not known for its motorcycle culture. Indeed, we only saw three others, one of which was rusting outside a garage. We'd bought the only oil available and hoped it wouldn't mess up the clutch.

Cruising along at seventy kilometres per hour, the scenery passed by in a blur. I only saw the intricate details of the flowers or heard the chirp of a bird when we stopped every hour or two to enjoy a cup of tea in the shade of a mopane tree and to bring back life to our numb backsides. If I had been travelling alone, I would have happily gone even slower.

Wild camping one evening while I pitched the tent and made tea, Kieran set to cleaning the engine. The oil leak was coming from the head gasket. Ensuring all the bolts were tight had done nothing to stem the steady outflow. Soon the rags were filthy, sand sticking to them. Kieran's hands were black. With limited water supply, we resorted to wet wipes. With little else we could do for the time being, we decided to limp towards Windhoek, Namibia's capital, one of the few places to buy replacement parts and where there was a Yamaha workshop.

We stopped where the small road from Molepolole to Motokwe joins the main trans-Kalahari highway, which runs between Botswana's capital and the Namibian border. The ailing bike was stuttering with malcontent. Kieran wanted to see if removing the air filter would help since we couldn't take the engine apart here, in such a dusty, sandy environment.

He now told me he'd known about the oil leak before we departed the UK and had even packed a replacement gasket. Why didn't he replace it before we left?

A small boy, who looked about eight years old, stood at a distance. I guessed he was older than his height suggested, stunted by poor nutrition with skinny arms and little flesh covering his ribs. His taut belly protruded over baggy shorts and looked about to burst like a balloon. He silently observed us with wide hungry eyes, gathering the courage to come closer. He answered, 'Yes yes' to every question.

Timidly at first, as though scared of his own voice, but then with more certainty, he uttered the words 'I eez hungree' and patted his pot belly. He looked at our tools and tried to anticipate which one Kieran would need next, picking one up and passing it to him. He was a thoughtful, helpful young lad who aimed to please and wanted to work. It was saddening to think that his prospects in life were limited by circumstances beyond his control. People had a hard life here living on the margins.

I'd wanted to take non-tarmac routes but Jimmy was reluctant. It wasn't prudent to head into remote territory with his bike leaking oil and the risk of a slipping clutch, he said.

My frustrated anger threatened to explode out of me uncontrollably. My fingers curled into a tense grip as I took a deep breath in. Then I exhaled with a long silent scream that pierced through my eyes, releasing the tension within. But it was only a temporary reprieve.

Kieran must have been equally irritated with me, could probably sense I wasn't happy, and it all came to a head one evening wild camping. I forget what sparked it. Perhaps I rebuffed his advances since I was sweaty and dusty and not in the mood or simply that, yet again, he had turned the gas stove on and left it burning with nothing cooking while he chopped vegetables.

Kieran said he couldn't go on like this, said it was as though I didn't want him on the trip and he would leave if that was what I wanted. If I needed space, he saw no point in the relationship. I couldn't have both. The silence of the bush grew heavy as we looked long and hard into each others eyes, my head whirring with thoughts.

I was torn.

Yes, just leave! I screamed in my head, but that would have been a rash response. I had many memories of good times together, of our adventures and moments laughing and joking. What's more, I cared deeply for Kieran even though I may not have told him often.

My emotions were a pressure cooker about to vent. The part of me that craved ... no, needed ... freedom and solitude had been subdued for too long and was rattling the bars of its cage demanding to be heard. For a year now, we had been in each other's company almost twenty-fours hours a day every day.

'Well?' he asked, because I still hadn't said anything.

If we split up, I would be free to go whichever way I chose whenever I wanted. I could take those rough tracks and hike those

44

big mountains. If I had to turn back, it would be due to my own inadequacies, not someone else holding me back. Travelling solo, I alone would be responsible for my successes and failures, without having to consider the needs or wants of anyone else.

I couldn't help thinking that by travelling together the risks when in remote areas were reduced, the stresses and burdens lowered.

'What would you do if we split up?' I asked.

'I'd get on my bike and ride for home as fast as I can.'

No, you can't do that! There is so much of Africa you haven't seen. You must at least take the time to explore it.

I saw it as him breaking off the relationship not only with me but the continent also. It made me sad to think he may never experience it with the depth of feeling and emotion as I had. I was certain that if given enough time, he would come to love Africa as I did; for surely, who could not love Africa?

And how would we divide our shared kit? Who would manage without essential tools? *Why do I have to be so damn practical and think through everything to the very end?* A chain breaker for the bikes really shouldn't have mattered when we were considering breaking the connection between us.

The situation remained unresolved. We could only agree that parting ways from a wild bush camp was impractical. So we said we'd see how we felt in the morning, but when morning came, we got up and made tea and I said that no, I didn't want him to leave. I wasn't ready to give up on us yet, even if he had been.

I had conceded again. But his words echoed in my mind; the ultimatum – for that's how I'd interpreted it – ringing in my ears, competing with the sounds of the bush long after the silence between us resumed.

We broke camp as we did every morning and, as the sun rose in the sky, we hit the road towards the Namibian border. I focussed on the feeling of awe and wonder that riding through Africa evokes. *Let's see how we feel when we reach Windhoek.*

The land became drier, the bush sparser with fewer mopane trees offering shade. The land beyond the roadside verges was no longer farmed but untamed bush. Only the delicate white butterflies and sometimes a red or orange one continued to cross our path. Then, as the road turned northwest, I spotted other wildlife. Vultures circled high, signalling dead game in the bush off to our right, a small dik-dik nipped into a thicket and the unmistakable outline of three ostriches silhouetted on the horizon. A single cloud, perhaps signalling a pan in the otherwise dry land, hovered in the pale-blue bleached sky.

As we crossed the border, the gentle rise and fall of the undulating countryside gave extensive views, bringing back fond memories of my time cycling through the Namibian wilderness. I couldn't wait to explore the parts of Namibia I'd missed last time.

First, we had to go to Windhoek to get the oil leak fixed but also to apply for a visa. I'd wanted to visit Angola for a long time. During my previous cycling trip, only five-day transit visas were being issued; instead, I had travelled through DR Congo. Now, coming from the south, rumours were that if you were lucky and had a letter of invitation, you could obtain a thirty-day tourist visa in Windhoek. Officially you were supposed to get them in your home country, an impossibility on a prolonged trip such as ours.

I'd sent messages to friends and had been given the name of a contact in Luanda. I knew nothing about him except his name: Lilio. He knew nothing about me except that I wanted to visit Angola on my motorbike. Nevertheless, he provided me with a notarised letter of invitation, his only condition being that we promise to visit his country. Keeping that promise would be easy if only the Angolan embassy would issue us visas.

I envisaged us getting Kieran's bike fixed, then exploring central Namibia while our visa applications were processed, then returning to collect our passports before continuing north.

It didn't go as planned.

05.

Windhoek Worries
Namibia

With calm determination, gentle persuasion and a warming smile on my part, the lady behind the counter at the Angolan embassy eventually agreed to take our visa applications even though we weren't residents in Namibia.

We paid the fee at the nearby bank and returned to submit our passports and accompanying paperwork. I didn't dare let myself get too excited, knowing how disappointed I would be if our applications were rejected. Straight-faced and without hint of emotion or indication as to our chances of success, the lady told us to come back in a week.

A week is a long time when a lot can change in an instant.

We located the Yamaha dealer and dropped off Kieran's bike at the workshop on the other side of town. Kieran volunteered to ride my bike with me as pillion back to the campsite.

Outside the dealership, I climbed onto my bike behind Kieran, wriggling into as comfy a position as possible, the bars of the rack digging into my backside. We exited the side road and stopped at the junction with the main dual carriageway. We needed to turn right across the oncoming early morning rush-hour traffic. Kieran rode half-way, to the intersection, and waited for another break in the traffic, feet planted on the ground for stability.

A black BMW pulled up alongside ... too close. The side doors pushed against my leg, squeezing it into the bike. I banged on the car but it was too late. Kieran yelped loudly as the front wheel rolled over his left foot.

I leapt off the bike and quickly put it on the side stand as Kieran stumbled to the floor, grabbing his foot and bawling expletives. He wasn't one to wince at pain, so I knew it was bad.

The car pulled onto the central reservation and a young suited professional came running over to help. Kieran was not receptive, anger and pain driving his reaction. I urged that he needed to get off the road or there'd be a worse accident.

The driver, Erastus, drove Kieran to the Roman Catholic hospital, which had a good reputation as one of the best medical facilities in Windhoek, as he had insurance and was registered there. I followed on my bike.

We helped Kieran hop into the immaculately clean reception. The nurses, dressed in pale blue with white apron and head scarf, exuded calm while going about their jobs quietly with no sense of urgency, only practical thoroughness. It felt more like a convent than a hospital.

We didn't have to wait long before Kieran was taken in a wheelchair to have his foot x-rayed whilst I stayed and filled out forms. Wracked with guilt, Erastus kept apologising. He wanted to make sure Kieran was alright but was very worried about being late and getting into trouble with work. I expected that good jobs with career prospects were not easy to come by. I told him to go because there was nothing more he could do. We exchanged numbers; he promised to contact his insurance company and return later. He sounded genuine, but I didn't expect to see him again. We had comprehensive travel insurance, so care should be covered anyway.

Kieran was upstairs, perched on a bed in a private consulting room. The colour had returned to his cheeks and, dosed up on strong painkillers, he had a manic grin spread across his face.

In an emergency, I tend to take a distanced view and act logically. I may appear unsympathetic, but usually it's better to deal with practicalities first. Kieran was in good hands; there was nothing more I could do at the hospital. When the doctor wanted to check his foot, rather than get in the way, I rode back to the campsite to collect his insurance documents and complete paperwork.

Soon after returning to the hospital, the driver reappeared. A work colleague, another young guy in shirt and smart trousers, was with him for moral support. He was worried about Erastus, who was still shaken by the accident. They couldn't stay long but had wanted to check that Kieran would be OK.

Erastus said his insurers wouldn't pay costs incurred so far as the treatment was not being done at their recommended hospital. If Kieran needed to be admitted, we could transfer him and the insurers would cover the ongoing costs.

Kieran was discharged with a hairline fracture to his outer metatarsal, severe bruising to his foot, a prescription for strong anti-inflammatories and instructions to change the dressing regularly.

It could have been a lot worse and it could have happened anywhere. I had found it hard to imagine that we would make it across Africa without a crash or injury. My hope had been that any damage would not be serious. If this was to be *the* crash, we had gotten off lightly, although Kieran may not have thought so. That said, we were only a few months into the trip with many thousands of kilometres between us and Egypt.

It was a nerve-wracking ride back to the campsite. I had only ridden with a pillion once before. Now I had to ride in lunchtime traffic through a city I didn't know well, the person I cared about on the back with a broken foot, holding the trainer that wouldn't fit over the heavy bandaging. We would always wonder if he'd been wearing his bike boots whether his foot would have sustained less damage.

——

Our relationship was still on rocky ground. I admit that I had been contemplating whether staying together was the right choice, for both of us. But I could not leave him now he was injured. It would take a heartless person to walk away from the one they care about when they need care the most. The decision, it seemed, had been made for me, for now.

After a couple of days, having been to the pharmacy for more painkillers, done our laundry, bought food supplies, taken a taxi to the Yamaha workshop and collected his bike, I began to wonder how long it would be until Kieran's foot healed?

He was gifted a pair of crutches by the campsite owner, so he could get about unaided. He rarely tried, content for me to go on errands and bring him beer. Ten years earlier with a serious knee injury, I had been on crutches for three months, unable to bend my one knee for two of those. I was single yet managed to look after myself for the most part, cooking my meals and doing my own shopping. Of course it was painful and inconvenient and everything took longer than normal, but it was possible. I played nurse to Kieran nonetheless, even doing his chores that didn't require two feet to stand on.

I wished I could head off for a week and explore central Namibia, giving me the space and time to myself that I craved. I could have done a multi-day hiking trip that I'd read about but had shelved because Kieran wasn't enthusiastic about walking in the heat. But I couldn't callously abandon Kieran so soon after his injury. Instead, I put my needs aside.

After a week I returned to the Angolan embassy. It was closed. I checked the time; it was well past nine o'clock when the embassy should be open even allowing for a slack attitude to punctuality.

The security guard told me it was Angola's national holiday today. *I should have known!* I always seemed to coincide my visits with the holidays, which embassies have a lot of since their staff often get to celebrate those of both their own and their host country. I returned the next day when the embassy was open. Finally I would find out whether our application had been successful.

The same stern woman handed me our passports with a poker face. I stepped aside and flicked through them eagerly. Both had a thirty-day visa stamped inside. *Yes!* Angola had eluded me six years earlier, but now I could go … as soon as Kieran's foot healed.

We agreed that as soon as he could get his bike boot on, we would leave Windhoek. Every morning, when his foot was least swollen, he would try. I watched helplessly as his face creased in pain, forcing in his toes but failing to slide in his heel.

There was so much of the Namibian wilderness I wanted to explore and I was trapped in a soulless city. There was a time limit on the Angolan visa. From the day it was issued, we had one month to get to the border before the countdown began on the thirty days allowed in the country. Every day stuck in Windhoek was a day less on the road in what I knew was a fabulous country.

Again I wished Kieran would suggest I go off by myself and meet him later but he didn't. Every day I looked on the map and mentally crossed off another part of Namibia I wouldn't have time to see and reformulated the route plan, hoping we would leave soon.

My latest idea was to ride to the coast through the Namib-Naukluft National Park. To travel there, we would need a permit.

Bike gear on and helmet in hand, I walked towards the front desk of the Ministry of Environment and Tourism. The confidence that had brought me here vanished, and I was overwhelmed with a strong urge to leave. *What am I doing?!*

'Yes?' The woman behind the screen asked.

You can't leave now … There's no harm in asking.

I stepped forward, took a deep breath and composed myself. 'I'd like a permit to visit the Namib-Naukluft National Park,' I said.

'Where is your form?' she demanded in a deep, serious voice that made the little schoolgirl in me want to cry.

'I don't have one …'

'Here,' she interrupted impatiently.

'Thank you. Is it allowed to visit on a motorcycle?' I quickly added. *See, that wasn't so hard.*

The woman immediately directed me to one of the back offices.

51

I had intended to travel through the park when I was cycling in Namibia, taking the chance without a permit. In the end, I had to bypass it over concerns that I was consuming my water supply too quickly in the intense desert heat. I *really* wanted to visit. Now, we had just enough time and could easily carry sufficient water on the motorbikes.

I sat down, placing my helmet on the empty seat next to me. I'd decided to come in my motorbike gear to make it clear what I was asking. I had imagined huge scope for misunderstanding. I didn't want to get a permit through deception; it would be harder to talk my way out if we later got caught.

The young man, new to his position, picked up the rules and regulations book and flicked through it.

'Hmm ... I don't know about motorbikes,' he said, confused. 'Do you think it's a problem?'

You're asking me?! I stifled a laugh.

'I don't think it's a problem.' I replied earnestly, because officials like to be taken seriously. 'We both know there are no big animals dangerous to people there.' I had no idea if he knew. 'It would be different if I were asking about Etosha where there are lions; that would be a problem.'

The young man listened intently from behind his desk. He seemed eager to glean new information that would help him in his job.

'Yes, you are right. See if you can find anything about motorcycles being forbidden in here,' he said, passing me the rule book.

He proceeded with my application on the computer, asking me what to enter: which park did we wish to visit? How many people? For how long? Where would we stay? I answered each question whilst flicking through the pages of the rule book.

I looked up to see him scrolling through a list of vehicles: small car, large car, 4x4, car with trailer, people carrier, minibus up to 16 people, bus ... It was a long list but did not include a motorcycle option. My heart sank. This was the moment he would refuse my request.

I reviewed the rulebook thoroughly for any motorcycle reference.

'It doesn't list motorcycle, but I have to select something,' he said, still scrolling through the list.

'There's nothing about motorcycles in the rules,' I commented honestly.

He scrolled up and down as though hoping the word 'motorcycle' would suddenly appear. I remained silent. *What are you going to do?*

He clicked on 'small car'. Then he printed out the form, crossed out 'small car' and wrote 'motorcycle' in pen alongside.

Brilliant! 'It's two motorcycles actually.'

He added '2 x'.

I handed over the cash and he passed me the official permit.

———

As the days went by, we preoccupied ourselves with various hobbies. Together we made bracelets and wine bottle holders out of paracord using some of the techniques that Andy had shown Kieran with leather. Kieran's foot slowly improved; he discarded one of the crutches.

Finally, one day, he announced over morning tea that his foot was less swollen and maybe he could fit on his walking shoe rather than his bike boot. It wouldn't provide as good protection, but we'd be able to ride. We were the same foot size, so I gave him my walking boot, which had ankle support.

He whelped as he forced it on, but it fit nonetheless, and hopped up on his good leg. Gingerly, he slid onto his bike and soon realised he couldn't change gear. Using his heel he could tap down, but putting pressure on the upper part of his foot was too painful to change up.

Not to be defeated, he found some wire and attached it to the gear shifter with a long piece of string tied to the end. When he pulled the string, the gear shifted up. We both smiled with relief.

Excited, I quickly packed our bags onto the bikes, and with Kieran secure in the saddle, wearing one bike boot and one hiking boot, I took his crutch, strapped it to the side of his bike, then lifted up his side stand. We were ready to ride.

Let the adventure continue!

06.

Namib-Naukluft Desert
Namibia

The stresses and strains of the last month evaporated as we rode out of Windhoek, the crush of city life lifting. With the shackles loosened, I wriggled on the seat, straightened my back and stretched out my shoulders, feeling the tension melt away. Memories flooded back of wild camping in the Namibian desert under a blanket of stars and listening to the caracal's call piercing the still air on dark nights. We were heading to a place I loved and felt at home.

I had forgotten about the endless kilometres of fencing along many Namibian roads. Whilst I could lift a bicycle over a fence and discreetly camp out of sight, this wasn't possible with a motorbike. But I've searched for wild camping spots on hundreds of nights and know when an opportunity is too good to turn down.

Where a section of wire fencing was flattened, I pulled off the road, ready to ride through. Kieran didn't follow. As someone who had spent years in the army, I was always surprised at his reluctance to wild camp. Instead we rode on, hoping to find somewhere more accessible.

Another hour passed. The sun set. Neither of us wanted to ride in the dark, so when we saw a sign to a campsite, we rode up to the farm and enquired. It was expensive, but we had little choice. We rode along a 4x4 trail that meandered through the scrub and chose our camp spot at the base of a rocky hill. With our tent pitched among the thorny acacias under the dark sky of a million stars, we could have been anywhere in the desert wilderness, except here we could have a hot shower before cooking our dinner and bedding down for the night.

I longed to show Kieran the Namibia I loved. Because he couldn't walk, we decided not to visit the iconic dunes of Sossusvlei. Instead, we rode down the Remhoogte Pass to Solitaire, the lonely one-man town. Last time I'd stayed, the 'local' farmers from up to five hundred kilometres away had gathered for their lively annual get-together. We had eaten braai and drunk beer and scoffed Moose's famous apple pie. Moose had since died and the place was eerily quiet with only a few passing tourists stopping at the bakery to buy pie served by a young foreigner. I don't know who made the pie now.

We rode north across the Tropic of Capricorn, stopping for a photo at the big sign plastered with overlanders' stickers, then continued to Rostock Ritz, a luxury lodge in the desert, nestled on a rocky escarpment. We drank a couple of beers, then moved down to the camping area. There seemed little point in putting up the tent; rain was improbable and we were safe on the veranda of the building from unsavoury animals. We watched the sun set in all its glory over a lunar landscape in humble silence. This was the Africa I love, the big secret between me and a million stars, and I was happy that Kieran was experiencing it too.

During my last visit to Namibia, the country experienced its wettest season in twenty-five years, a pale-green blanket of rain-nourished grass spread over the land and flowers bloomed, bright orange, pink and purple ones nestled in rocky crevices. It looked different today stripped bare, the flowers gone, the withered grass brown if it grew at all. The carnival had passed and the dullness of everyday life had returned.

When I'd cycled the Kuiseb Pass, yellow wildflowers had carpeted the riverbed and water flowed across the trail. I'd met a couple there camping with their 4x4 who had come out to see the desert in bloom for the first time in their lives. Now there was only a dry ford and barren hills. The contrast was stark.

Had I remembered wrongly? Surely this couldn't be the same place, yet I recognised the shape of the land and the winding road.

I tried explaining to Kieran what it had looked like before. I don't think he understood. How could he? I could hardly believe it myself. No wonder locals had been awestruck, as I was now.

Beyond the winding canyon, sun-bleached stone-littered plains stretched to the horizon. We turned left onto a faint trail, pale like unblemished skin, zig-zagging for no apparent reason without a tree or shrub or inch of shade in sight. There was nothing here, yet I felt some invisible force grabbing me, tugging and pulling me in.

We passed another sign for the Tropic of Capricorn, painted on a fallen slab of rock, cracked and forgotten. Without a single sticker plastered to it, there was no indication of who had passed this way before; yet, those who venture into these vast regions of emptiness interest me the most, not those who shout 'I was here!' from the highway. Further on – I can't say how far across this timeless emptiness – we came across another sign: Zebra Pan, the painted stone upright, defiant. But there were no zebras, only dry faded earth and burning blue sky.

Something whispered in the still, static air. *Don't leave, you can't go.* I didn't want to, but we wouldn't survive long where there's no water. A part of me would remain there like a silent ghost long after we'd gone and the lingering presence of the Serow's tyre tracks fade. We passed the striped desiccating remains of a zebra, the only other living thing, dead. *We must keep going.*

Past crumbling whitewashed concrete walls and scattered remains of old copper mines, we continued towards the hills emerging on the horizon. After riding through a wide canyon whose walls shielded us from the immensity of the open pan, we reached the dry Kuiseb River where trees grew tall and green. Beyond, an impenetrable dune wall of flaming orange sand rose up.

Homeb community campsite was nothing more than a designated place to pitch our tent. There were neither facilities nor water, only goat tracks and some wooden fencing.

I pitched the tent and went exploring on foot, leaving Kieran to rest. I tried to reach the dunes, separated from the camp by thorny scrub. I followed a path, but it narrowed to a meandering animal track, and soon I was creeping and crawling, ducking and side-stepping through the tangled maze, my bare arms scratched with every twist and turn. Occasionally the bush was clear enough to glimpse the orange glow, still far away.

Instead I climbed the nearside rocky riverbank and saw beyond the orange wall a sublime sand sea with wave after wave of ridges and troughs in sunlight and shade. The beautiful dunes of the Namib.

I wished we could have stayed longer, but we only had water for two days, the duration of our permit. We returned through the canyon and rejoined the main trail, rode past the research station at Gobabeb and then some shacks of corrugated iron and an ironic sign saying 'Car Wash'. The only vehicles were rusted shells of cars and pickups abandoned beside the trail.

As the bright orange dunes receded in the rear-view, the trail widened. A church appeared over a rise, a house here, another building there. A truck overtook, then another, and all too soon the solitude of the desert had disappeared.

Back on the main road, the ride via Walvis Bay to neighbouring Swakopmund, Namibia's second largest town, was quick. There I wrote and planned whilst Kieran worked on the bikes. Once rested and restocked, we set off again. The Skeleton Coast and Kaokoland beckoned.

———

'Loo roll!' I exclaimed through my helmet.

'What?' Kieran called back.

'Loo roll!' I repeated.

Trying to converse with our helmets on was like shouting in a care home to a deaf resident. Perhaps he heard me and wondered what had sparked my outburst.

'I forgot to buy loo roll,' I elaborated.

I always forget something. Usually I realise long after leaving town and have to manage without. I always make do, which makes me wonder how much of the stuff I lug about I could cope without.

'I'll be back soon,' I said, putting my helmet on the bike's mirror and taking the keys from the ignition.

We were parked in the middle of Swakopmund, a town which, in the local Nama language, means 'excrement opening'. Of all places, loo roll should be in plentiful supply here.

When I returned, Kieran was deep in conversation, talking about bikes to a middle-aged guy wearing a blue t-shirt with 'Yamaha' printed across it, who worked at the motorcycle shop around the corner. He had seen the Serows and come to chat.

Once I'd shoved the loo roll in my roll bag, I sat on the bike, arms leant over the handlebars, and waited impatiently. I wanted to escape town, ride trails and explore more of Namibia's desolate wilderness. *Get me out of here!* I put my helmet on in readiness, an unsubtle hint that went unnoticed.

I heard again how many litres our bikes' oversize fuel tanks can hold and how far that will get us. Retelling the same stories to the stream of people you meet when travelling can become tiresome. There are, however, a multitude of ways to tell a story; elaborate some parts, gloss over others. Hearing someone else tell their same story using the same words in the same tone over and over and over is enough to drive you crazy.

Keep calm. I exhaled a resigned sigh and removed my helmet.

'Which way are you going now?' the Yamaha guy asked.

Kieran mentioned we were going north to Angola.

'Yeah, we're going to head up the coast as far as ...' I started to explain. For the first time, the Yamaha guy looked to me. Then he turned back to Kieran and told him that motorcycles aren't allowed on the Skeleton Coast.

'Yes, I know ...' I interrupted.

He ignored me and continued to tell Kieran that permits are required beyond Torra Bay.

'Yes, I know that ...' I butted in again and kept talking, forcing him to pay attention. 'We know. We're going to turn inland at Mile 108 towards the Brandberg Mountain, then go north. We want to ride the trails around Kaokoland.'

The relatively undeveloped northwestern corner of the country is sparsely populated. I was attracted by the rough trails and hope of seeing more wildlife.

Perusing the map and reading about Kaokoland, I had discovered one route renowned in overlanding circles for its difficulty. Van Zyl's Pass is described in detail on the *Dangerous Roads* website. We'd already ridden several roads listed, none of which were particularly dangerous but either noteworthy for their roughness of trail or spectacular scenery. 'Legendary', 'notorious' and 'Namibia's toughest' were a few of the words used to describe Van Zyl's Pass to 4x4 enthusiasts. I wanted to ride it.

How challenging would it be on two wheels? The only videos I found online were of riders' attempts on big adventure bikes, which were dropped often amid a barrage of expletives. I was concerned it was beyond my skill level, but we could unload our lightweight bikes and walk them down if needed. We had nothing to prove.

I had asked Kieran for his thoughts, hoping he'd infuse optimism into my uncertainty, but he simply mirrored my attitude and opinion. Perhaps the Yamaha guy could provide reliable first-hand knowledge to counter the scaremongering naysayers on the web.

'We're wondering about riding Van Zyl's Pass. Do you think we'd manage on these bikes?' I asked.

The Yamaha guy stared at me in silence, then turned and said to Kieran. 'That's a really hard route. If it were just you, I'd say go for it. But it's not ...' Then he looked me up and down and, shaking his head, added, 'I mean, maybe you could *try* if you're a champion enduro rider or world class MX biker.'

60

You're right, you don't know me! How dare you dismiss me because I'm a girl!

Kieran looked at me and saw the raging fury in my eyes.

'Oh well, there're other routes,' I said calmly, betraying my loathsome indignation. 'Out of interest, what were you riding when you did it?'

'Ah, I haven't ridden it myself, but I know people who've done it in 4x4s.'

Kieran was wise enough to wrap up the conversation, put his helmet on, say good-bye and set off. In the Yamaha guy's eyes, I followed behind obediently.

I indicated to stop a few kilometres down the road, and Kieran pulled over.

'We're riding Van Zyl's Pass, aren't we?' he commented.

'Too bloody right!'

07.
Kaokoland
Namibia

It felt good to leave town. The wealthy orderly suburbs with large, clean compounds adjoining the coast gave way to corrugated iron and scrap metal homes sprawling into the desert, east of the highway. The Mondesa township, established during apartheid in the 1950s under the misleading name of the DRC, Democratic Resettlement Community, provides housing for the black workers and labourers who keep the wealthy homes clean. Beyond, past the salt works, the Skeleton Coast stretches north for hundreds of kilometres.

Somewhere past Henties Bay, I realised we were no longer on tarmac but a smooth salt road across pancake flat, sun-bleached earth. Where small orange-red hills rose up, we turned inland and, after camping in a sheltered spot since the wind had picked up, tracked northeast, the trail hard-packed through increasingly rocky terrain. Mirages of purple-blue pools reflected the hills, which gradually turned reddish brown as the day wore on, the sun intensifying until the track blurred into a shimmering heat haze. A lone thorny tree here, a Welwitschia plant there. Occasionally we passed a stripped rusting shell of an old car, bashed and battered and riddled with bullet holes. A faded sign leant against one read 'Wood Carvings For Sale. Very Beautiful!' Maybe once, not any more.

The track wound between low hills with wavy strata of dark grey and sandy coloured rock, following the course of an ancient riverbed, dry for millennia. At the dry Ugab River, khaki-coloured dome structures of the Save The Rhino Trust base camp looked like they had come from the *Star Wars* movie set. They were surrounded by reed walls to protect them from the desert elephants that regularly roam here. Rhinos, although highly territorial, have large ranges and so were less likely to be seen.

We rode on across open land, the meandering track visible for miles. As the sun lowered and the air cooled, wildlife emerged. Rutting springbok clashed horns and kicked up dust, a lone fox slunk off into the shadows of a hill, and the sound of our motorbikes startled a herd of gemsbok, who galloped off until hidden amongst the towering camel thorn acacias.

We pitched our tents in a lunar landscape nestled between low dunes where the sand had accumulated against small bushes, hoping this would be an unlikely path for roaming elephants. We'd seen their tracks criss-crossing the sand. I didn't fancy being trampled in my sleep because they hadn't seen our well-camouflaged green and sandy-grey tent. Although elephants have poor eyesight, I figured that their excellent hearing would pick up Kieran's snoring and their acute sense of smell would detect my festering bike boots.

We were undisturbed by animals. Only the wind whistling through the dunes woke me, and when I looked out of the tent, the light of a million stars lit up the desert arena.

Early the next morning we passed a watering hole, the sharp outlines of elephants' footprints overlaying all other tracks. We eagerly scanned the area through Kieran's monocular from a higher viewpoint but couldn't see any lumbering giants. I wished that I could explore the region in a 4x4. With capacity to carry extra fuel, food and water, it would be possible to stay for weeks at a time. *Next time, Namibia. Next time.*

The trail improved as we neared the main graded road towards Palmwag. Passing small communities, we saw more donkeys than zebra. We stopped for an expensive but ice-cold and refreshing Coca-Cola at a luxury lodge in a gorge. We looked out-of-place, unwashed and sweating in our dusty bike jeans and boots whilst the other clientele wore shirts and smart shoes or had manicured hands and make-up.

We stayed the night on the edge of Sesfontein at the basic, budget-friendly community-run campsite. We bought cheap cold beer from the bar in town to have with our instant noodles dinner at sunset while the camp guardian lit and stoked the fire for the donkey boiler, which in a couple of hours heated the water for a warm shower by torchlight.

It was two weeks since we'd left Windhoek. Kieran still winced with pain when taking his first step on his injured foot in the morning, limping until it loosened up. The break had healed enough to walk unaided, so we left his crutch with a lady at the shop. We were both glad that I no longer had to untie and hand it to him every time we stopped.

Out of town, soon after setting off across the tinder-dry yellow grass plain, we became bogged down in deep, corrugated sand. Struggling along in first gear, I strained with all my upper body strength to keep the handlebars straight and the bike going forward, my feet paddling the sand when the rear wheel slipped and slid and spun. I'd already stripped off my jacket and still the sweat streamed down my back, saturated my knickers and pooled in my padded bra.

Blistering in the open with no shade in sight, I was out of breath and in love with Namibia, the desert and the trails. I like nothing more than physical action to get my adrenalin flowing, heart pumping and a big smile spreading across my face. Much of my time cycling through Africa had been a test of endurance; yet on a motorbike, the challenging days I thrive upon had been few and far between.

Some people consider riding through sand purgatory. For me, this was the gateway into the remotest parts of Kaokoland, my kind of heaven.

I stopped to wait for Kieran. He looked like hell: red-faced, steaming like a vent about to blow. He crawled up behind me. He never coped well with the heat and his bike handled terribly in the sand. He was dispirited and ready to turn back. I passed him my water bottle and waited as he gulped it down and caught his breath.

There was no reason to believe the sand would continue; a few kilometres around the next bend, the trail could return to solid, hard-packed earth. I wasn't going to give up easily.

The trail did improve as we followed a dried-out riverbed, noticeable only by the line of green scrub in the otherwise sparse landscape. When we stopped because it was time to camp, we looked down at the trail and saw lion tracks. *Hmm … perhaps we'll ride further before camping.* Of course, lions roam far, and I couldn't say when this one had passed through.

We found a flat area in the shaded cluster of three camel thorn trees. I climbed up the riverbank and gazed at the view until the sun dropped below the horizon. Then, looking over my shoulder into the bush behind, I wondered if a lion could be lurking out of sight. It was time to retreat to the tent for the evening.

'I wonder whether that lion is nearby?' I said to Kieran in a quiet tone that shattered the silence as we lay in our sleeping bags.

'I dunno. Let's hope not,' he replied.

'Here kitty kitty kitty …' I whispered. 'Here kitty kitty …' I teased.

'Sshhh … stop it!' Kieran growled and gave me a sharp shove in the arm.

When I travelled alone, I often slept lightly, one ear open and alert to unusual sounds. If a lion was on the prowl, it seemed better to be awake and alert to defend myself should it attack rather than be ripped from my dreams and torn apart.

'OK, g'night!' I said with a smile and rolled over to sleep, content that Kieran would be my ears.

Or so I thought.

A sound jolted me awake in the middle of the night. Kieran was snoring. His rhythmic rumble resounding through the darkness didn't usually disturb me these days. Instantly alert, eyes open, not moving a muscle, I listened intently between breaths.

There it was: rustling in the bush behind.

Then silence. Except for Kieran's snores.

That rustling of the bush again, louder, prolonged.

Whatever the animal, it came crashing and barging, then stumbling and tumbling down the bank behind and ran heavy-hoofed onto the flat riverbed where it raced frantically in tight circles, slipping in the sand and tripping on rocks, galloping away, galloping back. Then it stood, exhausted. *Definitely not a lion ... Maybe being hunted by one?*

The silence returned. Except for Kieran's snores.

Then the animal snorted and started up again, wild and frenzied, hooves kicking rocks as it circled. Snorting, panic-stricken, it raced off.

The silence returned. Even the snoring had stopped.

'Did you hear that?' I whispered.

'Yep,' Kieran replied.

'What do you think it was?'

'I don't know, but I'm not going out to check.'

I peered out the tent porch but the stars sparkling in the inky-black sky couldn't tell me either. A lone, large antelope? Of all the images I conjured up, an oryx seemed to match the sounds. But what had spooked it? I was more concerned about the predator I couldn't hear. Gradually the stillness of the night changed from unnatural and unnerving to a peaceful serenity that wrapped me in a blanket, smothering the fear that darkness wreaks upon the mind.

A terrifying squeal echoed along the riverbed and transformed into a hair-raising wail.

Then silence. Except for my pounding heart.

Scenarios played in my mind. Perhaps the oryx had been caught in a man-made trap. I couldn't help thinking about the lion tracks we'd seen. At least it wouldn't be hungry for us now.

'Here kitty kitty ...' I dared to whisper.

Kieran was not impressed.

With daylight, I wandered through the riverbed. A fresh trail of sandy scree down the steep slope showed where the animal had fled the bush. The only prints were of a small antelope like a springbok. Noises always seem amplified in the dead of night. The animal's hooves had kicked up the soft sand as it wheeled about and fled. I couldn't find any big cat's spoor, but one could have stalked through the bush. I'll never know for certain what happened. I wished I could identify and read tracks reliably.

While searching the ground for clues, I watched large black ants with copper abdomens march across the flat sand. A striped skink scurried off, then stopped, head motionless, black eyes wide and long thin tail erect. I crouched down slowly to take a photo, then stepped away quietly.

As we sat by the tent sipping tea, a head emerged from behind the trees. In long, unhurried strides, a giraffe ambled by, pausing to look at us and then, curiosity satisfied, continued its journey.

Me and Kieran looked at each other. *Cool.*

Yeah, this is the Africa I love.

We were happy. The challenging terrain and trails were helping to reconnect us, and the Namibian wilderness was feeding my addiction, supplying me a dose of freedom.

We rode into Puros, a collection of simple concrete buildings spaced well apart from each other in the dust. We quickly filled our water bag to see us through to the next day, then continued west.

The land of soft sandy shades became harsher, darker and rockier. Even the grass thinned to nothing on the barren land. A shabby red windsock hung lifeless from a wooden pole. I couldn't fathom why an aircraft would need to land here.

Impatient yet daunted to ride deeper into this lifeless void where a breakdown could be fatal, we rode into this dead zone bounded by wind-battered ridges in bruised shades of purple. When we stopped to drink water from our precious supply, I almost dared not cut the Serow's engine in case it wouldn't restart.

We edged parallel to the desolate shoreline of the Skeleton Coast only thirty kilometres away, the hills receding until the faint trail snaked across a featureless faded-grey land. In the distance, I saw a trail of lingering dust from a 4x4 like a horizontal smoke signal; we weren't the only ones venturing here.

We passed a sign with 'Welcome to Puros Conservancy' painted on a vertical slab. The line drawing of an elephant seemed misleading. Surely no animal can survive where nothing grows. *What is there to conserve?* There are few places uninhabited, almost untouched by humans, like this remote corner of Namibia. Could this wasted desert be one of the last great wildernesses on earth? That is worth conserving.

Away from the coast, a few low scrubby bushes appeared along another ancient riverbed. Then a tree ... a small building ... a hand-painted sign saying 'Orupembe Shop 1. Cool Beer'. My eyes lit up and I licked my parched lips.

A buxom Herero lady met us at the doorway to her small Coca-Cola red painted concrete shop. Her colourful long-sleeved, full-length voluminous print dress with puffed shoulders, narrow waist, petticoats and sweeping hemline appeared an unusual fusion of African vibrancy and Victorian-era formality.

This dress style, influenced by the wives of German missionaries and colonists who came to Namibia in the early twentieth century, has become an important symbol of Herero culture, a reminder of the unsettling and tragic history of genocide by the Germans, which almost wiped them out.

Following uprisings against colonial rule by the Herero and Nama people, a German general ordered the annihilation or expulsion of the indigenous people. Unarmed men, women and children were marched into the desert where, prevented from leaving, they died of exhaustion and dehydration.

Rather than seeing the dress as a reminder of European oppression, the Herero women have modified it to create a traditional fashion that they fiercely defend and proudly wear. The accompanying horizontal horned headdress acknowledges the wealth and status symbol of cows to these traditional cattle-herding pastoralists.

The lady greeted us warmly and stepped inside, turning her head sideways so the wide horns of her hat fit through the door. Behind the counter, a few shelves stocked a limited supply of cooking oil, tinned sardines and Omo washing powder. She handed us two glass bottles of ice-cold Coke from the fridge, which we gulped down greedily. Then we bought another round to savour.

At the borehole and holding tank, men sat under a tree and cattle lingered. We refilled our water bags and bottles, then continued riding. Springbok watched from a distance, stationery in the shade of acacias, and a trio of ostriches ran across the track in long-legged strides. We passed traditional huts of semi-nomadic Himba. The low dome structures of mopane branches, some plastered in mud, had a battered oil drum and jerrycan at the entrance with blankets hung from branches stuck into the ground.

As the sun dropped, we stopped to camp. For the second night in a row we spotted big cat tracks in the sand. We were too tired to ride further. The long, hot, strenuous days had taken their toll. The cat was probably long gone.

'Here kitty kitty …' I called before bed.

Kieran was unimpressed.

We both slept through to daybreak. The only visitors to our tent were harmless purple-hued armoured ground crickets.

The track, taking a more direct route eastwards, criss-crossed the sandy Hoarusib River, another ephemeral river. Kieran usually rode in front, so I waited until certain he'd make it through the sand before plunging in. I didn't want to have to stop because getting moving again was always so hard. I could also park the bike without the side stand sinking into the ground in case he needed a helping shove, his bike weighed down more than mine.

When my Serow slowed in the sand, the rear wheel sinking, I'd leap off and run alongside, slipping, sliding, stumbling and determined not to stop. With throttle open and engine squealing, we'd pop up onto more solid terrain, sweat streaming down my face.

Makalani palm trees shooting straight up with their haloes of fan-like leaves gave the impression of being on a tropical island beach of blinding white sand, except for the lack of water. Fine dust lingered in the air and stuck to my clothes. Usually in Kieran's dust trail, too hot to ride with my visor down and because my sunglasses didn't fit under my helmet, my eyes became irritated and painfully sore. I overtook and rode ahead. I preferred riding faster on these trails anyway and felt the rush of freedom as I powered on at my own pace.

Before venturing further to attempt Van Zyl's Pass, we stopped to rest and resupply in Opuwo. The capital of the Kunene region, which encompasses Damaraland, Kaokoland and the Skeleton Coast, is where cultures congregate, converse and trade.

Lithe men in sandals, loose shirts and knee-length skirts stopped to chat, leaning casually against their wooden stick that every herder carries. Boys raced down the road and girls giggled; a stray dog slunk by in the shadows of the buildings. Ochre-covered bare-breasted Himba women walked past businessmen in suits. On the litter-strewn bare-earth backstreets, women sold produce under makeshift market stalls of wooden frames and wind-torn tarpaulin to shelter from the sun, and Herero men slaughtered sheep, the thick red rivulets of blood staining the earth.

The buildings were the same colour as the grey dust that spilled onto the tarmac and covered my bare feet as I strolled down the pavement in flip-flops. On reaching the main road by the fuel station, I headed to the supermarket for junk food I'd been deprived of and to the bottle store for Windhoek beer. The bank always had a long queue outside, money from the ATM never guaranteed.

Immediate needs attended to, I returned to the campsite to do my laundry. My bike clothes needed washing. Usually I cleaned them whenever I got chance for a shower, the water draining out a murky brown, which countered the smell but never got out the ingrained dirt completely.

'Do you think these need a wash?' I called to Kieran, bike jeans in hand. They could almost stand up by themselves. A cloud of dust enveloped me as I bashed them with the palm of my hand. The one set of clean clothes I was wearing was soon smeared in dirt.

'Ah, that'll do. Good for another five hundred kilometres,' I choked, giving the jeans another rough shake, more dust rising up. Washing my bike gear was as futile as sweeping the streets every morning, as every shop owner did on their patch of pavement. I never understood why when within an hour, all that work would come undone, the streets as dusty as ever.

I planned a circular route via Van Zyl's Pass enabling us to leave excess baggage at the campsite. We packed the bikes, loads lightened to essentials only – spare parts and tools, camping gear, food and water – to give us the best chance of making it through the pass.

As the pass is only supposed to be driven from east to west, we first travelled northwest to Okongwati, then onto the rocky jeep track. The bike jumped, jerked and jolted, the handlebars rattling and shaking. My forearms burned with the effort of keeping hold, and when the searing pain of tennis elbow became too great and the bike pulled violently to one side, I could only let go, the Serow dropping suddenly to the floor as though struck by a hunter's arrow. I began to crumble under the strain, doubts threatening to overwhelm me. I had needed more days to rest, but there wasn't time to hang around if we wanted to make full use of our Angolan one-month visas.

Kieran came to help as I struggled to lift the bike a third time. *Perhaps the Yamaha guy was right and Van Zyl's is too hard for me …*

'I'm not sure I can do this,' I confessed to Kieran.

How dare I think of giving up already!

'Perhaps I just need rest. We should camp soon,' I added. 'It's getting late anyway.'

71

Kieran helped banish my doubts and a good night's sleep renewed my energy, enthusiasm and optimism.

The pass is named after Ben van Zyl, the Commissioner for Kaokoland in the 1960s. He used game trails to mark a shortcut route between Otjitanda and Marienfluss. The 'road' was constructed in four months by a team of twenty labourers using hand tools. If van Zyl had travelled it in his Model T Ford, surely we could manage on our Serows. They were capable of going almost anywhere.

Getting down the pass is the hard part.

We reached the first steep section with jagged rocks to negotiate. Two 4x4s caught us up, and we let them go first. I watched with trepidation as they lurched from side to side, inching their way down. Kieran went next, and I walked alongside to offer a helping hand. Then it was my turn. My heart thumped and the muscles in my arms burned, but with Kieran's help holding the rear for stability, I made it onto level ground. We rode on elated, smiling and sweating in the sweltering sun. *That wasn't so bad!*

We took a break at a viewpoint with the golden-hued Marienfluss Valley outspread below. I don't know if it seemed more beautiful because of the difficulty in reaching it, but I thought I could sit and look at that view forever. I'm glad I didn't know then that the trickiest part was yet to come.

By going slow and steady and approaching the trail with patience and teamwork we made it down. With two wheels, we could pick a path through the morass of big rocks and drops and scree. The 4x4s had a rougher time, unable to manoeuvre width-ways for the sheer drop to one side, the trail needing to be repaired using rocks to smooth out the biggest drops.

At the bottom of the pass, we stopped in the shade together with the four friends in the their 4x4s.

'Here, have a beer,' one of the guys offered, holding out a bottle. 'You deserve it.'

'Thanks,' I said, not one to turn down an ice-cold, thirst-quenching beer.

Kieran politely refused, more concerned about dehydration, and supped from his bottle of lukewarm water instead.

I took several long gulps. 'Ahh ...' I exhaled, the cool liquid tracing through me, and I smiled. If only the Yamaha guy could have seen us.

'You should write your name on a rock,' the lady suggested. 'Here, use this. It weathers the wind, dust and rain better than pen or paint.' She handed me a small bottle of bright pink nail varnish. I'm not one to plaster my presence along the road either with stickers or painted rocks, but it seemed discourteous not to, so we added our named rocks to the pile.

The sandy trails in the valley were harder work than the pass. Eventually the ground rose towards Red Drum Pass. Named for the red oil drum originally put there by Ben van Zyl for fuel storage and resupply when he passed, it now serves as a distinctive way marker at a crossroads seemingly in the middle of nowhere.

The trail gradually improved as we worked our way back to Opuwo, where we collected our stored gear from the campsite before riding north. We thought Epupa Lodge by the Kunene River, which marks the border between Namibia and Angola, would make a comfortable, luxurious rest stop.

Luxury comes at a price. The restaurant was expensive, and there was no shop nearby to buy decent food. Our diet of biscuits and noodles on the trails had been insufficient for the calories expended. My body craved good food. There was no drinking water on tap either. I detest buying bottled mineral water for the plastic waste, never mind the cost. Boiling water to drink used our limited camping gas supply. We survived on overpriced beer. In the cold, shady campground under the makalani palms, surrounded by other holidaymakers in their well-equipped 4x4s full of supplies, I missed the searing sun and the solitude.

We rode eastwards, following the Kunene River past Ruacana Falls, through a couple of small towns with donkeys looking dejected and onto Oshakati, the main town near the Angolan border. A dusty campsite next to a modest hotel met all our needs. There was even a washing machine, the first our clothes had seen in five months.

We also soaked and scrubbed all our bike gear – armoured tops, jeans, boots, gloves, even removable foam inserts from our helmets. As suspected, this proved a pointless task when the following day we left town and within ten kilometres were covered in dust thrown up by passing cars along the dirt road.

During the brief period of wearing clean clothes, a 4x4 drove into the empty campground. The British-registered vehicle was the first we'd seen since South Africa. The couple joined us for beers. We enjoyed chatting and laughing with a shared sense of humour as only Brits can appreciate after a long absence from it.

Lizzie and James regaled us with tales of adventure from their last three months driving through West and Central Africa. Kieran mentioned that I'd cycled through that region.

'You're not Helen Lloyd are you?' Lizzie interrupted.

Not again! 'Err … yes, that's me. Why do you ask?'

'We read all your blog posts when planning our trip. We convinced our families that our journey wasn't so crazy by repeatedly saying that if Helen could cycle solo through Africa and be OK, then we'd be fine in our 4x4.'

I laughed. Sometimes the world seemed a very small place.

They said Angola was their favourite country and told us great things about it. We were heading there tomorrow. I couldn't wait.

08.
Iona National Park
Angola

The border crossing was a three-hour chaotic ordeal of misunderstanding or not understanding at all, of being directed with hand signals from one building to another, led by self-appointed fixers with a group of hangers-on who attached themselves to us like sucker fish under the misguided assumption that this was a symbiotic relationship. We passed in and out of the border zone and back onto the streets of Zambia for photocopies of paperwork and to Angola for photos of our bikes. Without our passports, which remained in the hands of the customs officer, I wondered if this was a scam and we'd be arrested and fined for entering the country illegally. Eventually our passports were stamped and temporary import permits issued. Welcome to Angola!

Within kilometres, we passed a rusted tank, abandoned and covered in graffiti beside the road. The 'Danger – Mines!' signs tied to the wire fencing were an immediate reminder to be careful riding off-road and wild camping even though the twenty-seven-year civil war had ended over fifteen years ago. Despite ongoing clean-up efforts, large parts of the country were still littered with landmines.

The guidebook to Angola had mentioned that mined areas were often marked, sometimes by an obvious skull and crossbones sign, other times simply by a tin can upturned on a stick. This struck me as unhelpful since tin cans on sticks were the sort of thing people used to indicate a path or entrance to a property. We agreed it would be prudent to stay in a village for our first night and pulled over at the first opportunity.

The lady behind the shop counter in the small wooden shack was busy serving a queue of young men in jeans and t-shirts. Beer was in high demand. I stood awkwardly and waited. No one acknowledged me, and I suddenly realised I had no idea what to say. I'd started to learn some Portuguese from a phrasebook I'd downloaded. Being able to converse makes for a more fulfilling experience in a new country. My repertoire of Portuguese words didn't yet extend beyond greetings and ordering beer.

Had I been alone, I would have joined the queue and had a drink. Who knows what would have happened next; that's the joy of travelling. But I wasn't alone, and I couldn't bear the prospect of having to attempt conversation and act as translator for Kieran. I lost courage and walked out unnoticed.

Kieran was still sitting on his bike across the road, leaning over the tank in a carefree, relaxed manner. His reluctance to learn any Portuguese gave him a free pass. Having been to Cuba ten years previously and learnt passable Spanish for small talk with taxi-drivers apparently qualified me to converse in Portuguese, Angola's official language. He wasn't going to be any help. I would have to take the initiative, be proactive and take responsibility, exactly like when I travelled alone.

I conjured up phrases in my mind with a mixture of Portu-guess, Spanglish and hand signals, hoping it would be enough to break the ice. With a calming deep breath, I turned and walked back into the shop.

One man was older than the rest with a neatly cut greying beard and kind eyes. He stood at the doorway with an air of authority and commanded respect. This time he told the young men to make space for me at the counter. I explained I didn't need to buy anything by pointing and repeating, 'No, no, no buy,' in Spanish. Then I explained my presence in a shop where all one does is buy things by saying that I was looking for a place to camp.

I think I said: 'I travel with motorbike' (Portu-guess). 'Need place to sleep' (Spanish). 'One night, have …' (Portu-guess again). Then I made a triangle with my arms indicating a tent or rocket ship, held my forefinger in the air meaning one night or a great idea and then placed my palms together against the side of cheek to imply sleep. However my ramblings were interpreted, the kind man suggested I go to the building across the road. I'm fairly sure he said it was a police station and not a psychiatric ward.

'Thank you,' I replied, exhaling to release the built-up pressure within me.

'No problem,' he answered. 'Can I buy you a beer?'

Oh, yes! A beer was exactly what I wanted. My eyes lit up briefly at the chance to get to know these people and this piece of Angola but glazed over with reality. 'Thank you, but no. My friend is waiting,' I replied, downcast.

'I understand,' he said, and I could tell from his eyes that he did, which made me more reluctant to leave. 'Good luck and safe journey.'

Three men in uniform were standing by the road. After giving my finely honed introduction, a junior policeman took me to speak with his commanding officer. We walked down a track around the back of the blue-painted building. Kieran remained with the bikes.

Under the shade of a tree, four well-fed men sat on bamboo stools playing cards on a low table. The big man with his back to us turned around and beckoned me over. With a smile warmed by beer, he invited us to camp on the ground and welcomed me to Angola. He told his junior to make sure we had everything we needed, then turned back to his game.

I returned to collect the bikes and Kieran, then we pitched our tent, cooked dinner and laughed about the lunacy of the earlier border crossing. When it was just the two of us like this, I couldn't be happier. It was unfair of me to compare our journey with how I travelled when alone. I couldn't have it both ways. Besides, I had to consider that perhaps, sometimes, Kieran chose to let me take the initiative because I usually knew how I would prefer to handle a situation.

As evening approached, the sky blackened and the stars emerged. With Orion overhead, I lay back in the tent and listened to familiar laughter and songs ringing through the crisp air as fires were stoked. It felt like I had returned home. *Yes, this is the Africa I love.*

Day 1

The everyday sounds of rural Africa, cockerels crowing and donkeys braying, roused me from a deep, dreamless sleep. I rubbed my dust-encrusted eyes in the dim light. After a relaxing morning coffee, I felt revived and excited for what awaited us on our first full day in Angola.

Unlike attempts the day before, I found someone to exchange dollars with on the black market in the next town. I had gone into a small shack selling motorcycle parts to look for a litre of oil. The young man couldn't help unless I wanted to buy five gallons in one go. I declined, but before stepping out of the doorway, I turned back and enquired where I could change money.

He asked how much I wanted to change and wanted to see the notes. His eyes lit up when I produced a crisp, clean, uncreased one-hundred-dollar bill from my money belt.

'Wait,' he ordered, pulling his phone from his pocket to make a call.

Five minutes later a large, well-dressed lady with a full head of gorgeous black curls arrived. With businesslike efficiency, she simply asked 'One hundred dollars?' to which I replied 'Yes'. From her faux-leather handbag she pulled out a stack of kwanza, the Angolan currency, and handed it to me. I passed her the one-hundred-dollar bill. Deal concluded, we shook hands and she left.

I had heard that Angola was expensive, unaffordable for the budget traveller. I expected we'd always have to camp and cook for ourselves while in the country.

Angola's economy was struggling. The official exchange rates were out of line with street prices. Whereas the banks offered 150 kwanza to the dollar, I got 400 kwanza on the street. By the end of the month the black market value was 600 kwanza to the dollar. Normally when travelling, I get money from cashpoints using my Visa card, but here with dollars in my pocket, I wasn't the pauper I appeared to be in my worn out, dusty bike gear.

Local currency in hand, we could buy supplies. The advantage of having a small bike is its fuel efficiency. I could ride over 700 kilometres on tarmac before refilling the 23-litre long range tank; although in Kaokoland, on rocky hills and through deep sand, the range was nearer 500 kilometres. There are not many places in the world with such long distances between filling stations.

Riding to the coast across Namibe province in southwestern Angola is one of them. In terms of climate, terrain and ecology, Namibe is an extension of Kaokoland and the Skeleton Coast in Namibia, separated only by the Kunene River.

To allow for unknown trail conditions and potential problems, it was prudent to carry extra fuel. We siphoned petrol from the tanks into a couple of large empty Coke bottles and an old four-litre water bag I had packed for such use. Then we topped up the tanks at the petrol station. At twenty-five cents per litre, the cost didn't make a dent in our kwanza cash pile.

Off the busy main road, we crossed a wide river interspersed with rocky pools where children played, jumping and diving and splashing. Women washed clothes. West towards Otinjau, the tarmac turned to a dusty orange laterite track flanked with golden dry grass. Beyond a towering lone baobab tree, the track disappeared into foreboding parched bush under oppressive sun-bleached skies.

It seemed as though anyone who entered would be lost forever to that forest of thorny thickets, trapped, unable to find a way through. Yet I felt drawn in, entranced by the promise of a magical world where every sight and sound and experience would be a first. It was so long since I'd first hoped to travel through Angola, it had become an unreachable, make-believe place in my mind. And now I was here, undaunted by and expectant of who or what I would find. Friend or foe, I'd greet them head-on with a smile and open heart. Grinning, I opened the throttle.

The guardian to this realm was an off-duty police officer. We'd stopped in the first village to get extra water. While I was rummaging in my rucksack for my water bag, the clean-shaven man in chinos and polo shirt walked over, surprised to see foreigners passing this way. With friendly concern, he wanted to make sure we had sufficient fuel, food and water to be safe on our journey. He disappeared with the water bag and returned shortly after with it filled, then he bid us goodbye and good luck. *Let the adventure begin!*

We rode at a leisurely pace, sometimes over hard-packed earth and other times in loose rocky gravel, constantly distracted by the changing landscape as the bush opened up and rocky hillsides rose to the south. The air cooled as we entered a grove of thick trees along a dry riverbed. Makeshift fencing from felled branches suggested a nearby settlement hidden from view. We rested in the shade, drank water and cooled down, then rode on, occasionally passing palisade wooden railings and a circular thatched hut. I never saw anyone.

The trees gave way to golden grasses and low scrub again, a few leafy trees offering elliptical islands of afternoon shade. We stopped where several footpaths through the grass converged on a water pump. Immersed in the ride I'd lost track of time, but the sun was already accelerating towards the horizon, the air cooling noticeably as the light faded.

Two bare-breasted women with braided hair and colourful beads around their necks and ankles stood facing each other on the large concrete block, hands on the large red painted wheel for pumping water from deep underground. They turned the wheel over and over without stopping or breaking sweat, their backs bending and straightening as their arms moved in full body circles. Water gurgled up through the pipe and into a trough where semi-naked children filled containers and washed in the cool clear liquid. A black pig and five piglets trotted over to take a drink from the run-off channel. Three young men sat together talking; one elderly man sat apart in silence.

I considered my irrational anxiety of introducing myself to strangers and asking for a place to stay, which in my opinion far outweighed the small calculated risk of stepping on a landmine. Namibe province has one of the lowest rates of injury and no recorded deaths from landmines. After significant mine-clearing efforts, it's now virtually free of them. Kieran was adamant about not taking the chance.

We rode towards the villagers and turned off the engines. These actions, which usually spark curiosity, were given barely a passing glance by anyone. It seemed odd, although I was unsure why; even my gut instinct, which I often rely on, was uncertain. After only one day in the country, there was still a lot I did not yet understand.

'Do you think we should ask to camp here?' I asked Kieran. If I couldn't trust my instinct, perhaps I could rely on my partner.

'I don't know. What do you think?'

Ugh. 'It's getting late, and we don't know how far the next village is,' I replied with logic. 'If we aren't going to bush camp, we probably need to ask here.' I paused, hoping that he would rise to the occasion and take the initiative. He stared back in silence. 'Do *you* want to ask?'

'You should. Your Portuguese is better than mine,' he replied.

Because I'm trying to learn!

It seemed unlikely that anyone in this remote tribal region would know Portuguese anyway. The trip was beginning to feel less like a joint endeavour and one where I was the guide responsible for its success or failure.

Realising that I would be our spokesperson for the next month, I removed my helmet and walked over to the elderly man with wrinkled skin covering a lean frame and sinewy muscles. He was naked from the waist up except for a chain of blue beads around his neck and

81

several bracelets on his forearms. My eyes were drawn to the knife tucked into his leather belt, which was stitched onto a simple skirt.

I said hello and shook his hand. His blank stare gave away nothing. I tried to ask to speak to the village chief as I had when I'd cycled across central Africa, but I didn't know the right words. It appeared we spoke no common language.

Since communication is predominantly visual, I mimed sleeping in a tent. His poker-faced gaze gave no recognition of understanding. I repeated my act and he remained a living statue of inscrutable countenance. He wasn't blind because the pupils of his eyes were shrunken to pin-pricks by the sunlight. I looked down at his knife and wondered if I should be concerned for our safety. But these were peaceful people going about their regular routines.

I wanted to explain that we wouldn't cause any trouble or intrude in their lives. Instead, I pointed to an area of scrub away from the water pump. 'We put tent there. We sleep now and tomorrow we go. OK?'

I noticed the slightest nod of his head. 'No problem?' I asked, giving a double thumbs up and smiling. 'OK?'

He gave a thumbs up in return, which I chose to interpret as agreement rather than imitation. If anyone took issue later, we could pack up and move on.

We pitched the tent in peace. As darkness approached, everyone dispersed through the dry grass and disappeared into the bush to their homes.

Cycling in West and Central Africa, I'd been viewed as an exotic curiosity and people seemed eager to hear about the world beyond their village or town or country. Here the Herero chose to ignore the march of progress and had no interest in our way of life.

Day 2

Kieran clambered onto the water pump's concrete platform and began turning the wheel round and round and round. Nothing happened. I stood waiting at the trough twenty metres away with the water bag and bottles. Three men wandered over. With no sign of water after five minutes, I asked the men if there was a problem. Have patience, they implied.

'Shall I take over?' I shouted reluctantly, feeling a tinge of guilt at not doing my share of the work.

'No, it's OK, it can't take much longer,' Kieran called back.

Oh good. I wiped my hand over my forehead. A bead of sweat trickled down the back of my neck. The sun was already beating down despite the early hour. No wonder the villagers collected water during the cool hours of dusk. Eventually a gurgling sound rose to the surface and water gushed out. Ten seconds later our water bag was full.

For hours the 4x4 trail weaved across otherwise untouched countryside. Sometimes the trail narrowed and split into separate single track paths. Pick one and hope it ends up where you want.

When researching routes online, I'd found little information on this region beyond a trip report on an adventure bike forum by a group of guys who'd ridden their motorbikes here. They made it sound tough, challenging, a 'real adventure', not something that just anyone like me could do. It took lots of planning and you needed big bikes and be experienced riders to cope with the terrain. I was almost deterred. Perhaps that was the intention.

I'd had similar doubts about riding through Kaokoland, had gone anyway and loved it. I'd struggle through somehow. If I didn't try I'd regret it.

Using my body to absorb the ruts and help the bike twist and turn through the featureless bush, loving every moment, I rode with no thought to the future beyond the next bend. The trail became rougher and was inconspicuous over large slabs of exposed rock. I accelerated up riverbanks and on open stretches where the trail was hard and smooth. Hitting third gear, I could take my eyes off the ground and look at the wide vistas framed by distant hills. Flesh-coloured plants that appeared to be upturned with their roots sticking out and cacti with delicate yellow flowers caught my eye.

I was riding across Namibe like those guys on the forum with replies saying how cool or crazy or tough they were and what an awesome adventure … *Oh yeah, look at me, I'm a tough adventurer too!*

With a warning toot of the horn, a cheap Chinese 125cc motorbike appeared, swerving around a bush onto an adjacent track at the last second to narrowly dodge a head-on collision. The rider and two passengers, squeezed together like segments of a caterpillar, clutching baggage and a jerry can of fuel, smiled as we passed. Somehow the guy at the back managed to free a hand to wave. I laughed, my ego quickly brought into check before it outgrew my battered bike boots. Riding a motorbike was part of everyday life here for some people.

We only passed one village, several houses built in grid formation. A sign indicated that it was a government housing initiative from 2005. Their straight, ordered impersonal alignment and uniformity were at odds with the irregularities of the surrounding natural environment. I had no desire to stop.

With no settlements in sight as dusk approached, Kieran conceded to wild camping. We pushed the bikes through a sandy gully of a small riverbed and rode up the bank onto a flat space in the bush. Old cattle tracks, which suggested we were not far from civilisation, convinced us there were no landmines. It didn't stop thoughts of being blown to smithereens as I scanned the ground and cautiously cleared a space for the tent.

'Hey, what's this? Come here,' Kieran called with a hint of caution that concerned me.

I walked over and peered where he was pointing with a stick expecting to see a metal device.

'Erm, I'm not sure. It looks like some old rag,' I replied. Dusty and sun-faded blue with a regular pattern, the rag had not been dropped but carefully laid out running back and forth like packed sausages.

84

All I could think about were landmines and traps and wondering what other man-made devices could harm us.

'It's not a landmine,' Kieran said and flicked it with the stick.

Mid-air, it sprang to life, the packed sausages whipping out into one long snake.

'Jesus!' We both jumped back.

The snake rapidly slithered away through the undergrowth, the dry leaves crackling noisily against its threshing body.

'Where'd it go?' Kieran asked.

We carefully swept the rest of the area, and I reminded myself to wear boots not flip-flops when I went to pee later.

Day 3
At Iona, the small village at the southern extreme of Iona National Park, we filled up our water bottles from the well in the police compound, then set off in a northerly direction. Two 4x4s passed us. The rangers driving officials on a guided tour would be the last people we saw until we reached the northern park boundary at the end of the day.

The sandy track wound through dry yellow grassland with conical hills towering in isolation. Stopping in the shade of an umbrella acacia, I took off my helmet and armour, the gentle breeze cooling my sweaty skin. Deeper into the park, the thorny acacia bushes disappeared until the only plants on the dry ground were the ancient Welwitschia looking like an invading army of alien organisms on the march. Eventually, even they dispersed when the sand returned and the yellow grass, the only vegetation able to take hold, spread out like a blanket to the horizon of foreboding hills. Jagged rocks, dark and razor sharp, thrust out of the bleached intolerably harsh and inhospitable land.

Beyond, the yellow grassland returned. Soon I was disorientated, weaving between thick acacia bushes that blocked the view. I ducked and dodged my body and pulled an arm to my ribs or shot it up above my head to avoid the thorns; still, they sometimes snagged my armoured jacket.

Wildlife in the park had been decimated during the war, many species wiped out. Apart from several rabbit warrens and fat crickets, I only saw springbok. At first these beautiful antelope, the national symbol of South Africa with a sable coat, distinct dark strip running the length of their body and a pale belly, appeared in ones or twos. Then I sighted large herds numbering at least a hundred. Spooked by the sound of our bikes, they raced off, leaping and bounding with graceful agility, unhindered by the bush, their white tails flashing in the sun. When they reached a safe distance, they stopped and turned their horned heads, staring as we passed.

At the Curoca River, we crossed the cerulean shallows where the water flowed gently between smooth ash grey rocks. The official park entrance was on the other side. Would we be fined because we hadn't bought a ticket? Never mind that this was the only place to buy them.

The tickets cost less than seven dollars each. I handed over the cash and received a receipt. An official receipt! I was gobsmacked. What about bribery and corruption? I quickly thanked the guard, waved goodbye and rode off before he realised his ineptitude in profiteering.

According to our GPS, there was a lodge further on. The last kilometres of energy-sapping sand through the park had been exhausting, but the prospect of a cold beer enticed us to persevere.

The lodge was surrounded by high-wire fencing for keeping animals and people out. The huge entrance gate was padlocked shut. Kieran pulled hard on the wooden stick attached to the end of a long suspended wire, which ran back a hundred metres. The wire rattled and shook, then a bell far behind the rocky outcrop jangled. No one answered. We rang again. Not even a dog barked. I resigned myself to a beer-less night.

We set up camp nearby. The giant boulder rock formations reminded me of Damaraland in Namibia where I'd been warned about hyenas when I had cycled there. *I wonder if there are hyenas here? Maybe there are lions too.*

Curled up in my sleeping bag and certain that Kieran was listening, I whispered into the darkness, 'Here kitty kitty kitty … Here kitty,' and rolled over to sleep.

Day 4

Rousing early in the cool hour before dawn, I pulled my sleeping bag over my shoulders. This darkest hour when the natural world sleeps, the most peaceful part of the day, was the only time I had completely to myself, and I treasured the rare moment. I didn't want to go back to sleep because when I woke again, it would be daylight and I would no longer be alone. But I was too tired and fell asleep anyway.

When I next woke, my eyes gradually adjusted until I could discern the dim outlines of my roll bag and helmet in the corner of the tent with my bike boots and the stove in the porch outside. I could hear Kieran's rhythmic breathing and hoped he wouldn't wake and shatter my precious solitude just yet.

A barking call echoed through the dawn, shattering the silence. I smiled. After hundreds of nights sleeping in the African bush, the raw, wild, distant animal calls no longer scared me but filled me with heart-warming wonder and made me feel like the luckiest person alive to hear such sounds.

Kieran woke instantly. He didn't move, only whispered, 'What was that?'

I didn't know. It didn't sound like a hyena or lion.

'Here kitty kitty!' I called mockingly, my voice sounding like a foreigner to the wilderness.

'Stop it!' Kieran barked quietly.

I giggled. 'Here kitty, kitty, kitty …' I repeated, taunting.

Waah-Hoomph. The call was much closer this time. I lay motionless, silent.

Another animal replied from the opposite direction. Waah-Hoomph. *A leopard, probably.*

A moment later the silence was filled by the high-pitched wailing of several cubs not far off.

The two adults kept calling. As one faded into the distance, the other got louder, closer.

I kept quiet and listened to my pounding heart.

'Not so brave now,' Kieran laughed nervously.

As the sun rose and long shadows stretched across the ground, the calls stopped, and when the sun's rays hit the tent, we felt safe enough to get up and make tea.

We rode through the boulder formations and turned west, crossing the open hard-packed desert. A huge cairn twice the height of our bikes and littered with hundreds of bottle tops was the only visible landmark for miles. Still without beer, we toasted our progress with a couple of juicy oranges and continued.

Sand dunes appeared in the distance, then a grove of palms and a lake surrounded by pink and golden layered sandstone cliffs eroded into beautiful curves. Beyond this colourful oasis, a village of basic corrugated roof mud huts blended into the monotone grey dirt; it looked a depressing place to live. We rode straight through and stopped only when the bikes tyres hit something unexpected: tarmac.

The smooth coastal road looked inviting after the bumpy ride of the last four days. We turned south. Soon cruising in top gear for the first time in five hundred kilometres, the cool sea air felt refreshing. Sand drifts spilled onto the road where small dunes had accumulated. Crumbling buildings spaced every few kilometres were covered with graffiti.

We rode to Tombua, the town at the end of the road. Beyond, there is nothing but the desolate Skeleton Coast. The low grey buildings with salt-stained windows, shut shops and dusty roads gave the impression that, on the edge of nothingness, the town had been forgotten. Meandering through the quiet streets on this sleepy Sunday afternoon, we found an open bar and bought beer. At twenty-five cents a can, it did little to reduce the size of our kwanza stash.

We refuelled the bikes at the new petrol station and rode north, back the way we'd come. In an old quarry near the dried-up Curoca River, we found a sheltered place to camp. We cracked open the cans of ice-cold Cuca beer – our first in Angola – and celebrated what had been an amazing introduction to the country. I couldn't wait to see more.

09.

Amigos da Picada
Angola

Leaving the coastal palm plantations behind, we turned inland. In the hazy distance, the highlands of Huambo reared up, the outline against the blue sky like the badlands of American western movies. The road made an arrow straight line across the dry savannah plain, then wound through increasingly lush forested foothills with hairpin switchbacks leading ever upwards. Where the hillside had been reinforced to prevent landslides, the concrete walls were covered in bright graffiti art. Up and up we went to the Leba Pass at 1,845 metres above sea level and there, in the cool, fresher air of the altiplano, we rode through agricultural fields and villages towards Lubango. A towering arms-wide Statue of Christ, gleaming white, overlooked the city sprawl in the valley bowl. Unlike the famous Christ the Redeemer in Brazil's Rio de Janeiro, this one's face is pockmarked with bullet holes and missing a few fingers despite restoration.

Beyond the N'gola brewery and Coca-cola bottling plant, we rode up to the flat volcanic rock plateau on the edge of the Serra da Leba escarpment. An abandoned ice-cream van in the large parking area suggested a popular weekend recreation place once. Today it was deserted except for a bored uniformed security guard and some birds flying around the exposed cliff-face. During the war, rebels and deserters plummeted to their deaths here with the aid of bullets. Wandering over the rocks, staring into the hazy distance and peering down the massive vertiginous fissure to the bottom of the cliffs, I felt vulnerable. No one would ever know if you slipped and fell.

The main route to the capital, Luanda, goes via the coastal towns of Benguela and Lobito. We descended from the altiplano to warmer, more arid land sprouting many baobabs. Near the coast,

90

the bush became scarce until only hard grey earth remained, harsh and uninviting. Isolated mud houses in cordoned compounds first appeared on the fringes of coastal Benguela, then agglomerations of houses formed villages. By the time street lighting appeared, the road was lined with automotive and Chinese construction business premises. The town was bustling, the roads busy, new buildings were being erected and megastores offered all modern conveniences. We stopped and shopped at Shoprite, the multinational supermarket chain familiar to us from South Africa and Namibia. In stark contrast, dilapidated colonial architecture from another era hid behind corrugated tin fencing in the shadows of palms and acacias along the seafront.

We rode on thirty kilometres to Lobito and through town to the Restinga sand spit lined with Art Deco buildings, cafes and bars. While stopped at the far end, a polished black 4x4 cruised around the roundabout and pulled up next to us. A good-looking guy with short hair and stylish sunglasses leant out the window.

'Hey man, you guys OK? I don't mean to bother you, but I'm a fellow biker. Bikers, we're all friends, right man? Are you looking for a place to stay? Maybe you're heading to Zulu right now.' The guy spoke fast with a smooth American accent without taking a breath as though he hoped that by talking rapidly he'd have more time in life to do everything he wanted. 'You can sleep there. Lots of foreigners camp on the beach.' He paused momentarily, raised his sunglasses onto the top of his head and thrust his arm out the window, then added, 'I'm Hugo.'

We shook hands.

'Have you heard of Alpha?' he continued.

'Er ... no,' I replied.

'Alpha's my bar. It's close by, on the beach too. You're welcome to stay at Alpha if you like ...' he paused again. 'Maybe you'll stay at Zulu? It's a good place too. But you're welcome to camp on the beach at my bar. Lots of people with motorbikes do that. Well, maybe you have plans. I don't mean to disturb you. Wherever you stay – Alpha, Zulu, somewhere else – I invite you for a beer at my bar, on me. You like beer, yes?'

I laughed. 'Yes.'

'OK, good. I'll leave you now to decide for yourselves, but see you later.'

With that, he pulled his sunglasses back over his eyes and drove off, the black 4x4 speeding off down the Restinga.

We had a beer at Zulu first, then went to Alpha for another and decided to stay, relaxing in the cool shade of the palm trees. Two beers turned to three, then Hugo arrived, and I quickly lost count as he did most of the talking and we did most of the drinking.

A lot of people rode motorcycles in Angola, predominantly small Chinese and Indian imports that are cheap to buy and cheap to fix. However, Hugo told us there was a growing scene of motorcycle enthusiasts who rode everything from Yamahas to Harleys and Ducatis.

'I run the motorcycle club in town,' he said. 'There's an even bigger club in Luanda called the Amigos da Picada with around 300 members. I am going there this weekend to meet up with Lilio, the club president.'

My ears pricked at the name. 'Say again?' I asked.

'Lilio Almeida. We are good friends,' Hugo replied.

The friend of a friend who had provided the letter of invitation for our visa application was the same Lilio Almeida. I'd had no idea he even rode a motorcycle. Now it all made sense.

The day we expected to reach Luanda, we stopped for a short lunch break by the roadside.

'I should message Lilio. Can you remind me when we get online?" I said to Kieran. 'It'd be great to meet him in Luanda. We can pay him for the letter of invitation.'

A truck pulled up alongside us. The driver also loved to travel and wanted to check whether we needed assistance in his country.

'I also ride motorbikes. I'm a member of a motorcycle club in Luanda.' the driver said proudly.

'Ah, the Amigos da Picada!' I interrupted.

'You know of it?' He asked, surprised.

'Yes, we were talking about it in Lobito with Hugo, the president of another ...'

'You know Hugo!'

'I don't suppose you know Lilio Almeida? He helped us get our visas. We hoped to meet him, but I only have his email.'

The driver was distracted answering his mobile. 'Yes, I know Lilio,' he replied to me, then chatted with the caller, explaining he was on his way now but had stopped to meet some foreign motorcyclists.' Then he handed me the phone. 'It's Lilio.'

Sometimes the world felt like a very small place.

———

The wide, multi-lane highway into Luanda was chaotic, noisy and congested. Traffic flowed freely without the need for traffic lights and stop signs, dangerous only if you tried to deviate from the surrounding flow. I invariably followed Kieran as he had the GPS, but he stubbornly refused to adapt his European riding style to more 'African' ways. I often feared one of us would be hit, and he always queued patiently in traffic, a model law-abiding citizen. What's the point when you can filter, weave in and out, rather than sit in the sweltering heat, sweating in your bike jeans astride a boiling hot engine, breathing the polluted air?

We waited amongst the stationary cars and *candongeiros*. Taxi drivers gave us thumbs-ups and ladies in the back of minibuses took photos. Several motorcyclists passed us on small Chinese bikes, big BMWs and Ducatis, the riders giving a nod and smiling.

We headed to the yacht club at the marina, which allowed overlanders to camp on their grounds for free. We couldn't afford an hotel in the capital. Lilio turned up soon after we arrived. Towering over us, he cut a much sharper image in his office suit than we did in our dusty jeans. He had popped out of work to greet us and invite us to the Amigos da Picada's club meet that evening.

We pitched our tent under the shade of some trees overlooking the gleaming white boats in the marina. Across the bay, a skyline of high-rises lined the Marginal. Tired from the long day, we lay down to rest in the tent.

'Hello? Sorry to disturb you,' a voice called.

I peered out.

'My friend messaged me earlier. He saw you on the way in and sent me a photo with the caption "Look at the only two educated bike riders in Angola – queuing in traffic". Whenever I hear that there are overlanders in town, I like to welcome them, so I come to the yacht club because that's where you usually stay; although, white foreigners are not hard to find in this city.'

We joined George and his partner for a beer at the bar. He gave us his home address and said we could stop by any time. If he was at work, the cleaner would let us in. We could have showers, do our laundry, make use of the free wi-fi. We spent the best part of the next day revelling in the comfort of his home and drinking espressos.

The hospitality shown by George was more than matched by the Amigos da Picada. Their usual club premises were being renovated, so we met some twenty other members in the dimly lit street outside for one of their informal gatherings held every evening. Across the road, we got beer on tap from the burger van and talked bikes and travel. During the coming days we met many bikers, who took us to sample the local fish on the Ilha do Cabo and showed us Luanda's sights. The hospitality of these apparently tough guys in their leather jackets and waistcoats was humbling and generous.

The club's mechanic did our bike maintenance and repairs. In a yard full of scrapped Jeeps, he worked using our tools to change the oil and clean the filters. While the tank was removed for checking the valve clearances someone noticed wear on the cylinder head side cover of my bike. The oversize tank had been rubbing against it, exacerbated by the last six weeks of rough terrain. He cut a piece from an old tyre that was lying around and attached it with cable ties to the frame, raising the tank clear of the engine. I was thankful our bikes were getting so much attention.

My bike had been handling badly since Swakopmund when Kieran had greased the headset bearings. I had to use excessive force to turn the handlebars from the centreline which resulted in oversteering. I had mentioned several times that it didn't feel right. Initially the headset had been loose, the handlebars wobbling as we rode out of town. When I'd stopped to tighten it, Kieran gave it another good yank. Then the stiff handling began as we rode up the Skeleton Coast. Kieran was at a loss as to the problem after making doubly sure the headset was tight. He had got defensive when I later wanted to take it apart.

My knowledge of motorbike mechanisms might have been inferior, but a part of my job as an engineer had been failure investigations and root cause analysis. I'd explained that the steering had been fine before he had worked on the headset, so logic suggested that the problem was with the headset. Unfortunately, he took this as a slight on his work. He joked again that the closest I'd got to being an engineer was shaking hands with one once; although, it had stopped sounding like a joke a long time ago. With an argument about to erupt, I gave up. I could handle a temperamental bike better than a temperamental boyfriend. Over time, I'd adapted my riding to compensate until it had become the norm.

When the mechanic asked if there were any other concerns, I casually mentioned the issue. He raised the front end of the bike and forced the handlebars from side-to-side. 'How long have you ridden like this?' he asked, horrified.

'For about three-and-a-half thousand kilometres,' I replied.

He raised his eyebrows in surprise, then undid the headset bolt, wiggled the handlebar and screwed the bolt down again. 'It was done up far too tight. It will ride like a different bike now.'

I kept my thoughts to myself.

———

On our last night in Luanda, we joined the Amigos for farewell beers at the burger van.

Lilio pulled me aside. 'Have you got a moment? There's something we need to have a talk about, me and you.' He spoke as though I were in trouble but his smiling face suggested otherwise.

'Yes, and there's something I need to talk to you about. Me first,' I said. 'I wanted to thank you for arranging the letter of invitation. We really appreciate it and love Angola. We owe you money. How much was the letter?'

'Oh no, don't you try that. You're in trouble, miss.' Lilio smiled. 'I hear that you paid the mechanic yesterday.'

'Of course,' I interjected.

'Yes, and you weren't supposed to. Here's the money back.' He held out the notes in his hand.

'No way. He needs paying for his time.' I shook my head.

'And he will be, but not by you.'

'I'm not taking it,' I said adamantly. For a moment we were locked in a stalemate.

'OK, fine. You win.' Lilio broke away.

'Good. So how much do I owe you for the letter?'

'We agreed you only had to pay me if you didn't visit, but you are here. You can't go back on a deal.'

That wasn't how I remembered it. 'OK, fine,' I conceded. 'Can I at least get a round of drinks for everyone?'

'OK, a deal.' We shook hands and smiled. Then Lilio added, 'But we are buying your drinks after that.'

I laughed. It was very difficult to part with cash in this country.

10.
Heart of Africa
Angola

Angola is a country of two halves: the coastal region made rich from oil and the rural east. As we left the urban sprawl behind, the forest grew thick and tall. Vines and creepers covered bushes and trees. Only the baobabs were big enough to break through. The road became badly potholed with craters that could swallow a car, making progress slow as we manoeuvred around and in and out of them. Then the forest thinned to an endless nondescript, arid miombo bush.

Tourist sites in Angola are few and far between, but we did detour a short distance south to the huge black rocks of Pungo Andongo, ancient geological conglomerates weathered by the wind and rain.

A place of myth and importance, Pungo Andongo served as the capital of the Kingdom of Ndongo, whose most celebrated ruler was Queen Nzinga in the seventeenth century. It is said that while bathing in a brook, she was seen by soldiers and fled, leaving behind her footprints in the rock. I didn't find any embedded footprints, although I did spot several cartridge cases. We didn't venture off the solid rocks for fear that there could be active mines.

Most Angolan National Parks are inaccessible to tourists with no information, tours or places to stay, the infrastructure broken, not to mention the land mined and wildlife populations decimated from war and human encroachment. I had hoped to visit Cangandala National Park close to our route. Mel, who we'd met in Hoedspruit, had told me it was founded to protect the endemic giant sable antelope. She had previously worked with a biologist who was heavily involved with their conservation. Mel gave me his contact details and I emailed him, optimistic that he might show us some of the park and his work, but unfortunately he was in Portugal at the time.

Instead we visited Calandula Falls and watched the 400-metre wide Rio Lucala plummet in a torrent of white water over a hundred metres into a pool spanned by a double rainbow. On the opposite side of the river, the shell of a former hotel peeked out of the tangled tropical confusion of trees and creepers.

Reminders of the war seemed to be everywhere. Armoured battle tanks overlooked a bridge and were abandoned beside the road; another sat neglected in a field. The remains of a rail bridge jutted into a river with a half-submerged oil tank car rusting in the murky water, the cylinder punctured with shrapnel wounds big enough to climb through. The rail wheels had been blown off and lay in the dusty grass.

During the midday heat of tropical Africa, I'd always seen children splashing in the rivers and under bridges, except where crocodiles were prevalent and, here, where unexploded mines remained a threat.

I had wanted to take the smaller roads to the south but was strongly advised by several of the Amigos da Picada to avoid them as they were so sandy. That it would be challenging and more of an adventure only encouraged me. Hard work, going slow and riding long hours didn't bother me.

Assessing other people's judgements of road conditions was always difficult. I could not easily dismiss the Amigos' advice since many had travelled extensively throughout their country. However, all had large, heavy bikes that struggled in the sand. We'd already made it through Kaokoland and Namibe. How much harder could it get?

Kieran was reluctant and reminded me how badly his bike handled in the sand and that the clutch was slipping again. Since he'd first come off his bike in Lesotho, he seemed to use the slipping clutch as a convenient excuse, particularly if he struggled more than me.

Why hadn't he got it replaced when his bike was in the workshop in Windhoek or when he was doing bike maintenance in Swakopmund? Both cities had Yamaha shops that could get parts for the next day.

Years ago when I was cycling in DR Congo, I had been persuaded to take the easier and safer route to Lubumbashi rather than head directly east as I had wanted. 'You'll have an adventure whichever route you take,' Charlie had said (I'll tell you about Charlie soon enough). I remembered that sentiment years later when I made the decision to cycle the Kolyma Highway in Siberia rather than the tougher, riskier route north over the snow-covered tundra. It was true. Adventure lies in every direction.

So we rode east towards Saurimo on the main road connecting Luanda with DR Congo. Then we turned south to Luena. The thin layer of tarmac laid atop the earth with no foundations had crumbled at the edges and sunken into ruts from the weight of trucks, the main albeit infrequent traffic. The dry miombo woodland rolled on endlessly. Trails of smoke from bush fires wafted into the hazy air, the bush intentionally burned to produce charcoal and to clear it for agriculture.

Sometimes smoke billowed across the road. The crackling noise of dry undergrowth burning rapidly was disconcerting. We'd dash through with visors down to shield our eyes and minimise smoke inhalation. I could feel the heat through my armour as flames leapt into the air and lashed out like searing tendrils in the cross-wind.

We camped in small villages. Whether beside a shop or within the wire-fenced compound of a policeman's home, we were warmly welcomed and brought cans of Cuca beer, bottles of Fanta and given fresh pineapple as gifts. We finally succeeded in spending money in Saurimo, the last major town before the DR Congo border. The black market economy made us feel like kings.

This region is rich in diamonds. They are panned from the rivers by hopeful individuals who come from neighbouring DR Congo with nothing to lose. They are also mined on an industrial scale in open-cast mines by large multinational companies, which bring in foreigners from further afield. Towns rapidly spring up from modest villages. With diamond money fuelling the economy, the roadsides between the concrete shops trading diamonds were filled with stalls and produce.

The town also had decent hotels. Still with a large stack of kwanza but limited days remaining in which to spend it, we could afford the most luxurious one. The fresh white sheets, air-conditioning, TV and en-suite bathroom were all too enticing, never mind a bed! I could count on one hand the number of times I'd slept on a mattress during the last five months of travel. We stayed another night. I spent the day sprawled on the bed day-dreaming.

Lunda Sol reminded me of the mining regions I'd travelled in DR Congo. I reminisced about the people I had met and wondered if I could return. I always said I would go back. How were the friends I'd made and what were they doing? We had stayed in touch sporadically for several years, but I'd not heard from any of them for some time. I naively imagined that neither they nor the country would have changed, but situations regarding security can rapidly deteriorate in Africa, particularly in places like DR Congo where regional stability is fragile.

Kieran had become so embedded in my life over the last two years that I hadn't met up with any of my friends without him coming too. Sometimes it felt like I didn't have my own life any more. Over time, I simply assumed he would be beside me in anything I did. Only my memories from before I knew him belonged to me alone. They were my escape and refuge. I wanted to hold onto those feelings of being single, independent and self-sufficient that I'd had when cycling through Africa.

I'd already shown Kieran many places I'd been. Couldn't I keep DR Congo for myself? If we went there together now and met with the friends I had made, I feared his presence would tarnish my precious memories. Perhaps I was being selfish.

100

And there was Charlie. How could Kieran with his insecurities ever be ready to meet the first man I fell in love with? It was an irrational, all-consuming, inexplicable love.

Charlie was a planet orbiting the DR Congo star, and I was an asteroid travelling through space whose trajectory happened to come within his field of gravity. I was unable to stop myself being pulled in. We circled the star together until I was knocked off course, ejected from his orbit to continue my journey. A piece of me had broken up in that violent wrenching apart of two powerful entities attracted to one another by an unseen force. Pieces of my head and heart fell from space into DR Congo's core where they continued to burn. Initially hot and bright, they were now little more than gently glowing coals; all they needed were a light breath of air over their surface to reignite my burning desire and set fire to my whole world again. The broken fragments left me with scars, reminders of the love I felt.

It could never have worked between us. We were two fiercely independent individuals living in different worlds whose paths once crossed. It is strange because even if Charlie and I had led compatible lives, we were not right for each other. We fought as hard as we loved. It was exhausting and exhilarating. Neither of us had the power to tear ourselves away from the other, even though I think we both knew it could never work. In the end, it was other people that forced us apart.

Before Charlie, any romantic notion of love came from movies and books. I had thought it was all fiction, although a part of me always clung to the hope that it was real. And I used to think that, if it did exist, nothing else mattered.

We had remained connected emotionally by an invisible thread over thousands of miles, but once I passed beyond Charlie's gravitational pull, I could look back rationally on our experiences and my feelings. I concluded: yes, love is beautiful, but it is not always worth the hurt and the pain, the difficulties and impossible decisions, and sometimes there are other forces beyond our control that prevent love from flourishing.

This realisation, together with my later experiences in Siberia, led me towards a relationship with Kieran. During the winter I spent cycling solo in the Russian Far East, I had struggled at times with my sanity in the face of, ironically, so much time alone. I met Kieran soon after I returned from Siberia. He was great company, which I had sorely missed after so long adrift in the wilderness.

I didn't go looking for a relationship, didn't particularly want one, but I got together with Kieran anyway. I let 'us' happen because it felt good, so I figured why not. I fell in with Kieran; I don't think I fell in love with him. I naively thought that by holding back on that last word I was protecting myself from getting hurt again.

I was, however, in love with the us that enjoyed doing stuff – hiking, biking, travelling, laughing, joking, drinking, eating – together. Every time we met up was an adventure, whether heading down to Cornwall on our motorbikes for a week, walking part of the Thames Path, or travelling around Wales in my van. I never tired of the experiences, and I loved sharing them with Kieran.

Now I longed for some time alone but whichever way I turned he was there. I knew that if I suggested again going my own way for a short while, he would go the other and that would be it. Despite my yearning for solitude and compromised dreams, I wasn't ready for that.

I opened my eyes and stretched my body across the fresh cotton sheets like a cat upon waking and when Kieran came out of the shower, I mentioned that I was hungry, so we wandered to the hotel restaurant together and ordered some food.

———

On the way to Luena, we helped three guys whose motorcycle had a puncture. They'd found the split in the thin worn tube but had no way to fix it. I don't know how they would have repaired it had we not come along and provided patches and a pump. They seemed unconcerned, used to uncertainty in the same way I never know where I'll be sleeping at the end of the day when travelling. Whereas, once, this may have seemed a daunting prospect, I soon learnt not to worry, knowing I'd always find somewhere to sleep.

When a petty-minded old policeman at a provincial checkpoint took our passports and tried to prevent us from continuing without a payment, I smiled, knowing it'd work out in the end. Two could play this game.

I had encountered many men in West and Central Africa who thought their uniform entitled them to demand additional payments to enhance their meagre salaries. I couldn't blame them, but I refused to give in either. My arsenal of patience and a sense of humour always trumped bribery and corruption. Sometimes, though, you had to stand up to them first with strong words and a forceful demeanour, make them realise that you won't be easily defeated, make them doubt whether the fight is worth it.

My raised voice at the barrier brought out two young officials from the nearby building to see what the kerfuffle with the old policeman was about. They cottoned on quickly; one prised our passports from his sweaty grip, and the other led him away by the arm.

The young officer handed us back our passports. 'I am very sorry. That man is old, from another generation. That is how it was done then. But Angola is a modern, progressive country. That behaviour is no longer acceptable. We do not tolerate it. You must forgive us.'

He wished us a safe journey with grave warnings about the heavily mined region. 'Do not leave the road for any reason.'

This made for inconvenient toilet stops. Men stand by the roadside and pee discreetly. As a woman, I have to squat beside the bike. I could almost guarantee that as soon as I pulled down my pants a kid would appear from nowhere or a car would round the bend. Propriety came second to being blown up.

Too dangerous to wild camp, I'd been trying to gauge which of the several villages we rode past would be good to enquire about camping. Kieran showed no sign of stopping even though it would be dark soon. I indicated and pulled over, ready to suggest that we ask the men sat by the hut with the Angolan flag raised.

The shy introvert in me found groups intimidating to approach. I prefer to struggle linguistically in front of a single patient, understanding person.

Then a lady marched purposefully towards us, wiping her hands on her apron and retying the knot around her waist. I took off my helmet and strolled over to her. She greeted me with a warm handshake and two kisses on the cheek, then hugged me as though we were long-lost friends. I asked to speak with the *Soba*, the head man, and was whisked away with our arms interlinked in a shared moment of female intimacy.

Ronda showed us behind her father's hut where we could put our bikes and place the tent away from curious eyes. She sat us on plastic chairs beside her elderly father as honoured guests. His youngest grandchild perched on his bony knee and several others sat around him. We each took a handful of ground nuts from the bowl that was passed round, and when the empty shells littered the dusty ground, one of the teenage girls swept them away. Feeling that our duty as guests had been upheld, I drew the line when a bucket of putrid-smelling fish was offered, happy to explain that we had our own food for dinner, even though it was only instant noodles.

In Luena, the last sizeable town until we reached Zambia, we bought food and fuel, then headed east with the rail line on our left and simple concrete homes and shops to our right. The tarmac road soon turned to hardened earth. Crumbling station buildings lay in ruins and old overturned carriages rusted in the dirt, victims of the war. The railway sleepers had been removed from the line and recycled into bridges across ditches and for fencing in villages. Rusting wheels and engine parts had been placed like garden sculptures beneath palms or beside clusters of flowers.

By late afternoon I was tired and suggested we stop at a clean, well-kept village. Our friendly and peaceful stay with Ronda and her family had boosted my confidence. I led the way. A tall, thin woman emerged from the nearest hut. I removed my helmet and gloves, and we shook hands.

In broken Portuguese, I asked to speak to the soba. As with Ronda the evening before, the lady invited us in without hesitation, indicating that we could stay in her compound. We wheeled our bikes in and sat on the plastic chairs she provided, indicating with hand signals that we should relax. A gentle, unassuming man arrived and sat on another chair opposite us. Then three other elders joined him. All except one were attired in trousers, shirt and suit jacket. Although well-worn, the clothing implied they had self-respect and honour. The other wore a sloppy, grubby t-shirt and ill-fitting sandals cut from old tyres. He took the lead asking us questions.

I struggled to understand him, only a few words decipherable through his slurred drawl. He asked what we wanted. I explained as best I could that we only wanted a place to camp for one night. And then he spoke long and fast to the other men, all of whom were quiet and passive. They said little but spoke calmly and quietly.

The drunk interrogator leant towards me and raised his voice. 'What do you want here?'

I explained again and said we would be gone in the morning.

'What are you doing here?!' he shouted, a bully who ruled by intimidation and threat.

I tried to explain that we were tourists travelling by motorbike because we wanted to see Angola.

'But what are you doing?' he barked.

I described our journey and where we were going, and he asked the same question again and again.

'Is there a problem?' I asked.

'The problem is that you do not speak Portuguese. Why do you not speak Portuguese?' he demanded angrily.

'I am *trying* to speak Portuguese, but I am English.' My Portuguese *was* limited, but that was not the problem. My grasp of the language had improved significantly over the weeks and other people understood me.

Frustrated and tired, the back of my throat constricted as I fought to control my anger and growing upset. I could not let him see me break down; I wouldn't give him the satisfaction. Running out of ways to explain ourselves, I looked to Kieran for help. He shrugged his shoulders; he hadn't learnt any Portuguese.

I tried communicating once more using simple words and hand actions.

'Yes I understand "sleep", "to camp", "one night", "tent",' he growled. His face screwed up, the muscles in his neck taut, and he leant forward aggressively until his face was directly in front of mine. With clenched fist he prodded me in the chest with his forefinger and spat, 'What are you doing here? Explain yourself!'

I stood up, the chair kicking back in the dirt.

Kieran came to my defence. 'Don't you ever speak to my wife like that!' He was furious and commanded in a tone that even the drunk bully couldn't fail to understand.

The tall thin lady, Fernanda, came to me and put her pacifying arm on my shoulder. 'Please sit,' she said calmly and politely.

I took a breath. Finally, I had support and with this small sense of relief, my guard lowered and a tear rolled down my cheek; yet I couldn't help think wryly, *I'm not anyone's wife.*

Fernanda told us to wait and be calm. Then she turned to the drunk elder and fired angry words like bullets, and with both barrels told the other three exactly what for. Admonished, one of them sent for someone who spoke English whilst the others helped push back the growing crowd.

Five tense minutes later, a Zambian man arrived. I had already got out our map of Southern Africa and laid it on the floor. He listened to our story and then to the old man.

'He wants to know where you are going and what is your job?'

I realised the elder had no concept of what a tourist was. I told the Zambian man that we were not here for work but still the same questions were repeated. I despaired, exhausted.

Kieran looked to me, 'What should we do?'

'If it were just me, I would have left a long time ago,' I replied. 'I know it's almost dark, but we should go. This might not be resolved for hours, and I'm not comfortable here.'

'OK,' he agreed.

We started to walk to the bikes but the old man grabbed me by the arm. 'Where are you going?'

'Get off me!' I demanded and pulled my arm away. I feared the situation could quickly become dangerous as the crowd of onlookers pressed in again and voices were raised. They wanted to know what was happening. They didn't want us to leave.

'Please, please,' the Zambian man implored. 'Please, you must stay. It is OK.'

'No,' I replied adamantly. 'It is *not* OK!'

'Please, don't go,' he pleaded, then spoke to the crowd and told them to give us space. The elders took the drunk by the arms and led him away.

Fernanda shepherded us towards her hut. 'Don't worry, you are safe here. My home is your home,' she consoled as I wiped the tears from my face.

Only the one man had an issue. Unfortunately, no one seemed able to allay his concerns. It seemed a shame that one person could have such a disproportionate and negative effect. Human history is littered with such people.

'I'll be fine,' I said, my head pounding, exhausted from being interlocutor, translator and decision-maker all the time.

Realising that I had reached my limit, Kieran made dinner although I had lost my appetite. An hour later, a truck pulled up outside, headlights beaming brightly across the compound, the only illumination except for the stars and a small fire bowl that Fernanda had brought to us for warmth.

Several men in combat fatigues carrying weapons leapt out. One peered into the tent.

What's going on now?

'Your passports,' he demanded.

Here we go again. 'Why? What's the problem?' I asked defensively, already getting out of the tent.

I was greeted by a large man in a smart suit. He was from the local administration. 'There's no problem. I am the communications officer and am here to help,' he said in perfect English. He said he hadn't been sure what to expect when he'd received a call to say there were two unknown people in the village who didn't speak Portuguese and wouldn't say what they were doing. He laughed when we explained about our travels and nodded energetically when the Zambian man explained the confusion.

'You must excuse the old man. He does not understand what tourism is. He doesn't know about the world like you and me. He only remembers the war, when strangers brought trouble.'

The war may have ended fifteen years ago, but it lives on in people's memories. For some, war never ends.

Once the officer had confirmed that we were OK, he gave us his mobile number and email address. 'You must contact me if you have more problems. I will help if I can.'

Kieran thanked him while I smiled and nodded, too tired to fully appreciate his help.

Five hours after arriving in the village, we were able to relax. I went straight to bed but sleep was a long time coming. The next morning we made tea and, as usual, the children and a few adults gathered at a respectful distance to watch us take down the tent, have photos taken with us and wave as we rode away. It was as though I had dreamt the whole saga from the previous evening except I was physically more tired than normal and felt emotionally drained.

Within a few kilometres, the hard-packed track had deteriorated into a sandy mess, but my fears that we were in for a tough day were waylaid when the rickety school bus drove past. The deep sand was short-lived and soon we were eating up the kilometres, not needing to constantly watch the track but able to look around. The wide drainage channel was full of fish, a food source that attracted bird and man alike. Pelicans flew overhead, egrets gathered on bushes, fish eagles assumed their lofty perches atop the infrequent trees, and the ugly marabou storks walked awkwardly through the long grass. Makeshift tables were covered in drying fish, and sun-faded sheets and ragged clothing hung from the bushes under the fierce African sun. Chest-high huts of bent branches covered in dried grass, looking like little haystacks, provided scant shade or shelter. They were a similar construction to the traditional huts of the Himba in Namibia and, as I saw later, of the Turkana in northern Kenya and the Afar in Ethiopia's Danakil.

In Leua we stopped to buy a fizzy drink at the shop. A confident, smartly dressed man approached us. Justin was a truck driver, had learnt English whilst travelling throughout Southern Africa, and wondered where we were going.

'East to Jimbe. It's a remote border post with Zambia,' I explained. Not many people had heard of it.

'I know it well,' he replied. 'I often used to drive that way, but there is a new road to the south via Cazombo. Why don't you take the good road?'

'We like a challenge.' I replied hesitantly, not expecting him to understand.

'Ah, you like adventure!' he exclaimed. 'Then you must go to Jimbe.'

It's not often I am surprised by people, but the most surprising people are often those who have travelled.

'The route is bad. In places, it is as though there is no track at all,' Justin explained. 'On bikes though, you can do it. No problem,' he added with bright optimism and a hint of envy.

When someone says 'no problem' in Africa, they mean 'not impossible'. 'Possible' has many levels of difficulty.

'The route is overgrown and you might think you've gone the wrong way,' Justin continued. 'Don't worry, you haven't, just keep going.'

'OK,' I replied.

'Even when you think you've reached the end of the trail ... keep going.'

'Alright.' I smiled.

'And when you think you're not even on a trail any longer ...' he continued, 'don't worry, you're on the right path. Whatever you think, just keep going. You will get to Jimbe eventually.'

I laughed. If appearing we weren't on a trail meant that we were, it seemed highly likely we were going to get lost in the bush and end up who knows where but probably not Jimbe. *What could possibly go wrong?!*

11.

When the Road Ends

Angola

The shop on the wide main tree-lined boulevard in Luacano was run by Omar Rachid according to the sign painted on the wall. He had a steady stream of customers; kids buying sweets and women buying bread or rice. Surprisingly, Omar spoke excellent English. A young Somali man, he had fled his country because it wasn't safe and moved to Angola, who had welcomed him. He had known no Portuguese when he arrived and said it was tough at the start. Six years later, he felt happy here. With a hard work ethic, he appeared to be thriving.

The only fuel available was sold in glass wine bottles outside one family's home. We bought all sixteen bottles, the tops stuffed with old rags like Molotov cocktails. The young boys took it in turns to empty one after the other into our fuel tanks.

Beyond a rusty armoured tank at the edge of town, the sandy 4x4 track wound like a river through the long grass. Instead, we followed the hard-packed path alongside the railway line, wide enough to walk or ride a motorcycle on. Where the ground had subsided, we inched our way around the large gaps in the gravel embankment.

Stopping for a break at a dusty junction, two motorbikes approached from opposite directions. The men stopped to chat. Based on their gesturing, they were discussing their bikes, Chinese 'Kawaseki' ones with ineffective brakes. One man asked where we were going and where we were from.

I explained. Mr Kawaseki furrowed his brow in confusion and looked at me closer. He turned to inspect Kieran, then our two bikes and proceeded to scour the bush as though something were missing from the equation.

Unsatisfied, he turned to me, 'There are three of you, yes?'

'No, just two' I replied, failing to see how two people and two bikes didn't add up.

'But, you ... you ride?'

'Yes,' I replied matter-of-factly.

A surprised look washed over his face, which then filled with a bright smile. Giving me a high-five, he laughed out loudly and exclaimed, 'Very good! A girl!'

It was the only time that someone expressed surprise at me, as a woman, riding a motorbike. Surprise and respect were common reactions when I had cycled on the continent. I am not sure whether the difference was that attitudes about women had changed or that previously I had been travelling alone.

No other traffic passed apart from three young men walking single-file in full army combats, carrying backpacks and sweating profusely. At the village of Mucusueji we refilled our water bottles while our passports were inspected at a checkpoint. On the opposite side of the rail line, we continued, skirting around the corner of the DR Congo that juts into Angola.

The solid trail degraded into a churned-up sandy logging track through the forest. Sweat soaked through my clothes in the heavy air. Then the forest opened up, and we wound our way across dry land where the bush had been recently burned. Small clumps of vivid green grass were already sprouting through the blackened earth.

Following the pale-veined single track, we rode on to where the fires hadn't reached and tinder-dry grass above head height obscured any view, the grass seeds sticking to our armoured jackets as we brushed through.

'It seems the path has run out,' I remarked. 'I guess we just keep going.'

We felt our way along the bumpy rutted track. Progress was slow and uncertain, but continuing into the unknown was more enviable than turning back. Unexpectedly, we emerged onto the newly tarmacked road that Justin had described. He'd been right, no matter that the track had apparently disappeared, we had gone the right way!

With the dying light of day, I went through the habitual process of stopping at a suitable village to stay. When someone asks how I choose a good village or place to camp, I dismissively call it intuition, nothing more than a neat word to describe the sum of subtle observations and nuances based on an accumulation of past experiences.

I would look at the size and layout of the village and whether it was well kept and clean. Big villages were too intimidating and impersonal; smaller villages were preferable, ideally with a shop, church or school, somewhere I'd likely find a trustworthy person of responsibility. I would observe what the adults were doing and how they spoke to each other, and I'd watch the children, whether playing raucously or sitting quietly with the adults. Approaching a polite village elder or a child with respect for adults and asking to speak to the village soba usually elicited a helpful response.

The soba of Tchitunda I (we'd already passed Tchitunda II) was a quiet, unassuming man of few words and seemed wiser for it. He never raised his voice and appeared well-respected. We were provided plastic seats outside his round thatched adobe home. The soba's son placed a bucket in front of us. Under the scrutiny of a score of villagers, I set to washing my hands and face. The soba said something to a young girl, who rushed off, returning moments later with a bar of soap.

Do I look that dirty? I checked in the side mirror of the motorbike and hardly recognised the blackened face with dirt etched into every crease and wrinkle, bright white eyes shining back at me.

After a peaceful night in the tent and lots of photos with the children as we packed the next morning, we continued our journey. The tarmac became laterite and, where it headed south towards Cazombo, we turned onto a heavily overgrown track that should eventually take us to Jimbe.

Deep ruts meant we couldn't lose the way now. Instead, we battled endlessly in the sand, fighting to keep the bikes going in a straight line. If the front wheel veered into the edge of the rut, the bike jammed to a halt. Riding on the raised ground in-between was impossible; the rear wheel always slipped off.

The rough trail parallel to the invisible yet impenetrable Congolese border a few kilometres north reminded me of when I'd cycled there. I wished I was on my bicycle, able to lift and push it. The motorbike required monumental exertion and brute strength.

Dirt clung to my sweat-soaked skin and I regularly gulped my water. As the minutes turned to hours, with barely a few kilometres won, I began to wonder if we could make it.

Just keep persevering; it's not a race. But as I drank more lukewarm water and realised the bottle was rapidly emptying, I began to doubt whether I had enough fluid to last. How long to reach the Zambian border? What were the chances of finding water before then? According to the map, the Congolese border followed a small stream. In an emergency we could beat a way through to it, but I feared it would be dry and the bush impenetrable without a machete.

With no desire to backtrack, going forward appeared the only real option. As a last resort, I would walk, a less energy-consuming task than riding across this terrain, to the next village for water and return for the bike. Experience told me there would be more villages than were shown on the map.

We continued battling forward, the deep ruts swallowing the bikes. I rode with my knees raised towards my ears trying to keep my legs clear of the narrow sides.

When my foot got caught on a protruding root, the bike instantly halted. A branch rammed into my shin, already bruised from an earlier bike drop, bringing tears to my eyes, despite my boots offering good protection. The bike toppled and I stepped away, an overwhelming pain shooting up my leg whenever I tried to put weight on it. I collapsed to the ground, my vision blurred, the pain searing.

When Kieran caught up, he suggested we take a break and have lunch. Unusually, I had no appetite, but the pain gradually subsided to a dull nauseating ache. Within minutes though, the no-see-ums, pesky little biting black flies, began plaguing us.

The next section was the hardest as we fought our way along more deep sandy tracks. The only vehicle we saw had been abandoned, blocking the route. Still with wheels, engine and seats intact, nothing had been permanently 'borrowed'. It was a sure indicator of how few people passed this way. We later heard that this was the last vehicle until us to attempt passing six months ago.

Shortly after, a single meandering footpath appeared through the bush, the ground hardened by footfall. We were approaching civilisation again. I licked my dry lips and summoned enough saliva to swallow in anticipation of water. The solid trail also made riding easier. A few quick kilometres further, we reached a military checkpoint where water and a place to camp were forthcoming.

From thereon, the track improved, solid trails diverging and weaving around the trees and scrub, passing one village, then another until we reached Caianda, where we bought Fanta and glucose biscuits from the shop and overpriced, but still very cheap, fuel from wine bottles.

The trail split in two at a metal hand-painted sign informing us that 'Jimbi' was fifty-seven kilometres further. One arrow pointed right: Zambia. Another pointed left: Congo.

Oh, how I'd love to go back to the Congo.

If I had been travelling alone, I would have taken that left track. Who knows where it would have led, but something was tugging at me to go that way. Was it my heart calling, urging, beckoning; the piece of me I had left behind now drawing me in like a magnet? Seven years ago, I'd fallen in love with Congo and with Charlie. Seven years ago, I had also realised that love alone is not enough.

Never mind that Kieran would not cope meeting Charlie. I wasn't sure *I* was ready to see Charlie. Would I have the willpower to ride away from him a second time?

Before I had left, Charlie had promised with passion that if I ever came back, he would never let me leave again. I believed him and suspected he had the power to stop me, which scared me, but the rush of excitement and surging adrenalin thrilled me equally. Together we could have been unstoppable, but I would not have wanted to make an enemy of him. Everything in Congo was a game and Charlie loved playing with high stakes to win through charm, wit and intellect. I think we both thought we had met our match and both wanted to pitch our wits against the other. Yet I could also see he had the capacity for ruthlessness, perhaps born out of survival.

What if I went to look for Charlie? A hunter in search of a lion, whose power and beauty they admire and fear simultaneously, can never be sure they won't become the hunted. All I could think was that if Kieran came too, he might unknowingly be like the lamb led to slaughter.

I put my thoughts aside. Charlie was in my past. I couldn't say which way my future lay, but right now it was heading to Jimbe with Kieran.

———

We reached the Zambian border late in the afternoon. It came upon us so suddenly and, being nothing more than a small village, we had soon ridden right through it to the police post. I wished we could backtrack to camp in the bush one last night before getting stamped out of Angola.

A smartly dressed young woman spoke to us, asking where we'd come from and where we were going with friendly curiosity and courtesy. 'My name is Martha. I am the officer here. You can camp here tonight and we will process your documents in the morning.' she said without presumption or order, but as though she understood our reluctance to leave, hoping that we would enjoy our last night in her country.

'Do you want a wash?' she asked me.

Of course, I did.

'OK, you can come with me to the river. You have a towel, yes? And soap?' she enquired.

Abandoning Kieran, I gathered my towel and wash bag and followed her down the path. At the wide bend in the river, we stripped off and put our clothes down on the rocks, then slipped into the clear water. There were several other girls already washing, while others chatted on the bank.

Martha asked how old I was and whether I had children and what I did for a job. Then she spoke to one of the girls staring at me naked in the water and turned back to me. 'Sorry, I speak no good English,' she said and tried to explain their conversation. 'It is funny,' she smiled. 'She never see whole white person body. I don't know what she think to see. But I say we are all the same.' We all laughed together at the innocence.

The water was so cool and refreshing after the hot, sweaty day. I held onto a rock and let my feet flow in the stream. When back home I relish a powerful hot shower but nothing beats washing in a lake or river surrounded by nature, uninhibited and calm.

Martha pointed to the bridge downstream. I guessed we'd be crossing there in the morning. 'The boys wash on the other side. Have you finished? Good, let's go. It gets cold now.'

Back at the compound, I cooked noodles for dinner and talked with Martha's co-worker. He was tall, slim and clean cut. Well-educated, he spoke freely and clearly, 'I am six months here. I have six more to do. Is too long. Always officers are one girl, one boy. But girls only do six months, then go different place. Is not fair for us men. There is too little to do here.' He paused in thought, then added with optimism, 'It will get better. Can I give you a tour?'

We stepped out of the thatched lapa and leapt over the dry drainage ditch to the concrete building behind.

'A new building will be put here with electricity, telephones, internet. Everything very modern. Even new flush toilet.' It seemed hard to believe. 'But everything in this country takes long time. I will not see it finished. Come.'

I followed him back across the ditch.

'It is sad. This country have much – how you say? – potential. The land is very rich.' He bent over and picked up a handful of earth. 'But people in villages do not know how to work. They too lazy.'

'My father is farmer,' he continued. 'He know much on growing vegetables. I try here to grow potatoes.' He pointed to the ridged lines of cultivated soil. 'I plant only now but they grow for sure.'

I hoped his youthful energy, enthusiasm and initiative were not drained out of him before he finished his placement. He was his country's future.

That last evening in Angola, talking with the bright young officials who radiated optimism and hope, summed up the last month I'd experienced in the country. Their futures seem to be like the trail we'd just ridden: sometimes rough and rocky, occasionally unclear and without apparent direction, but they just had to keep going, keep persevering, and they'd reach the brighter place they hoped for eventually.

12.

The Africa I Love
Zambia

'Do you want a single or multiple entry visa?'

'Single.'

'Good. We can only issue a single visa at this border.' *I wonder why he bothered asking.*

I read the anti-corruption poster on the wall while the immigration officer completed the visas and stamped our passports. Then I handed over payment.

'Welcome to Zambia,' he smiled warmly as he handed back our passports.

'Thank you. Now, where is customs?' I asked.

'No customs here,' he replied.

'But we need our carnets stamped,' I explained, placing the A4 booklet with its distinctive yellow cover onto the desk between us.

'That is a problem. No customs officer here.'

'There has to be. Every border needs a customs officer.'

'Normally two customs officers, but one was sent to cover at busy border in south and one is not here … is, er … in training. I cannot help; I do not have the correct stamp.'

I suspected 'in training' meant 'at home'. At a border with so little traffic, it seemed likely that the officers took it in turns to go and spend time with their wives and families. It was unfortunate that on the one day there was work to be done, the remaining officer had been sent away.

I stared into the eyes of the middle-aged officer, hoping to convey my steadfast patience and resolute intent to not leave without a solution to this impasse. A long silence ensued while I let him ponder his predicament. He knew he'd been caught out.

'Maybe I *can* help,' he offered.

He picked up the phone to contact his superior, who told him to contact the customs office at Katima Mulilo where we intended to exit the country. The plan was to make our way back to Botswana to ride across the salt pans now that the rains had passed.

He picked up the phone again and, put through to the border officer in charge, explained that our carnets had not been stamped and that we should be allowed to export the bikes with no paperwork and no problem. Then he wrote out a letter for us in case we had to show documentation to any officials whilst in the country.

'How long since the last vehicle crossed the border?' I asked casually.

'A few weeks ago,' he replied. 'Many local people walk across though. There is a mission hospital in Kalene Hill, the next village. People from Angola and Congo visit it for healthcare.'

I waited while he neatly folded the handwritten letter and passed it to me. 'OK, good. Now you must pay the carbon tax.'

'What tax?'

'Yes, carbon tax. To offset vehicle emissions.'

'Are you serious?' He was serious. 'OK, how much?'

'Five dollars. But you cannot pay here. You must pay customs officer and get receipt. But customs officer not here.'

'Yes, we've clarified that already; so, where *can* we pay this tax?'

'You must go to nearest customs office. Which way do you go to Katima?'

I produced the Michelin map from my tank bag and showed him a route directly south.

'Ah, yes. Then you must go to Solwezi customs.'

He traced his finger over the map and stopped over the town far to the east.

'But that's miles out of the way!' I exclaimed. 'Can't we just pay at Katima?'

'Solwezi – small detour. You must pay tax. You do not want a problem on the journey.'

I sighed at his finest logic. I explained the irony of making a five-hundred-kilometre detour to pay a five-dollar tax to offset our carbon emissions.

He shrugged his shoulders.

We're going to Solwezi.

Barely a hundred metres on from the border we were stopped at a barrier and wire fencing. A deep voice boomed from inside a building. 'You! Come Here!'

I recognised the aggressive tone of misguided authority and was sharpening my tongue in contempt and anticipation of the inevitable showdown. Sure enough, he demanded money.

He didn't get any.

Later that day we had an altercation with a corrupt traffic officer. Zambia, it seemed, was going to offer a very different experience than we'd had in Angola.

Despite our best efforts to spend money there, we had a lot of kwanza left. Beyond Angola's borders, the currency was useless. Fortunately we were able to exchange it for Zambian kwacha with a local in Kalene Hill. I went straight to the market, which had more fresh produce than we'd seen since Luanda, and bought lettuce, tomatoes and onions by the bagful.

We could have gotten away without paying the carbon tax. Had we been stopped, a back-handed bribe would have solved the problem if good old charm and persuasion hadn't. Our route was unimportant. I was content to take an alternative, longer way that gave us more time in Zambia.

Solwezi was a busy copper mining town bordering DR Congo. Oh how it reminded me of those crazy, dusty, chaotic towns I passed through in West and Central Africa. Most towns in Southern Africa have an ordered modernity to them. Passing off as westernised, they have an almost European feel to them. Not here, where we rode past the churches on the outskirts, the auto spares compounds with tyres stacked outside and on through the market where vendors set up shop on the pavement: second-hand clothes and shoes piled up on tables, bright handbags hanging from hooks, stacks of fresh fruit and veg looking so ripe and full of flavour. And there were people – hundreds of men and women – walking shopping talking laughing hustling bustling. The city was brimming with life. *Yes, this is the Africa I love.*

We passed a Shoprite supermarket and pulled over near the police station and multi-storey council offices. I presumed we'd find an office at the border crossing to DR Congo and had expected to see a main road going north. The only roads looked like side alleys. According to my Michelin map, the border was only a centimetre away. In reality, this equated to some forty kilometres.

'I'm not sure where we need to go,' I commented to Kieran.

'Shall we get some lunch first?' he replied.

It was Friday afternoon. 'We should probably find the office in case it closes for the weekend.'

While Kieran was searching on his GPS for inspiration, a young man approached. 'Are you lost? Can I help you?' he asked.

'Which way is it to the border?' I asked.

He seemed confused, then replied, 'Ah, you go to Kipushi?'

'Er, no.' I'd never heard of the place. 'We've come from Angola, but need to find the customs office here.'

'Ah, you must go to Chingola then.'

'No, no,' I knew Chingola was further east; it was the first Zambian town I had come to after I'd cycled out of Lubumbashi in DR Congo years before. 'We were definitely told there is a customs office in Solwezi.'

'I do not know. Maybe you can try the government offices at Napsa Hai Telecoms. It is close.'

We thanked him, rode on, found the building, asked for the customs office again and were directed to the Zambia Revenue Authority building opposite.

Told to wait by the receptionist, we obediently sat on the plastic chairs lining the characterless cream walls that made it seem like a shabby dentist's waiting room, placed our helmets on the floor and rifled through our tank bags to find our passports and paperwork.

A large man greeted us. 'Hello. My name is Mr Joseph Nyirenda. How can I help you?' he began and shook our hands. He had a caring, thoughtful demeanour. I could imagine him as a family man with several children vying for his attention when he returned home each evening.

He laughed in big bellyfuls, finding it hilarious that we'd made such a big detour. 'But why did you not pay at the border?'

We explained about the official being on training.

Suddenly he seemed serious. 'There should always be one officer on duty. That is bad.'

I hoped we hadn't inadvertently got anyone in trouble.

He put his hands on his leather belt to adjust his trousers over his paunch back up onto his waist. 'This is the domestic tax office, not customs. But I will try to help. Come.'

We followed Mr Joseph Nyirenda down a cream corridor to his office with a large wooden table covered in paperwork and a desktop computer that looked like it was from the nineties. He made a phone call, then looked directly at us. 'There is a problem. The customs officer is not in today. He is on training.'

'Everyone seems to be "on training",' I commented in jest.

He leant back in his chair and chuckled nervously.

'I'm beginning to wonder if this customs department is real.'

We all laughed.

'I will see what I can do,' he replied.

We waited patiently back in reception with only the clock on the wall as a distraction. As the hands neared five o'clock, I began to fidget. The receptionist appeared to be tidying up for the day. 'I hope you like the town,' I said to Kieran. 'We might be staying for the weekend.'

At two minutes past five, Mr Joseph Nyirenda returned. 'Follow me ...' We walked with some urgency down the cream corridor to another office where he introduced us to a clean-cut man with grey flecks in his short hair, a blue-checked shirt and trousers that matched the colour of the walls. 'This is my boss, Mr Kaluba. He will help you. I must go. I am late for my wife ...'

Mr Kaluba had emailed the head office and was waiting for their reply. Eventually, several phone calls later, he received approval to take our payment and stamp the receipt. He wrote a covering letter by hand for us to give to the customs office at Katima Mulilo when we exited the country.

It had taken a lot of fuel and man-hours to pay a five-dollar tax. We might not have decided what route to take through Zambia, but we were certain which border we would be leaving through.

We found a simple guesthouse on the outskirts of town. It was clean and, far from the tourist route, very cheap. Once again we had the luxury of a bed and a shower. Relaxing without time constraints for the first time since Windhoek, we both succumbed to fatigue and disinterest in moving further than the bar. We stayed two nights.

———

Travelling south, we passed people strolling along the roadside to church wearing their Sunday best. Homes here were larger with patterns painted in natural red and black. Beyond Kasempa, the tarmac turned to laterite, which eventually petered out after a few villages until we were riding on a dusty forest trail, cool in the shade of the canopy.

We were plagued by tsetse flies that followed us with dogged persistence, biting us wherever they could. We put on our jackets, zipping them up to the chin for added protection, and still they managed to bite through them. Our armour gave some protection but they found the gaps. My worn jeans posed no barrier. I was thankful not to have suffered this torment while cycling, when hot and sweaty from the exertion makes layering up more uncomfortable, and the slower pace makes you an even easier target.

We crossed the river on a pontoon with warnings of lions and leopards on the other side now we were entering the boundary of Kafue National Park. Prudently, we camped by the park warden's office.

An A4 sheet of paper pinned to the building listed the park's hunting fees. Every species was fair game. The permit for a foreigner to legally shoot an elephant cost $10,000; a lion cost only $4,200. The prices were much less for various antelope. Separate charges for local residents were listed parallel. The vervet monkey was at the bottom of the list. Locals were welcome to dispose of them at no charge whatsoever. A wry smile crossed Kieran's face when he read that. He was still bitter from when they'd stolen our stove and smeared shit on the tent. It was as though the Zambian park authority approved of his personal vendetta.

The following day, there were two more river crossings. The man taking payment at the first explained that we were supposed to pay the price for vehicles with foreign plates, ten times more expensive than local vehicles. No distinction was made between the size of a motorcycle and a 4x4. Being charged the local rate yesterday had been an oversight, the man calmly explained but let us pay the local price too. The boat captain for the final crossing was less flexible. Having travelled all day and with the only alternative to go back the way we'd come, he knew he had us trapped.

Dual pricing was prevalent throughout Zambia. The park authorities were particularly keen on fleecing tourists to the extent that we were usually deterred.

Soon after crossing the border from Angola, our route had taken us near the source of the Zambezi River. Reputedly not much more than a marker in the ground, it was supposed to be a pleasant location to camp. An official notice attached to a green sign at the turn off from the main road informed us that, as a foreigner, the fees for visiting were twenty dollars per person and five dollars per vehicle in addition to fifteen dollars each to camp at a site with no facilities and, ironically, no water. We bush-camped a few kilometres further on for free.

Exhausted from the non-stop day with the tsetse fly bites itching to distraction, we checked into a guesthouse. We ordered chicken and chips for dinner and drank Zambezi beer in the bar while we waited. I was ravenous by the time the tiny chicken leg and undercooked chips were served three hours later. I devoured it all in thirty seconds. Stripping every last morsel of meat from the bone did nothing to stem my hunger. There was no point getting angry, so I ordered one last beer before crashing on the bed and falling asleep, glad it was our last night in Zambia.

The road to Katima Mulilo was easy-going tarmac and the border exit formalities went without hindrance. There was even a customs officer present (and not 'on training') at the customs office. The woman behind the counter took the hand-written letter explaining why our carnets were not stamped and waved us through without a word. I couldn't work out whether she simply didn't care or we'd caused such havoc that everyone knew we were coming.

Across the river, in Namibia, we found a lodge with camping. While Kieran put up the tent and cooked, I made a run into town to source beer supplies. Our jobs were done just in time to crack open a Mosi beer as the sun set over the Zambezi River.

Every day for a week I woke up at first light, stepped out of the tent onto the lush cut grass sodden with dew and waited for the sun to come up. I looked forward to the moment when the first rays touched my face and felt their soft fingers of warmth on my skin. The nights were cold now and my lightweight summer sleeping bag poorly insulated.

In that first hour of light, I enjoyed the subtle warmth that swept away the chill of the night, forgotten for another day. Mist floating ethereally above the calm surface of the water soon evaporated and little wavelets, shimmering and dancing in the sunlight, rhythmically lapped at the shore. A pied kingfisher perched on a branch, tipping its tail back and forth for balance, and a graceful white bird flew upriver so close to the water its wing tips sliced the surface. If we were lucky, we'd hear the happy honking sound of the hippos as they returned upstream to their daytime place of rest.

By nine o'clock in the morning, the heat was intense, and I'd take shelter in the shade of a tree and read or write my journal. Everything was still again. The sun shone brilliantly, and the river, a mirror of calm, rolled languidly past. The fishermen in their dugout canoes, having checked their traps, returned to shore, their work on the Zambezi done until evening. Only the ring-necked doves, out-of-sight high in the branches of the tree behind, continued to repeat their mantra 'work harder, work harder'. All ignored their call. ·

In the evenings as the sun inched towards the horizon and the sky burned brightly in the dying light of day, I heard the distinctive call of the hippos again. Once, I saw them swim downstream towards their grazing grounds, their glistening black heads and round twitching ears just above the water, huge bodies submerged and hidden. About the same time every evening, four hadada ibises flew upriver, crying out 'haa haa-de-dah, haa haa-de-dah' as they went, their prehistoric form silhouetted against the water.

The calm riverside campsite was too appealing and we were too tired to leave. It was a haven of tranquillity, isolated from our journey in time and space. Having been on the move almost every day since Windhoek two months ago, it was the perfect antidote. Unlike our ever-changing days on the road, this place had its own regular and predictable rhythm, nature running like clockwork. It was easy to fit into its routine and required no thought or planning.

While on my cycling journeys, I regularly stopped for several days at a time, my body demanding rest from the physical exertion of pedalling. Travelling by motorbike did not require such effort, so we didn't stop as frequently. Daily life on the road, spending hours in the saddle, finding a place to camp, pitching the tent and often sleeping fitfully, still took its toll, and I needed the downtime to process everything I'd seen and experienced.

After a week, though, we were well rested, our clothes washed, our bikes clean, my journal up to date, and my hunger for devouring good books sated in one sitting. I was happy to move on before this haven of ease and comfort became replaced by familiar indifference.

Besides, on some afternoons, if the wind picked up, I had a sense of unease, murmurings of discontent in the wavelets on the water's surface that belied the peaceful setting. For the first time in months I had instant access to the internet. I had not missed keeping up to date with global affairs but had now become obsessed by two events: the rise of Trump in the run-up to the US elections and the EU referendum at home. The first was a source of humour and entertainment, the second of little note until the morning of the result. Leave. I was in disbelief, but I hadn't been in the UK for almost a year and had little comprehension of the discontent in my home country. As 'Brexit' entered mainstream vocabulary, I buried my head in the sand the only way I knew how: pack up and ride.

———

We spent the day making a loop following the Botswanan border. At the junction rejoining the Caprivi Strip, a couple travelling in their 4x4 stopped to talk and recommended we stay at a nearby lodge worth visiting for the view.

From the upper floor of the lodge, wooden stairs led to a viewing platform that towered above the wetland delta. The sprawl of tall grasses dried golden spread for miles below us, almost concealing the water channels, which bring life to this region. They were two feet lower than normal for this time in the season. Apparently it had not rained for four years.

The campsite was back up the sandy track next to a small stream winding through the bush. A group of four Afrikaners, two couples each with a Land Cruiser towing an off-road trailer, had their camp already set up.

Originally from Jo'burg but now retired, they split their time between home on the Garden Route and camping in the bush. They'd been here two days already. They were sitting on canvas chairs around a campfire waiting for the bread to finish baking in the potjie, the cast iron Dutch oven wedged in the embers.

Looking up from the meat on the braai, Johan said, 'I could spend my life on the road and in the bush and never go home.'

'Look, this is all we need,' Adriaan spoke up, waving his beer can in the air. 'Fresh air, good food and beer.'

'Ja, but we have grandchildren at home. I could not live without seeing them grow up,' Marieke added without looking up from the bowl of salad she was mixing.

Ava smiled and nodded.

Johan and Adriaan kept quiet. I think they knew better than to disagree with their wives if they wanted their contented lives to continue.

'You eat meat, ja? Will you join us for dinner?' Johan invited.

The smell emanating from the marinated meat was mouth-watering. It'd beat the hell out of our instant noodles. 'Sure, that'd be great!' I replied quickly.

'Lekker. Adriaan, don't be so rude; get them beer,' Johan ordered.

Adriaan hauled himself out of the chair, went to his trailer and returned with cold cans and spare chairs for us.

'Listen,' Ava whispered.

Marieke stopped mixing and tilted her head towards the river. 'Sshhh ...' she exhaled sharply when Johan kept talking.

A contented grunt from the river disturbed the still air.

'There …' Ava spoke quietly.

'Hippo,' Adriaan said and, as if in reply, a happy honk-honk-honk rippled through the dusk to our ears. The sound like a deep belly-aching laugh always brought a smile to my face.

We all stood up and crept towards the bank. On the bend in the deepest part of the stream, the hippo splashed. After a moment, Johan went back to the braai and the rest of us watched in silence until the hippo disappeared into the shadows of the tall grass as darkness descended and the first pinpricks of light pierced the black canvas above.

When the *boerewors* and *sosaties* were cooked and Marieke had sliced the bread, we piled the food onto plates and ate around the fire. Through the darkness, our faces lit up red in the flickering flames, we each told stories of our experiences camping and travelling through southern Africa. It was a scene from the bush not dissimilar to when our ancestors lived. I looked up through the clearing at the tranquil sky awash with stars, feeling privileged to know and appreciate such peaceful contentment.

'Do you ever think about quitting?' Johan asked.

'Quitting what? I asked.

'Your journey,' he explained.

I laughed at the absurdity of it. I couldn't quit; this was not a single journey that could be stopped; it was my life. I had chosen to be here, now, travelling like this. I was living exactly how I wanted.

The hardships people saw did not bother me much. The cold mornings and sore hips from my mattress that continued to deflate overnight were a small price to pay for this life of simplicity and freedom; because, when the sun rose and I stretched lazily on the banks of the stream, my aches and any worries evaporated with the morning mist. When people questioned my choice of lifestyle, I wished I could transport them to this moment and see if they still failed to understand.

'Why would I want to quit this?' I exclaimed and spread my arms out.

'Very true,' he said and smiled.

When morning came, the only disturbance on the glassy water reflecting the reeds and clear blue sky was a gentle ripple as a small fish surfaced near the lily pads. A little brown bird balanced on a reed tip, then swooped down to catch an insect; swifts darted through the air; bee-eaters chattered in the branches; and a yellow weaver bird perched on the handlebar of my bike, peering and pecking at its image in the mirror. I sipped my cup of tea slowly, savouring every drop of a new day.

If I could freeze this moment in time, I would be happy forever.

Yes, this is the Africa I love.

13.

Okavango Delta and Salt Pans
Botswana

With only a few days remaining on our original visas for Namibia, we had to get a move on. Knowing the bikes would soon need new chains and sprockets, we'd arranged for the parts to be posted to Maun in Botswana. I'd convinced Kieran to order replacement clutch plates too. I wasn't going to let a slipping clutch prevent us from riding across the salt pans.

Unfortunately, the parts were stuck in customs. I had been unable to make contact to pay the charges. Hopefully visiting the DHL office in person would progress matters.

We reached the office late on a Friday and paid the bill. Nothing would happen over the weekend or Monday, because – I should have known! – it was a national holiday. The earliest the parts would arrive was Wednesday. Despite advance planning we would still have to wait. At least in Botswana we had no time constraints; the ninety days allowed visa-free was plenty of time to ride across the salt pans.

For Kieran's upcoming birthday, we booked an overnight guided trip into the Okavango Delta, wetlands thriving with wildlife. A motorised boat took us upriver with other tourists in the early chill of morning. We had travelled a long way south over the last couple of weeks, and now it was July, mid-winter in the southern hemisphere.

With the background drone of the engine drowning out all noise, I watched the riverbanks slide past like a silent motion picture. Fish eagles looked down from their high thrones, crowned with gleaming white heads and yellow razor-sharp hooked bills. Kingfishers, giant and pied and the colourful malachite, swooped between bushes along the water's edge.

At a sandy bank, we transferred to *mokoros*, traditional dugout canoes, to navigate further. We loaded our rucksack and clambered in, the mokoro wobbling from side to side until we were sitting centrally, one behind the other. Titi our guide pushed the mokoro clear into the water, nimbly stepped on and, standing at the back with a long wooden pole, propelled us forward. We glided into the wetlands with a carpet of green reed tips a few inches tall peeking above the water's surface. Storks waded, slender white herons and egrets fished in the shallows, and a formation of wattled cranes flew overhead, while the smaller chestnut coloured jacanas called incessantly from amongst the grass.

Despite a stiff breeze making the open water choppy, the slow, silent travel made a relaxing, peaceful contrast to the motorbike. I wasn't used to sitting back and having someone else do the hard work, which always made me feel uneasy. Even though we were paying for Titi's services, I didn't like the obvious inequality, especially when he answered with the subservient 'yes, baas'.

After a couple of hours we reached an island that would be our home for the night. From the beach, a well-trodden path led through a narrow opening in the bush to a small clearing.

Titi was a man of few words, although I think this was more because he only knew basic English. I imagined he would be quite talkative in the company of his friends and family.

'Baas, this is where we camp. Relax. Have a siesta. This is Africa time. You must be tired after a long journey. It is too hot. Later, we go out again.'

What? I thought we'd only just started.

I shrugged my shoulders. There was no point in getting frustrated, better to enjoy the slower pace of life and let my mind slow down. I'd have brought a book or my journal had I known.

It's surprising how quickly time can pass. We put up the tent at a leisurely pace, which still only took a few minutes, made tea, had lunch, dozed a little. We swept the fire pit, collected some dry grass and kindling and piled them precisely in the cleared pit, perfecting the art of building a fire even though the wood here was tinder dry and would light instantly. Then we gathered larger branches, neatly assembling the different sizes into separate stacks.

Making jobs that can be done quickly take a long time is an art form I have reluctantly mastered. I prefer to work with methodical efficiency to ensure a task is done in the most time-effective manner. I'm used to waiting for others.

I was pottering about on the sandy shore taking photos when Titi suddenly announced it was time to go. We'd been doing nothing for five hours, but now there was not a moment to lose. I already had my camera with me so clambered aboard the mokoro. We waited while Kieran disappeared to the tent in the bush.

'Where is your friend? We must go.' Titi said after five minutes, with an agitated edge as though we were in a race against time.

'I think he's getting his video camera,' I replied, although I had no idea what could be taking so long. 'Don't worry,' I added. 'This is Africa time.'

Titi poled us with long determined strokes, racing the setting sun. When he got to where he'd been wanting to reach, he stopped and let the boat glide silently towards thicker grass. He didn't say anything, but I knew we should keep quiet. He crouched down while trying to see beyond the reeds, then he moved the boat back a little, forward a little. *What's he looking for?*

'There,' he whispered and pulled on the grasses, sliding the boat forward until the front was peeking out of the reeds, revealing an open pool of water.

I waited, silent, expectant.

And then I saw them: a pair of round pinkish-grey ears surfaced. Then another pair, and another. *Hippos!*

A huge angular head emerged from the water and stared directly at us, then it snorted through its large nostrils. The dark shadows in

134

the eye sockets lent a malevolent look, a contradiction to the happy honking sound I'd heard from hippos before.

A head sometimes sunk out of sight while another surfaced, so it was hard to tell exactly how many there were. Just once, eight pairs of ears were visible at the same time. The family bathed and played, sinking and surfacing and sometimes crashing out of the water and other times opening their powerful jaws in giant pink-flesh gaping yawns that could crush a man.

I took a few photos, then when Titi pulled the mokoro back for safety – you don't want to anger a hippo – I sat back and listened. Kieran seemed frustrated that he couldn't get a clear shot on his video camera. There was nothing I could do to help and instead focussed on the sound of grasses rustling as the cool air wafted through.

After the sun set, turning the sky to evening shades of pink and purple, we returned to camp and lit the fire. We baked flatbreads with the flour we'd brought along. At the last moment we'd found out that food wasn't included on the tour and we needed to bring our own. If we'd have known that we'd be sitting around a fire, we would have brought meat to braai. Instead, we cooked up some noodles and cracked open the bottle of red wine we'd picked up to celebrate Kieran's birthday.

Titi sat on the opposite side of the fire, the flames flickering between us and lighting our faces through the darkness, the cicadas buzzing in the background.

'Are you not eating?' I asked Titi.

'I finished my rice at lunchtime. I was hungry,' he replied.

'You have no more food? What about tomorrow?' I asked, unsure if I was more surprised that he'd managed to eat a carrier bag full of cooked rice in one sitting or that he'd not thought to ration it for the duration. If we'd have known, we could have brought extra food.

'I will manage until I get home,' he replied.

Me and Kieran always ate out of the same pan, taking turns to spoon a mouthful. I think it started as a weight-saving initiative by not needing separate plates, but I liked it. It reminded me of the many meals I'd shared with people I met on my travels in Northern Africa, where a large plate of food was placed on the floor and we'd all sit and eat from it with our right hand.

Kieran emptied a third of the noodles onto the lid of the pan and handed it to Titi. 'We'll share,' I said and passed him my spoon. Then, slightly grudgingly, passed him my mug of wine too. One thing I've learnt through the generosity of even the poorest people is that, however little, there is always enough food and drink to share with one more person. I suspected Titi was used to clients with more lavish tastes than us. Still, he thanked us and devoured the meagre dinner.

We were up early to go on a walking safari before it got too hot and while the animals would still be in the open, not hiding in the shade. Although you cannot get as close to the wildlife on foot as in a 4x4, the experience is more captivating. On foot and unarmed, senses heightened, you are just another animal slotting into the natural order, no longer at the top of the food chain but exposed and vulnerable. It gives perspective on what survival in the African savannah once meant.

As we walked, I scanned the ground for spoor and scat to indicate what wildlife had passed recently. Sometimes Titi pointed to a print or poo: giraffe, zebra, buffalo, porcupine … We noted the direction of the faint breeze and kept downwind from a herd of grazing antelope to mask our presence.

Titi bent down and pointed to a scattering of giraffe droppings, round and hard like rabbit poo only bigger and more spread out having fallen from a greater height. As Titi stood up again, he stopped abruptly and ducked his head down, his eyes transfixed on something in the bush. I followed his stare and saw a bull elephant behind a tree using his trunk to pull off the leaves. It always amazed me how such big animals could be so well camouflaged in the bush. They had given me the greatest cause for concern when I'd cycled in Botswana, together with lions.

Without breaking his gaze, Titi reached out to touch my arm and put his finger to his lips. Then he beckoned with his hand to step away slowly and silently. Kieran was oblivious, engrossed in filming something else on his video camera.

'Kieran,' I whispered.

He didn't hear me.

'Kieran!' I hissed louder, concerned for his safety.

He looked to me. I pointed towards the elephant and beckoned him to follow us. He spun the camera to face the elephant and started creeping closer to it.

What's he doing?! 'Kieran!' I growled.

He ignored me. The elephant stopped eating and turned towards us.

'Your friend needs to move away,' Titi whispered to me.

'I know!' I replied.

Agitated and feeling threatened, the elephant fanned out his ears and took a step towards us.

'Kieran!' I growled, louder.

He glanced over but continued filming.

Titi crept over and tapped Kieran on the shoulder, eventually persuading him to back away.

'So Titi,' I asked later, 'did you know the elephant was there and showing me the giraffe spoor was part of the show?'

'No, it was a surprise,' Titi replied. 'That is why we must always be alert.'

We continued meandering along game trails, always in a northerly direction. Through Kieran's monocular I could make out the herd of impala, some zebra and wildebeest, and several tsessebe, which I'd not seen before but were distinctive horned chestnut-coloured large antelopes with humped shoulders and sloping backs.

Titi spotted the giraffes he'd been looking for. We picked up our pace and, keeping downwind and out of sight, crept closer. Some thirty giraffes, tall and proud, nibbled on the leaves of the highest trees. When they ambled off, we skirted the bush and headed back to camp along different trails across open country where scattered bones and the massive skull of an elephant lay bleached by the sun.

Earlier that morning, only a few hundred metres from our camp, I had spotted a vervet monkey clinging to the trunk of a palm tree. It had stared at us with that mischievous look they have. I had glared back at it, remembering the monkeys that had stolen our stove and thrown shit at our tent in the Baviaanskloof. *The cheeky little bugger had better not invade our camp!* We'd cleared up and closed the tent; it would be fine.

It was not fine.

Three hours later, I wandered back down the small path into the clearing in the bush where our tent was.

What the..?!

The ground was covered in a greyish-white ash, too much for it to be from last night's fire; besides, the pit was untouched. I looked over to the tent and saw a long rip along the back. Fearing the worst, I unzipped the outer and peered inside. The mesh inner was ripped and the zip partially undone.

I'd already packed away my gear into the rucksack, which looked untouched. Kieran's side of the tent, however, was a war zone. It didn't need an investigative journalist to figure out that the vervet monkey had forced its way inside, discovered the bag of flour and gone wild. Kieran's roll mat and clothes, strewn around the tent were covered in a heavy dusting, topped with a smearing of monkey shit.

'What's going on?' Kieran asked as he leant over and peered into the tent.

I stifled a laugh. 'Happy Birthday!'

We had vowed the last time to never leave the tent unattended in the bush. We continued to grow older but apparently not wiser.

138

The tent I had taken when I cycled to Cape Town had at least made it to Namibia from the UK, having survived repeated ant and termite attacks, the persistent dust that clogged the zips and the daily storms during West Africa's rainy season, before finally succumbing to a hungry jackal at Sossusvlei. For this trip, I had insisted on not spending lots of money on a top-of-the-range lightweight tent. Durability was more important. Even so, it was looking increasingly unlikely that this tent would survive until Egypt.

Kieran removed his contaminated items from the tent whilst I filmed this birthday surprise for his later viewing pleasure. He wiped off as much crap as he could, then tipped the tent upside-down and shook it like a giant sieve to empty the flour.

Back at the lodge that evening, we drank pints of Windhoek draught, laughed a lot and told travel tales round the fire with the other campers. Then someone brought out the liquor. The birthday boy couldn't resist. I left him with the other revellers and went back to the tent to sleep.

I awoke in the night, not to snores but moans of pain interspersed with hiccuping.

'You OK?' I asked.

The only response was the rustle of his sleeping bag and sound of the tent being unzipped, followed shortly afterwards by retching. A sickly sweet aroma permeated the air. I rolled over to see Kieran with his head out of the tent, vomit dribbling down his chin. I opened my side to let fresh air through. Then I silently passed him a mug of water and went back to sleep with my head tucked deep into my own bag to filter the lingering smell.

I next woke to the dawn chorus accompanied by the deathly groans of someone suffering an almighty hangover.

'Morning! Fancy a cup of tea?' I asked cheerily.

The response was unintelligible.

I refilled Kieran's mug of water and watched the lodge's dog wander past the tent. 'Don't you dare ...' I growled at it, suspecting it might pee on the tent. Instead it trotted over to the tree where Kieran's monkey-shit-covered clothes were piled awaiting washing and cocked its leg.

I laughed and heard a mumbled curse flung in the dog's direction.

Six hours later Kieran emerged to begin decontamination proceedings, cursing the vervet monkey under his breath and waging war on the species. By the time the tent was clean, Kieran had conjured up the perfect monkey deterrent: Tool-in-a-Can. Testing confirmed that, when combined with a lighter, the multi-purpose lubricant spray made an effective flame-thrower.

Let me get one thing straight: I'm an animal lover. Yes, throwing rocks at vervet monkeys is a detestable thing to do, but so is shitting on someone's tent. It seemed we weren't the only people to face the vervet monkeys' wrath. They made enemies everywhere. Locals tended to hurl pebbles at them, although I'd met some South Africans who had potato guns and Super Soakers. Just as cats always land on their feet, so monkey's always dodge incoming artillery. It was a game for both sides. Months later in Ethiopia, the shoe was on the other foot and we, the foreign bikers, were the targets of rock-throwing kids. Karma, perhaps. Both times, we were outwitted by an opposition who'd had a lifetime of practice.

———

We collected the parcel of parts, which had arrived at the DHL office. At camp, Kieran finally replaced the clutch plates on his bike. We did oil changes, and I checked the valve clearances on mine while I had the tank removed to check that it was still not rubbing on the cylinder head side cover. I noticed an unusual shape along the frame and peered closer.

A chameleon!

The slender chameleon, mottled grey like the dusty bike, was motionless. Its pincer-like feet clasped the throttle cable and its tail was curled into a spiral. I only noticed it because I knew every inch of my bike.

I ran my finger down its ridged spine. Its skin was rough as a pumice and its stomach squidgy like a cupcake. It opened its mouth wide, gulped, and shifted its black pin-hole eye.

I carefully put it onto a tree branch. Almost imperceptibly, it changed colour to a variegated army green and khaki. After ten minutes it blended perfectly with the bark and leaves in the dappled sunlight. Stationary, with tail unfurled and legs bent as though halfway through a press-up, I struggled to see it.

Chameleons are one of my favourite animals. Sometimes I think of myself as a kind of chameleon, able to adapt to different environments as I travel, blend into each until a part of them. It means I can feel at home anywhere in the world amongst almost any group of people. Although connections and fitting in have as much to do with empathy and understanding. When it came to Kieran though, I'd been modifying my behaviour for too long. Too often I seemed to be fighting myself and camouflaging my needs to keep us together.

With clutch plates replaced and chameleon displaced, we set off towards the salt pans, passing within 1,500 kilometres as the crow flies from Cape Town. I could have walked that distance during the six months we'd been travelling. If we were to reach Egypt, we'd have to stop circling southern Africa and start heading north soon.

——

In Mopipi, we refuelled and got water, albeit distasteful and brackish. Then we turned onto the next track north and followed vet fences, which segregate the bush into disease-controlled sectors. At the first control point, a ranger told us to beware of elephants and to not rev our engines or toot our horns if we did come across them.

The next gate was guarded by an impressive six-foot-plus hulk of a man. 'Where are you going?' he asked with cheery bounce and charm.

Kieran looked to me. I hesitated, shrugged my shoulders and mentioned vaguely about going north towards Gweta and then turning southeast towards Kubu Island. I hadn't looked in detail at the route, my only intention being to wild camp somewhere on the pans, although I wasn't sure if we were allowed; I wasn't even sure if we were allowed on the pans on our bikes.

The guard seemed unconcerned. He pointed to a newly erected board mentioning a private lease. 'That was put up by the owner of a camp, but we took down the one saying no camping. That man is a *matatu* – a worry – and strict. But we don't work for him; we work for the government and the government owns this land. Camp if you want, but maybe not too close to the signs or Chapman's Baobab. Don't be scared if you see the warden. You are fine to go.'

'OK,' I smiled.

'I hear that the baobab tree fell down three months ago,' he continued. 'I do not know how true it is. Maybe you can message me when you see it? I will give you my number.'

'What is this baobab?' I asked.

'Chapman's Baobab is a giant tree many thousands of years old, maybe the oldest baobab in Botswana. You could see it a long way off. It was used as a way marker by hunters and explorers; now tourists visit it.'

We located it on the GPS. It was as good a place as any to head towards.

The bush cleared to golden grass, which became sparser until there was only a pancake flat dirt-white salt pan under the vast blue sky and relentless sun. On the far side, I could make out the stubble of faint golden grass. We followed the tyre tracks running straight across like a scar.

Is that the end so soon?

Following the GPS, we turned east, riding through grassland grazed by cattle until we could see our waypoint.

Chapman's Baobab had fallen, split vertically through its trunk and burst open like a star. It lay like outspread giant fingers on the ground, the roots reaching skyward. The sections of trunk towered above us. No wonder it was a marvel when it stood.

We pitched our tent beyond some wooden kraals by a secluded cluster of trees. Domestic and wild animals coexisted on the same turf. Cattle wandered by, returning to the villages where they'd be safe at night. Darkness brought the sound of the jackal, sometimes a dog barking and, in the early hours, a stampede of hoofs, which daylight showed to be zebra.

We rode along a sandy track through grassland grazed by hundreds of zebra and wildebeest who galloped off at the sound of the bikes, kicking up dust clouds into the atmosphere. A wild wind blasted across the land, turning the air white.

Where the hazy bleached sky merged with a featureless flat pan, it was impossible to tell earth from air in the bright midday light when even the shadows had vanished. We stopped to take photos, then Kieran rode off to record some video.

A blissful feeling washed over me. I was alone, at last. The world beyond ceased to exist. The white-out reminded me of the vast nothingness of Siberia under snow. With the lack of sensory stimulation, I had struggled there with isolation. Now, deprived of time alone and space to myself, I wondered, could this peaceful nirvana of solitude be frozen in time?

Then I saw the black spec in the distance raise an arm, signalling me to catch up, and the moment was gone. I put my camera back in my tank bag, started the Serow, which shattered the silence, and rode on to my present reality.

Soon we were riding sandy trails through golden grass, thorny bushes clawing at my arms. Alongside another vet fence, a hare leapt out in front and darted through a gap, forcing me to brake suddenly.

143

Clouds of white dust billowed, choking and blinding me. Then the air cleared, the grasses receded, and we rode out onto another desolate expanse. Ahead, the low rocky Kubu Island, sprouting baobabs like a scraggy beard, broke through the monotonous white horizon and touched the cloudless blue sky.

Kubu Island campsite would have been an impressive place to spend the night. At twenty dollars for the privilege of no facilities, we rode on and found a place beyond the pan to sleep in the bush where the starry sky comes free of charge.

We reached the tarmac road just sixty kilometres east of where we'd departed it. Heading towards the capital, Francistown, I began to wonder where we would go next.

Reading guidebooks and government websites, researching political situations and security warnings, determining visa and other red-tape requirements, scrutinising maps and interpreting weather charts all takes time.

Although I'd explored some of the pans before, I'd been happy to plan a three-month loop enabling us to return to Botswana in the dry season when travelling on them would be possible because they were one of the few places about which Kieran had expressed real enthusiasm. Seeing that he was content to rush through the salt pans in less than forty-eight hours and frustrated that he left all the planning to me, I decided the direction I took us next would be where I wanted to go.

Mozambique, another ex-Portuguese colony, interested me as much as Angola. The security situation, however, wasn't good for travel. I remained hopeful that it could improve as we neared its borders. First we'd have to travel through Zimbabwe, another troubled country I wanted to see.

14.
Corruption and Kindness
Zimbabwe

News from Africa is not often printed in British papers, but the protests against corruption around the time we neared the border did. Following violent clashes between taxi drivers and the police, a national stay-away day had been declared. News of the idea had spread on social media and led to one of the largest peaceful protests in a decade. Most Zimbabweans missed a day's wage to stay at home, whilst foreign banks and businesses closed in the capital.

With an entire nation a potential tinderbox, I kept abreast of the news with baited breath. At least the risk-averse foreign office advice was only to avoid large cities and crowds. For now, it was peaceful.

The Zimbabwean economy was in tatters with no way for foreigners to access money within the country. All funds had to be brought in. Hyperinflation of the Zimbabwean dollar a decade ago meant that trade was now done in US dollar notes. The only valid coins in circulation were a recently introduced Zimbabwean bond coin. The smallest denomination was worth one US dollar.

On the streets, fresh fruit and veg had to be sold in dollar quantities. If I wanted tomatoes, I had to buy a dollar's worth. *But that's like two kilos!* If I wanted onions, a dollar's worth no less. *That bag is half the size of my rucksack!* Chillis, the same.

'I only need a couple of tomatoes and an onion!' I exclaimed to one street seller. And I laughed because this was the Africa I loved, illogical and confusing in all its absurdities, guaranteed to amuse, frustrate and infuriate in equal measure.

The smallest bill I had was ten dollars, as we'd only just crossed the border and this was the first chance to spend any money. I went from vendor to vendor until I found one who had enough change. I picked out a selection of vegetables and fruit and handed over the ten dollar note. He counted out nine bond coins in return, then added several more vegetables to the bag.

'No, no, it's enough. We don't have space!' I exclaimed and, thanking him, took the bag.

Struggling to fit the produce on our loaded bikes, I received a tap on the shoulder. 'A gift,' he smiled and gave me some apples.

Any doubts I'd had about Zimbabwe vanished. *I think I'm going to like it here.*

——

Matobo National Park, between the border and Bulawayo, was the first place we visited. Matobo, meaning 'bald head' in Ndebele refers to the massive granite *kopjes,* rounded by the weather. We hoped to explore the recreation area with kopjes and caves containing San bushman rock art, the largest concentration in South Africa. We camped nearby and rode without our luggage to the entrance.

'Motorbikes are not allowed in the park. I am sorry,' the man at the ticket office told me.

'We only want to visit the recreation area, not the game park, ' I explained.

'No motorbikes. There is dangerous wildlife. You can walk or cycle,' he added. 'We have bicycles for hire.'

'That makes no sense!' I exclaimed. 'Anyway, there are no dangerous animals in the recreation area here.'

'There could be …' he said.

'Then you shouldn't be allowed in on foot or bicycle,' I argued.

'Motorbikes are noisy and scare the animals. 'I am sorry. I do not make the rules. No motorbikes.'

A large school bus pulled up outside. Black smoke and acrid fumes wafted our way. A row of heads peered from the windows, and a few school kids took the opportunity to get off. The driver shouted at them to behave and get back on board. Laughter and shouting rose above the roar of the engine. It could have been a school bus anywhere in the world. Several minutes later it drove off through the park entrance gates. I can categorically say that two small motorbikes are less intrusive, less noisy and undoubtedly less likely to scare off wildlife than a decrepit ten-tonne bus with fifty unruly school kids.

I suggested to Kieran that we go back to the campsite and get some other clothes, then return to hire bicycles. He was reluctant; it was hot.

A group of white middle-aged ladies in running gear walked out of the park and stopped to chat, curious about what we were doing. I explained about our trip, and we joked about the park rules regarding motorbikes.

'You need a car,' one lady said. 'We have a car. You can borrow ours if you don't mind coming to Bulawayo first.'

I couldn't quite believe what I heard. These ladies were prepared to loan a car to complete strangers. Kieran appeared as surprised and confused as me.

'Er, sure …' I replied.

'OK, great. Because there are six of us we can't all fit into one car and we need to get back to town. Come with us now, borrow the car and bring it back at the end of the day.'

The ladies were convinced this was our best option, so we helmeted up and followed them towards town.

The car slowed at a checkpoint and stopped. After a brief chat with the policeman, they moved on. Then Kieran was stopped; a prolonged conversation with the officer ensued.

I pulled up alongside. 'Is there a problem?' I asked.

Kieran hadn't got his headlight on. The law stated that you must always drive with lights on. Kieran had now switched it on, but it was too late. *What else might he find to fine us with?*

'Your documents,' he demanded.

Oh shit. We had only planned to pop round the corner to the park. Our carnets were at the campsite with the rest of our belongings.

I handed over our passports poker-faced, hoping that would suffice.

'And the import papers,' he demanded.

Busted.

I explained with the most apologetic face I could muster that we didn't have them.

'You, park there and speak to that man,' he ordered, pointing first at the kerb, then at another official further on.

Sigh. I looked towards the black car, feeling guilty for making the ladies wait.

The second officer was more amenable. I persuaded him to let us through, promising we would return the following day with the carnets. I could give no guarantee except my word. Why he agreed I've no idea, but I didn't hang around to question him. I suspect he didn't want his life complicated by wrangling with an obstinate tourist. His time was better spent focussing on the locals, who knew the rules of engagement and grudgingly paid up.

Later we were stopped for not having regulation reflectors on our bikes. The officer tried to fine us forty dollars. New legislation required larger cars like 4x4s and commercial vehicles to have strips of reflective tape to a detailed specification on the bumpers and along the sides of longer vehicles. All machines capable of producing the tape had been bought by a government minister weeks before the new law came into effect. Nobody was fooled; it was a money-making scheme, not for improved safety.

The officer insisted the law applied to us because our bikes were commercial vehicles. He slipped up by agreeing with me that we were tourists because we were in the country on tourist visas, and since tourists were forbidden from conducting business, our bikes couldn't be commercial.

When he changed tack, saying motorcycles must still have regulation reflectors on the front and rear, I insisted that he show me the legislation in writing. Rather too eagerly, he brought out a well-used 'law book' of printed sheets of A4 stapled together from the police car and flicked through the grubby, thumbed pages.

'See here,' he pointed.

I read the rule and replied, 'This only refers to red reflectors on the rear and doesn't specify the type. We are in compliance.'

He slammed the book shut and ordered us to go. I quickly rode off with a smug grin on my face. *Oh, this is the Africa I love!*

These games never lost their appeal. I should have been outraged by the corruption but couldn't help being impressed. He was a worthy opponent, less amateurish than many. Kieran was unimpressed.

We pulled up to a modest house in the leafy suburbs, locked our bikes and were handed the car key.

'It's very trusting to loan us your car,' I commented.

'It's very trusting to leave your motorbikes on our drive,' the ladies joked.

We could have chatted all day about our exploits on the road and their adventures of daily life, but they told us to go explore while there was daytime remaining and to post the car key through the letterbox when we returned.

The ticket officer at the park entrance was unsurprised by our new mode of transport and, wishing us a good day, handed over the tickets. The tarmac drive wound between steep granite rock faces towering to either side. It was strange being so low down in the car, the view inferior compared to the motorbike.

At Maleme dam we parked and set off on foot, wandering over open rocks and through a wooded grove, stumbling clumsily on roots in our bike boots. Sweating through our jeans in the heavy still air, we came to the cool shade of Pomongwe cave, with drawings by San bushmen who lived here over 2,000 years ago. Red painted hunters with bows and arrows and spears leapt like dancers with hundreds of animals – giraffe, elephant and kudu – migrating across the walls.

Baboons, absent from the cave paintings, were prolific in the park. Whilst stopped for lunch at a picnic area, a young baboon sneaked up

149

behind me, leapt onto the table and tried to grab my sandwich. With a lightning reflex, I swiped the bread but was too late to save the juicy ripe tomato. It seemed the baboons were in collusion with the vervet monkeys. We ate quickly, indigestion preferable to hunger.

As well as baboons and bushmen, the British mining magnate, imperialist and politician, Cecil Rhodes spent a lot of time in these hills. He is buried on the summit of Malindidzimu, a sacred place to indigenous groups meaning Hill of the Spirits, but simply known as World's View to tourists. We walked around the smooth inselberg and clambered over the giant rounded rocks, which seemed as though they could topple and roll at any moment.

All too soon we were driving back towards the main gate, baboon-spotting as we went. We needed to return the car. Neither of us wanted to ride back to the campsite in the dark when the risk of hitting animals is too great.

It wasn't until a couple of days later that we saw any wildlife close-up again. We'd gone to visit the ruins of Great Zimbabwe, the archaeological site of what was the capital of the Kingdom of Zimbabwe between the eleventh and fifteenth centuries. They are some of the oldest ruined stone buildings in Southern Africa, and its imposing eleven-metre high walled Great Enclosure is the largest ancient structure south of the Sahara.

The campsite next to the ruins was devoid of tents, 4x4s or overlanding trucks. The economic state of the country and recent protests were detrimentally impacting tourism. A note at reception warned campers to lock their vehicles, keep windows closed and not leave belongings unattended.

A band of thieves was operating in the area.

Thieves with long tails, who swung from the trees.

Vervet monkeys.

We'd seen them on our way in; thirty or so, sitting about as though they owned the place.

We were wise to their ways now.

150

If it had been up to Kieran, we would have foregone seeing the ruins and continued riding, not willing to risk the monkeys wrath again. He had assessed the battlefield like a commander, deemed the opponents too numerous, determined that loss was inevitable despite superior weaponry and that it would be safer to flee than fight. I was the dissenter in the ranks.

We unloaded our roll bags, panniers and tank bags and, with our helmets and boots, put them all in the secure reception area. If vervet monkeys can unzip tents and open car doors, they can probably unclip a bag or kickstart a motorbike. I locked the bike and, with the key clasped tight, I thrust my hand deep into my trouser pocket as I walked across enemy territory. They weren't stealing my Serow.

The vervet monkeys sat and watched us go, biding their time.

When we returned, the monkeys had all vanished. Weary of ambush, we hauled our bags across the campsite and selected our spot, not for the view or flattest ground but because it provided the best place to defend, far from any trees and scrub. In the open we could see the marauders approach.

The youngsters appeared first, fearless and bold. They approached and retreated in turns as though playing a game to see who could get the closest. The adults attempted plunder when we lit the stove, approaching from the rear and using the tent to hide from view. We took turns standing guard.

Kieran had been learning new skills with his nunchucks, which he'd made whilst we were hiking in South Africa. Without knowing, he'd selected knobwood, often used to make knobkerries, a short stick with a rounded bulge traditionally used as a weapon. My bo staff was a long stick we'd picked up in Lesotho to fend off aggressive shepherds' dogs.

Swinging the bo staff and nunchucks initially held back the monkeys until they realised that we lacked the skill or intent to place a hit. Kieran's Tool-in-a-Can flamethrower sent them scarpering temporarily. In the end, the setting sun sent them away, peace descending with the darkness.

The ceasefire lasted until first light.

Unzipping the tent, I caught sight of spindly tails and long back legs leaping away to a safe distance, where they turned about and sat on their heels, a wide-eyed, eager audience waiting for the game to resume.

———

We rode to Chimanimani National Park on the eastern border, parked our bikes at the ticket office and set off with a rucksack and a couple of days of food. After an initial scramble up the steep rocky face, the land opened onto a plateau, and we followed the trail between gnarled rock formations that sprouted out of the ground like giant warts. We left our overnight supplies at a mountain hut and crossed the wide valley to the mountains forming a natural border with Mozambique. At the top of Skeleton Pass, with a foot in each country, we looked east towards the horizon, over rugged ridgelines and swathes of forested valleys that looked so much wilder and untouched than the Zimbabwean side, which was being lost to felling for timber and burning for agriculture.

This was as close to Mozambique as we'd get; the embassy in Mutare was only issuing expensive transit visas. We had no interest in rushing through just for another passport stamp. We needed a new direction.

We were indifferent to riding north through Zambia. I scrutinised the map for alternatives. There was the DR Congo. *Oh how I'd love to go back!* We wouldn't risk bumping into Charlie or his friends if we rode along the eastern border towards Kalemie and crossed Lake Tanganyika. Maybe that would satisfy my irrational craving. *No, lay these fantasies to rest.* The remaining option was to transit to Malawi and then ride north. Often referred to as 'Africa for beginners', Malawi is an easy country to travel through. It's safe, has a decent tourist infrastructure, and has many beautiful sandy beaches along its lake.

Beach holidays are not my style, but it was better to approach the country with an open mind and look for the opportunities afforded by ease and comfort. A slower pace of travel and staying in backpacker lodges and campsites might give me the chance to focus on my writing. Kieran said he would find ways to occupy his time on this holiday from the rigours of the previous months.

15.

No Place Like Home

Malawi

To write in Malawi, I wanted my laptop. But my laptop wouldn't charge because I'd left the charger at a campsite in Zambia. I'd also left my towel and a pair of underwear there, but neither of those stopped me typing, only lightened my load.

Finding a replacement charger in Lilongwe, Malawi's capital, involved a hectic but fun morning dodging tuk-tuk taxis. We went from M1 electronics to Consumer Solutions, Computer King, a couple of stores near the banks and finally Radio Exchange, where the fellow behind the glass counter with soldering iron and circuit board in his hands took up the hunt with enthusiasm. Surrounded by hundreds of boxes of IT equipment and computer parts but no complete computer on the shelves, he rifled through containers of chargers but came out empty-handed.

'Do not worry!' he exclaimed. 'I will call my other shop.'

Ten minutes later an out-of-breath Indian, who looked like he ran a lot of errands, entered the shop and handed over three chargers. One was the correct voltage but the adapter was too big.

'No problem!' he exclaimed. This man was in the problem-solving business. He filed down the end a little, wiggled it and gave it a good shove to squeeze it into the laptop, then plugged it in. It worked!

We went back to the bikes triumphant. One of my panniers was unzipped, some food we'd bought now gone. You win some, you lose some. Now all I needed to write was a peaceful scenic spot.

Senga Bay was not that place. The campsite, at the budget end of a compound beyond the resort hotel, resembled a dusty parking lot more than a sandy beach and was full of more families than Brighton in the school holidays. The combination of children and loud music was not conducive to literary creativity. We suffered through one night, then rode further up the coast.

At Nkhotakota on a farm, the private spot under palm trees on the edge of the expansive sandy beach was more to our liking. The beach was usually empty except at first and last light. In the hour before the sun rose above the calm water, young boys walked the shoreline and searched the rock pools for stranded fish, men launched their boats onto the lake, and the women walked from the village to wash clothes and spread them to dry on rocks in the sun.

Peace and serenity were temporary. When the wind whipped up at night, blowing sand through the mesh inner of the tent, I had to bury my head in my sleeping bag to breathe. By morning, with sore eyes, I was too tired to write. But what made us pack up and move on were the daily visitors to our camp.

They arrived through the treetops and settled in the palms above our tent.

They looked curious and cute and cuddly, but we knew better.

Vervet monkeys.

A woman who worked at the farm was hanging out laundry. They weren't going to get her fresh linen. When she spotted them watching her, in one slick manoeuvre, she picked up a pebble and hurled it with sniper-like precision. The monkey leapt to another branch. They'd both played this game before.

She saw us looking up in the trees, picked up another pebble and launched it directly at the little one. The monkey ducked, the missile missing its head by inches, then sat back up unperturbed. The woman didn't like being dismissed so readily and marched over, bending down every few strides to scoop one pebble after another, hurling them on the move. The monkeys scarpered through the trees, fleeing the bombardment. And when the woman reached us, the monkeys, Kieran and I all stopped and stared at her. She smiled, gave a satisfied nod and returned to her laundry. But the monkeys soon plucked up courage and encroached on our pitch again. It was time to move.

Continuing north, the tarmac was smooth, the winding road fast and flowing. I felt as one with the bike until, suddenly, the back end felt loose and started to wobble. Flat tyre.

The tyres had done 20,000 kilometres since Cape Town and, whilst they didn't have a lot of grip in wet and mud, we were hopeful that they'd get us to Nairobi, where decent new tyres were easy to get. New tyres wouldn't have stopped the six inch nail, which had hit the rim and bent ninety degrees.

I unloaded the luggage and dug out the tyre levers and went in search of something with which to lift the rear wheel off the ground. In less than forty minutes we had the wheel off, tyre removed and offending nail pulled out, inner tube replaced, the tyre back on the rim helped with some shampoo as lubricant, and had pumped it up and put the wheel back on the bike.

It was dark by the time we reached the base of the hill to Livingstonia and began attacking the rough rocky bumpy track. I hugged the inside, fully concentrating on every rock and rut and not riding too fast. With the Serow's dim headlight, I found it hard to see where the trail suddenly changed direction as it switch-backed upwards. I was nervous that one wrong move could send me plummeting into the pitch black, down the vertiginous escarpment, but I loved the rush of adrenalin and thrill of the ride. The trails since Angola had all seemed tame.

After a couple of nights camping at a backpackers lodge, we relocated to a community guesthouse at the top of the hill, with friendly staff who cooked us dinner each night. Our private room had a comfy double bed with fresh white linen sheets, a functioning light and plug sockets. It was a simple wooden hut but luxurious compared to sleeping in a tent.

Spending time indoors had become a rarity. Privacy, safety and security are all luxuries easily taken for granted. I hadn't missed them, but here I could let my guard down. I enjoyed not having to pack our bags or pitch a tent every day, or be disturbed by mischievous meddling vervet monkeys, loud music or howling winds.

Places I stay more than the few days often take on a familiarity that begins to feel like home. Home is also where friends are.

A happy-go-lucky South Korean girl arrived on foot with a huge backpack. She had left her 125cc Honda motorcycle at a campsite and was now hiking. We'd originally met in Botswana, then more recently stayed at the same campsite in Zambia and later overtook her on Malawi's lakeside road. We also received a message from Lizzie and James, the British couple in the 4x4 who'd driven through Angola, saying they were also on their way. Sometimes the world seemed a very small place.

That night we had a fire, braai and beers late into the night as the rest of the village slept. It felt as though we could have been the last people on earth with only the stars to see us, our stories lingering and laughter melting into the air by the flickering flames. It was like old times, even though we'd only ever spent a few days together. Making friends quickly is the nature of travel.

The days passed quickly. I wrote in the mornings, then took a leisurely stroll with Kieran through the village along tree-lined avenues. The market was at the centre of a quad of small shops. The many concrete tables and wooden frames suggested a thriving place once. Now, piles of tomatoes and onions, rice and ground nuts, and small bowls for measuring out portions remained untouched; only the bananas hung from hooks seemed to sell. We bought bread from one shop and Castle beer from another. It didn't take long before the owner knew what we wanted on our daily visit.

Having rarely stayed in one place in the UK long enough to feel part of a community, days like this made me long for a more settled, less transient lifestyle. Sometimes I envied people who are satisfied with a conventional life of routine, but I know that I would not remain contented in a permanent location for long. My roots never spread deep enough to overcome the nomadic urge that surges through my core, sustaining me and making me feel alive.

After a few days, once Kieran had nothing left to fix on the bikes and with his journal up to date and videos edited, there were only so many cups of tea he could drink while I wrote. I felt guilty for making him hang around. So this unsettled feeling drove us from the ease and comfort that Livingstonia provided. Besides, I was ready to wake up not knowing what the day would bring or where I would sleep that night.

Rather than riding the featureless bush of the interior of Tanzania, we'd heard about a boat that regularly transports people and goods up and down Lake Tanganyika. We could embark at Kasanga, a small village in the south of Tanzania, which had a quay, the waters deep enough for the ferry to dock and enable our bikes to be loaded.

Schedules in Africa are more like rough guidelines than strict timetables. The one I'd found on the internet was of uncertain provenance. Unsure exactly how long it would take us to reach Kasanga from Livingstonia, I allowed a couple of days leeway for unforeseen problems. We had a border to cross, and they always represent some uncertainty. Having a couple of days to relax by the lake seemed preferable to arriving late and having to wait two weeks while the boat made the round trip to Kigoma.

Deadlines are rare on overland journeys, the advantage of having your own vehicle rather than relying on the vagaries of public transport. Now, for the first time since boarding the plane to Cape Town, we had a date with a fixed destination.

Life tended to progress smoothly when I had no direction; add a deadline and something would inevitably go awry. At first, delays are inconsequential because I like to allow plenty of time, but as the clock counts down and small problems add up, anxiety bubbles to the surface. *Will we make it on time?*

16.

The MV Liemba

Tanzania

'I wonder what it is we should have done?' Kieran pondered the evening before we intended to leave Livingstonia. Rhetorical question or not, it got me thinking. We always forgot something.

'Ah, I know! You were going to change the inner tube on your back tyre. The one with the valve that's started leaking,' I said.

'Nah, I'll wait now until we get new tyres.'

'Really? You'll be pumping it up every day!' I exclaimed. 'Don't expect me to.'

'That's OK,' he replied.

Pumping up tyres with a bicycle pump is exhausting and only serves to make you feel hot and sweaty, out of breath and unfit. We'd already proved we could remove and refit a tyre in minimal time.

'OK, your decision. But you're not allowed to complain about it,' I said mockingly.

'Of course I'm allowed to complain about it!' He exclaimed and we laughed.

The next morning, we packed our belongings that a week ago had fit into our roll bags but had expanded to fill an entire room. I'd loaded up my bike and was sitting on the balcony, waiting for the ladies to bring our breakfast.

Kieran returned. 'Ugh, that tyre I pumped up first thing has already gone down!'

'So you know that thing we should have done before we leave ...' I joked.

The ride to the border went smoothly. The bureaucracy of exiting one country and entering another was efficient. I wasn't entirely sure whether the fees for visas, tourist tax, vehicle insurance and road tax were all genuine. For a hassle-free crossing, we paid up and got receipts.

Across the border, we rode to ever increasing elevations, the hillsides covered in tea plantations. Towards Mbeya, the biggest town in southern Tanzania, the roads became congested with big trucks, whilst Bajaj, little auto-rickshaws named after the Indian company who manufacture them, tooted their horns, nipping and weaving chaotically between the lorries like ants. I felt grimier being held up with the old vehicles churning out dirty noxious fumes than after a week without washing in the desert.

We camped in town on the grass volleyball court in the Catholic Mission compound for an exorbitant price, which we hoped would guarantee the safety of our belongings. After a much needed shower, we went in search of food. Rice and beans leftover from the lunchtime trade was all that remained.

Cold beer, however, was in plentiful supply. We took a Kilimanjaro and a Safari from the fridge in a wooden shack, paid the unsmiling lady and took a seat on the plastic chairs outside. As the sun set over the small tin-roof stores with secondhand car parts and accessories for sale, men rolled massive truck tyres down the dusty street to be safely locked up. By the end of the second beer, I was straining my eyes to make out shadowy figures moving between the shops on the unlit streets.

Occasionally a ragged-clothed, unkempt man stumbled into the store and bought a fifty millilitre sachet of cheap whisky, gin or Konyagi, the Tanzanian liquor distilled from sugarcane. Costing around twenty-five cents, the plastic sachets of intoxicating spirit were affordable to even the poorest. In 2017 a ban on these alcohol sachets was introduced to curb youth boozing (the sachets are easily concealed between the pages of school exercise books) and help protect the environment (the sachets are regularly discarded on the street and clog up drains).

Unfortunately, we started to attract attention from the less salubrious patrons, our white faces standing out under the low-wattage light bulb in the store. It seemed prudent to return to the safe confines of the Catholic mission. We had a long ride to the lake.

Out of town, the main road descended from the lush plantations to vast expanses of stubble fields. Where Bajaj drivers hustled for trade amongst the roadside stalls selling fruit and vegetable imports near the Zambian border, we took a right turn onto a quieter road headed west.

In Laela, the guesthouse was characteristic of East African accommodation with loud music blaring from the bar and rooms with ensuite squat toilets. The shops, also typical, sold mostly confectionery and fizzy drinks, catering for the sweet-toothed Tanzanian kids. They wandered down the road with large lengths of sugar cane over their shoulders, habitually ripping off and chewing strips to extract the sugary juice before discarding the remnants and leaving a trail of destruction underfoot.

In the next town, we stopped for breakfast. The coffee was made with granules so old they didn't dissolve in the hot milk. The young man serving us shrugged his shoulders as if to say, you ordered coffee, I gave you coffee, and walked off. I laughed, shrugged *my* shoulders and gave it another stir.

I was so content, immersed in each moment with no thought to the past and allowing the vagaries of travel to erase my anxiety about reaching the port on time. *So what if we missed the boat?* We could wait two weeks or ride north instead. We passed more small villages on yet smaller roads through the bush on dusty tracks. Even struggling in the sand couldn't dampen my mood.

Then Kieran got a puncture. The wear on his rear tyre was accelerating, raising fears that it wouldn't last until Nairobi.

'Why does this have to happen now, here?' he vented.

His reaction of frustrated anger took me by surprise.

'Never mind, it's happened,' I said nonchalantly, which irritated more than pacified.

We moved the bikes to solid ground and began the familiar puncture repair process. Kieran soon relaxed into it. Kids appeared and watched from a distance until confidence and curiosity about our tools overwhelmed their reserve. I got out my camera and took photos, which sent them scarpering like vervet monkeys, laughing as they fled. Then the older kids led us to a man with a compressor in the village, which made re-inflating the tyre and seating it on the rim easy.

Even with the flat tyres, we arrived a couple of days before the boat's expected arrival. The lodge on the outskirts of Kasanga village allowed camping on the beach under the shade of the palm trees. The owner served us grilled locally caught tilapia and rice al fresco in the evening as the sun set over the lake, the water gently lapping at the shore. The next morning, he told us the boat had not yet left Kigoma but was expected to depart that afternoon and take two days to travel here.

I wrote my journal, read a book and intermittently made cups of tea on the stove. The owner's six-year-old son played contentedly alone in the camp with only an imagination for company, except when he came over to us, babbling non-stop as though we understood the language.

Everyday, children took the path between the lake and the camp. Schoolgirls dressed smartly in white blouses and dark pinafores walked past quietly and orderly. The shirtless boys in secondhand shorts laughed and joked, calling out 'Mzungu! Mzungu!' and 'What eez ma nem?'

One time, a tiny girl walking with her mother called repeatedly to us 'Wah-yu! Wah-yu!' To which the mother, carrying a bucket on her head and speaking the queen's English, precise and clear, said to her daughter, 'No, it is "how are you?".' The girl repeated 'Wah-yu! wah-yu!' and the mother looked over and returned my smile. 'Now say "Good afternoon",' she said to her daughter, and the daughter called out, 'Good af-ta-nun!' Both the mother and I laughed. 'Good afternoon,' I replied.

Some afternoons, sweating in the intense heat, we walked along the lakeshore in flip-flops, the sand too hot for soft bare feet. Boys fished with rods made from branches and splashed in the shallows. Where the reeds opened out, fishing nets were spread out along the beach, the small catch from the previous night's excursions drying in the sun.

Children continued to call out 'Mzungu!' and 'What eez ma nem?'

'I don't know, what is your name?' I replied, knowing that wasn't what they meant, but it confused and kept them quiet for a few seconds longer.

In the village itself, we found a cafe-shack nestled under the trees and sat inside with the flies for company. Partially hidden behind the curtained doorway, we were out of sight of the young men playing table football in varying states of inebriation. Invariably, the menu consisted of locally caught tilapia fish, beans and rice. The food cost a fraction of the lodge's prices, and here we could get cold drinks. The lodge only turned on the generator for an hour in the evening, never long enough to chill the beers stacked in the fridge. We'd drink beer anyway and watch the lamplights of fishing boats flickering on the lake under the starlight.

Finally, one afternoon the call came that the boat was expected. We packed up, rode to the port and waited in the shade. More people arrived and waited. At midnight, we were informed that the boat had been delayed again due to the high volume of goods being loaded at another village and were told to come back early in the morning. Someone mentioned six o'clock.

There seemed little point in going back to the lodge. Instead, we rolled our bikes down to the far end of the quayside, a patch of wasteland, and pitched our tent. I slept little. The wind howled all night and by morning everything was covered in orange dirt. There was no sign of the boat.

Several hours later, a boat appeared on the horizon and sounded its horn, gradually drawing nearer and looming larger until we could make out its definable shape: the *MV Liemba* that I had seen in black and white photographs. *Finally!*

Formerly known as the *Graf von Goetzen*, the boat was originally built in Germany in 1913, then dissembled, packed into 5,000 boxes and shipped to Dar es Salaam on the Tanzanian coast before being loaded onto trains and transported inland to Kigoma, where it was rebuilt.

During World War I, it was converted into a warship and, with two other ships, was used to launch surprise attacks on the Allies, ensuring the Germans controlled Lake Tanganyika. The British Royal Navy launched counterattacks with two armed motorboats, *Mimi* and *Toutou*, brought from England via the Belgian Congo using roads, railways and rivers. With air support, the British boats bombed Kigoma where the *Goetzen* was in harbour. When the railway was attacked, cutting off the town, the Germans removed the guns from the *Goetzen*, loaded it with sand, covered the engines in oil and scuttled it.

In 1918, the Belgians salvaged the ship by filling the holds with empty barrels and, with cables passed underneath and attached to two purpose-built barges, lifted the ship enough to float. A storm in 1920 submerged it again. Finally, the British raised and reconditioned the ship, renaming it the *MV Liemba*, which has operated since 1927 as a passenger and cargo ferry.

With the boat docked, we waited as bags of cement were lifted out of the hold by a huge crane, then moved to the warehouse by a team of local men, who carried the sacks on their shoulders. Working fast, they'd carry a sack to the harbour building and dump it, clouds of cement dust filling the heavy air as it hit the ground, then they'd return to the dock for another sack without stopping.

An hour passed with no sign of any worker slowing. Hour after hour passed until I thought there couldn't be any sacks left on board, but the sacks kept appearing and the air became cloudier and greyer. My throat got sore even though we watched from a distance, and I hated to think what the workers' lungs were like.

The afternoon wore on, more passengers arrived and waited in the shade, bags and belongings tied up in blankets. Then a call went out over the tannoy, and gradually people began moving.

We wheeled our bikes towards the ferry. A deckhand indicated an old cargo net lying on the ground. Kieran pushed his bike onto it, attached cable hooks to the four corners of the net, the ropes thicker than my arms. The ship's crane slowly winched up the net until it enveloped the bike.

'Wait, wait!' Kieran called.

The deckhand shouted to the winch operator to stop. Once satisfied the bike wouldn't topple out of the net, we gave the go ahead and watched nervously as the bike was lifted through the air onto the forecastle. My bike was next.

The harbour master approached. He didn't look like a man of authority in his slouchy jeans, baseball cap and unkempt beard. His thick hands and creases on his face suggested he'd once had a harder life than his current position of barking orders and taking bribes. 'Come with me,' he ordered.

'Why?' I asked, more interested in making sure the bikes were secure. Kieran went on board to lash them down.

'Now you must pay the loading fee'. He pointed at the crane on the dock, then put his thick hands in his pockets, causing his jeans to slide below his belly.

'No way,' I said defensively but ready to fight my position. 'I paid you last night.'

'That was the embarkation fee,' he explained.

'I don't care. You overcharged us then. We paid more than enough to cover all fees for the bikes too.' I was still annoyed at myself for having conceded, but I'd had no leverage and was tired. I wasn't going to let him keep milking us.

He quoted an extortionate rate. I sniggered and hardened my stance. I had the upper hand now because our bikes were already on board.

'I'm not paying you more. No one on the dock helped. We had to do it ourselves because no one takes responsibility, and the crane on the *Liemba* was used to lift our bikes, not the one on the docks.'

He gave up. He liked easy money, not hard work.

I walked up the gangway, under the crane, across the platform and climbed the steps onto the forecastle where Kieran had finished tying down the bikes and was talking to the ship's navigator.

I was still on edge, wondering what other issues I'd have to resolve. Travel by independent means was a luxury I had started to take for granted. Now, I remembered the underlying disquiet of being reliant upon and at the mercy of others to get about.

As white people, the captain spotted us and came over to welcome us aboard, treating us royally despite our grubby, unwashed and tired appearance. He asked whether we wanted standard or first class tickets. I'd never travelled first class anywhere. We splashed out.

The captain showed us to our small but clean cabin with a bunk bed, wardrobe, sink and a tiny table top fixed to the wall. It was hot and airless, but the front-facing window had a mesh covering, which the captain promised would let a cool breeze filter through once we got underway.

'Cabin number one is the best,' he assured us.

I suspected he said the same about each of the four cabins. I was content because our luggage would be safe, and I could escape from the public eye anytime I wanted.

We shut the door, drew the curtains, and I lay down on the bed. Finally, I could relax. The tension seeped out of my shoulders. 'Wouldn't a beer be good right now?' I said with a sigh.

When no one miraculously appeared offering cold drinks, we got up to explore. The boat had looked huge from the outside but took barely five minutes to walk around. Most people were squeezed on benches or the floor at the back amongst their bags and belongings. I was more used to roughing it this way and felt glad and guilty for our cabin.

In the dining room, we sat with Michael, a South African who was also on a motorbike for his holiday, and Arthur, a backpacker from Belgium. We had little in common except for being white people travelling in Africa, which gave us enough to talk about, and for having cabins, which also set us apart; isolation, the price of luxury.

René, an easy-going, affable Congolese guy, told us to get comfortable. He worked on the *Emmanuela*, which was docked alongside. He knew neither boat would be leaving until all the sacks of millet from his boat had been transferred to ours.

I bought Kilimanjaro beers and relaxed into the slow pace of African travel, which mostly involved waiting.

Tired from the previous restless night on the dock, we went to bed early only to be woken around midnight by the deafening blast of the ship's horn. The sound of the engines increased, the gentle vibrations becoming juddering shakes as the boat pulled away from the dock with the rudder on hard. When the noise dimmed to a background hum, I felt the gentle sway as we glided over the lake. *We're underway!*

I spent most of the next day reading peacefully in the cabin, coming out only for the meals served at set times, the food forgettable except that it wasn't tilapia and rice everyday.

The boat stopped at villages to load and unload people and goods. Where there was no jetty, the ship remained in deep water. When the horn sounded, dozens of wooden dugouts left the distant shore of golden sand, palm trees and giant rounded boulder formations. They motored out, pulling up and jostling for position abreast the *MV Liemba*.

A melee of people in a multitude of bright colours lingered on the deck and leaned over the railings. Sacks of maize were offloaded, whilst chickens and apples and who knows what other fruit and vegetables and fish were thrown on board. Men clambered up and down with bags and buckets, women were given a helping hand, and babies were passed unceremoniously by an arm or dangling leg between boats. One lady fell inelegantly into the water when the wooden boat she was stretching to reach separated from the *MV Liemba*. Several hands quickly came to her rescue. Her initial look of wide-eyed surprise turned to smiles and laughter as she rang out her dress and wiped her face with a cloth someone passed. When a lad nimbly darting between boats, whose confidence and ego dwarfed his small frame, misjudged a leap and ended with a drenching, several of his friends cheered. When the horn gave its warning blast for imminent departure, a frenzy of last minute trades and transactions were completed.

As the *MV Liemba* began to pull away, the wooden dugouts turned about and set for shore until another two weeks' time. Even though the open water held no boundaries and they were free take any route they pleased, each boat followed the course of the one in front, so that they spread out in a straight line as though fettered by some unseen chain.

I returned to the cabin and wondered which direction we'd go next once back on land, reunited with our bikes. We were not free to go in just any direction, constrained by roads and regulations, guided by hopes and fears.

I pored over the map, tracing my finger in loops and circles past lakes, over mountains and across borders, but whichever way it went, my eyes were drawn west to DR Congo. I couldn't help it. I knew there was a boat that crosses Lake Tanganyika from Kigoma to Kalemie.

I had planned to leave DR Congo that way when I had cycled there, but that was before other events overshadowed my plans, forcing me to leave by other means.

Where, I wondered, might we get a DR Congo visa? Of the people I knew, who would I contact for a letter of invitation? These seemed mere formalities. If the three months I'd travelled there had taught me anything, it was that when it comes to the Congo, anything is possible if you know how to play the game. The country is like a chessboard, and you make the choice to be a pawn or the queen. Do you let others take control or do you tactically plot your moves in advance?

I had always wanted to take a barge down the Congo River to Kinshasa. If we did that, we'd be on the west coast again, and I wasn't sure how to get back east. Alternatively, we could ride to Kisangani, then head to Rwanda, which involved the added risk of regional instability. I could justify going if it enabled me to reach my destination, but this was going for travel's sake alone.

I knew I could look after myself and deal with corruption and bribery, daily interrogations by the police or immigration, and the endless attention of hundreds of children in every village.

If I were travelling alone and could have got a visa, I probably would have gone. But I had to consider Kieran. I wasn't sure how he would handle everything or how I would handle Kieran.

The only times I have been genuinely concerned about my safety have been when travelling with a male, whose aggressive response made compromising situations worse. I never understood how they failed to see that they're reactions were inflammatory and counter-productive. I prefer flight over a fight and plan escapes in anticipation. When the male response is to attack – especially when they see themselves as my protector, albeit not needed and unwanted – I'm unsure how best to react.

I remembered the fury, anger and desire for revenge in Kieran's eyes when we'd been scammed by money changers at the Zambian border. He had strutted away red-faced with shoulders tensed and barely contained rage threatening to spill out of him and into trouble. I could not trust that he would remain calm when faced with real danger. I would have hoped his military training would ensure he kept control of his emotions, but I couldn't be sure. Unpredictability is a dangerous trait.

In the end, I chose Kieran over DR Congo. My dreams of returning would not come true on this journey. I told myself to never regret my choice or hold this decision against him. Some things are easier said than done.

I'd been in touch with Claire Elsdon, who had set up and now ran MJ Piki, an organisation based in Mwanza, Tanzania, championing community-safe motorcycling by training women to safely ride and maintain motorcycles. I'd hoped we could visit and help out for a while, but Claire was in the UK at the time.

As we'd already got our visas online for Rwanda, another country I longed to visit and one that was safe to travel through, we decided to head directly there through Tanzania. I was more like those boats departing the *MV Liemba* than I realised, apparently free to go where I wanted but constrained to one direction by the reality of invisible forces.

17.

Refugees and Reconciliation
Rwanda

Many places I have visited on my travels are linked to wars. After all, humanity has always fought, and war tourism is not a new concept. Whilst death and suffering horrifies me, I find it fascinating to see what emerges in the aftermath of war: rebuilding, reconciliation, the rebirth of dreams like a phoenix rising from the ashes. Often the best and worst of humanity are closely aligned.

Even though the genocide synonymous with Rwanda happened over twenty years ago, when Hutu extremists were incensed to commit atrocities against the minority Tutsi population, tension remained high. Whilst Rwanda was seen as a beacon of hope and light, the problems had shifted across the border to Burundi.

The dusty orange laterite road from Kigoma towards Rwanda runs parallel to the Burundian border, always about twenty kilometres away. People fleeing danger spilled across this border. Aid agency signs erected at the end of each side road indicated where the refugee camps were, out of sight, where it was easier to pretend they didn't exist. The camps, originally set up for refugees fleeing civil war in DR Congo, had recently become the destination for over 100,000 Burundians fleeing their country. It was hard to imagine so many people in temporary shelters close by.

The road was being upgraded with the bush being cleared and the ground prepared. Thick clouds of dust filled the air, our nostrils and lungs, and coated us in an orange layer like Oompah Loompahs. Fortunately we found a cheap hotel and bucket washed the dust off before presenting ourselves at the border.

Rwanda's new immigration building resembled a modern airport departure lounge. I don't recall seeing litter on the roadsides or in the gutters as we weaved along the winding green hills past flooded rice paddies in the valleys, banana plantations and countless villages on the way to Kigali, the capital. Rwanda appeared to be leading the way in Africa both economically and environmentally.

Once every month there is a community day when everyone collects rubbish and cleans the streets. A ban on single-use plastic bags helped reduce litter. The lack of suitable alternatives for street vendors and market sellers has led to a thriving black market trade. Between the DR Congo border and Kigali the price of plastic bags triples. The risk if caught is severe with up to six months imprisonment.

Murky shadows often linger behind shining examples. There are rarely heroes without villains, rebels with rules, light without darkness, or pleasure without pain. An homogenous one-dimensional world would be plain and boring. Africa is a loveable rogue full of contrast, where the very best and worst sit side by side, and sometimes it's hard to tell them apart.

—

I'd been in touch with Benjamin, a contact from another overland traveller, as someone who could get new tyres. He told us to meet him at Car Wash in Kigali. He mentioned the bar with the casual assumption that *everyone* in the city knew it.

Car Wash was next to a petrol station in a large covered area, empty except for one couple in a dark corner and Benjamin, sitting at the far end near the pool table, lit by green, pink and purple disco lights.

We ordered Primus beer and joined him. I was taken aback by the young guy with tightly braided hair and silver bling on his wrists and thick rings on his fingers. I'd expected a mechanic in grubby overalls not a graphic designer in trendy shirt and smart trousers. Even after decades of travel, I am guilty of falling into the trap of stereotyping.

'Have you eaten yet?' Benjamin asked. 'This is the best place in town for *nyama choma*. It translates as grilled meat and is usually goat.'

I loved grilled goat. Together with Primus beer, memories of Kinshasa's nightlife and eating at city street cafes came flooding back. I'd not consumed either since I was in DR Congo.

Our days of cooking supermarket food in Southern Africa were long gone. Now we ate cheap meals in street cafes. Each region or country had its speciality. In Tanzania our main meal in the south was tilapia, rice and beans, then as we moved north, *chips mayi*, Swahili for chips and egg and made by throwing a handful of pre-cooked chips into an omelette to reheat them. Ugandan Rolex, vegetable omelette rolled up in a chapati, was delicious, but goat kebab, our staple in Rwanda, was my favourite.

Smart couples and groups arrived, and the tables filled with beers and wine and plates of mouth-watering food. Car Wash was a popular place amongst the burgeoning middle class. Chatter and background music added to the ambience, which made the bar staff in their crisp white shirts and ties look less out of place.

Benjamin was a biker and asked how we found riding in his country. We explained that the winding country roads were great, but the city was another matter. We'd got lost on the myriad of main routes and smaller roads criss-crossing the hillsides. On the map, they appeared almost on top of each other, the distance between them more vertical than horizontal.

I knew it was hard for Kieran to follow the GPS while navigating the chaotic melee of traffic, but there'd been little I could do to help. I hadn't had chance to memorise where we were going beforehand, as the city chaos had come upon us suddenly.

The heavy traffic moved fast; slowing down or hesitating risked collision. We attracted moto-taxis in swarms, the young riders curious to see our bikes. They rode close and stared at the luggage, the other traffic forgotten. Only the beep of a car horn or Kieran's angered

173

shouts when they swerved too close brought their focus back to the road. Then they sped off, darting between the cars and buses, and other moto-taxis took their place. I loved the chaos but Kieran was furious at them.

Benjamin laughed and sympathised. Despite being heavily regulated – each driver was required to wear a coloured bib with their registration, license and mobile numbers on it, and every passenger was obligated by law to wear a helmet – there was no minimum riding standard or test to pass. Anyone who could afford an imported 125cc bike could register as a taxi. The moto-taxis were the greatest cause of and casualties in traffic accidents, but they were cheap and convenient, so many people used them in preference to taking a bus.

'You know we call Rwanda the Switzerland of Africa,' Benjamin joked. 'It's a small, landlocked, green and hilly country with lots of rules and regulations where everything's expensive.'

The waiter brought over our grilled goat kebabs. We ordered another round of beer and changed the topic to tyres. Benjamin could get Vee Rubber tyres delivered overnight from Kampala, Uganda's capital. We weren't sure how durable they would be. For the same price we could get tyres in Nairobi, which would definitely get us home. I was certain my tyres would last until Nairobi. Kieran was reluctant to buy the Vee tyres; I didn't want worn tyres to prevent us from riding the routes we wanted. As a compromise, we agreed to continue but get the Vee tyres sent to us if needed. Benjamin gave us the name and number of his contact in Kampala.

The next day we visited the museum about the genocide. Benjamin had advised us to take a moto-taxi rather than walking in the heat.

The ride across town was terrifying. I've been on the back of 125cc moto-taxis all over West Africa. I'd hop on them in my shorts, vest top and flip flops without a second thought. With one hand on the grab rail, I'd peer round the rider's head and admire their quick reactions and reflexes as we rushed through city streets.

174

Now, with an ill-fitting, battered plastic helmet strapped loosely under my chin, I sat with butt cheeks clenched tight, holding on with a double-handed white-knuckle grip, my heart racing every time my rider hit the brakes or overtook. This was the first time I'd ridden pillion with a stranger since I'd learnt to ride. Kieran looked whiter than usual by the time he arrived at the museum entrance.

'Perhaps we can walk back,' he commented dryly.

We watched an emotional introductory video, summarising the genocide and showing interviews with survivors. A woman came round at the end of the screening with a box of tissues; several people took one.

The next few hours were sobering as I tried to digest all that had happened during the hundred days that the genocide had lasted. Eighty per cent of the population knew someone who was murdered, ninety per cent thought they would die at some point. I cannot imagine living in that state of fear.

I searched the info boards and artefacts in the dimly lit rooms for answers. What can incite a person to commit such violence against their fellow man? How can people hate with such savage intensity? And how can others watch the suffering with indifference?

The museum didn't say how many people murdered, whether through extremist ideology or pure survival in a moment of kill or be killed. As we walked back across town, I couldn't help but look at the face of each person that passed. Had they committed a crime? Was their family killed? Not one person in Rwanda today is unaffected by what happened.

I wondered what I would have done? We never know how we will react until put into a situation. It's easy to say I would never kill, but I'm sure most Rwandans said the same before 1994. Self-preservation usually triumphs altruism, and everyone has their breaking point.

18.

Congo-Nile Trail
Rwanda

We'd not done any multi-day hikes since we'd left South Africa, beyond which hiking was limited by climate, terrain or time-restraints. Our excursions on foot had since been predominantly limited to strolling around markets and searching for places to eat in town. I was looking forward to another long-distance walk, to see Rwanda at a slower pace and to get some exercise.

The Congo-Nile trail is a 227-kilometre walking and cycling route, launched and opened in 2009. It's not near either the Congo or the Nile, Africa's two longest rivers, of which neither are in Rwanda. Arguably, the sources of both rivers are around the mountains and Great Lakes of the East African Rift where Rwanda is situated. The reason for the misleading name is pure marketing. Both rivers are famous beyond Africa, have attracted explorers throughout the centuries, and evoke romantic images of raw power and savage beauty.

The Congo-Nile trail follows existing footpaths and tracks along the eastern shore of Lake Kivu, which may not be record-breaking in size but is geologically fascinating. It is one of three lakes known to undergo limnic eruptions, a natural process whereby dissolved carbon dioxide in deep water erupts, forming a gas cloud and possibly a tsunami. The other two lakes, both in Cameroon, experienced such eruptions in the nineties. The resulting gas cloud from one killed 1,700 people and 3,500 livestock by asphyxiation.

Lake Kivu is densely populated with some two million inhabitants along its shores; a limnic eruption here could have disastrous consequences. Geologists have found evidence of local mass extinction events around the lake every thousand years or so, which are attributed to this volcanic activity.

Carbon dioxide, being heavier than air, hugs the ground and does not disperse in valleys. Lethal pockets of carbon dioxide-rich air are known as a *mazuku*, a word from a Rwandan dialect meaning 'evil spirit'. Mazuku indicate areas where people and livestock 'mysteriously' die in the night. For a long time the perennial cause of deaths was unknown but has since been attributed to dry gas vents in depressions where the gas accumulates.

Lake Kivu also contains significant methane, estimated at sixty-five cubic kilometres, which could generate a hundred gigawatts of constant power for a whole year. Until now, the use of trapped methane for energy has been limited to running the boilers at the Bralirwa brewery by the lakeshore. As more is understood about limnic eruptions and the potential disastrous consequences, the Rwandan government has been looking at large-scale extraction projects to meet the countries energy demands while reducing the risk of future eruptions by lowering the concentration of dissolved gas.

We rode to the northern end of the lake, stored our bikes at a lodge, picked up supplies and packed our rucksacks. Past the Bralirwa brewery, the trail followed winding orange earth tracks halfway up the hillside, rising up and down and skirting in and out with the lay of the land through an endless series of settlements. Occasionally we caught a glimpse of the lake.

The entire area was farmed, the hills divided and terraced to grow bananas, maize, beans and cassava. Men and women worked with adze or carried bundled branches of firewood. Some children joined us for short distances or waved from the steps of a hut; most remained out of sight, like the birds. Hidden amongst the leaves and trees, we only knew they were near from their excited calls, 'Mzungu! Mzungu!'

When our feet got sore and our legs were tired because the bikes had made us soft and lazy, we'd mock each other with the ring-necked dove call we'd heard so often in southern Africa, 'Work harder! Work harder!' And I'd look across my shoulder at Kieran and smile. These were the times I loved being together. Though, I couldn't help thinking that I would probably be just as happy were I walking alone.

We stayed at community camps, outside a teacher's hut, and at a coffee washing station. Coffee is one of Rwanda's main exports. Whereas we'd seen tea grown on large estates, coffee is grown by some 400,000 small-scale farmers, each on land a third of the size of a football pitch. The farmers join co-operatives, each with its own washing station, and combine produce to improve the quality.

After three long days we arrived in Kibuye after a stretch on tarmac. We checked into a hotel and took a day off to rest before continuing. The tarmac continued out of town, the sore soles of my feet aching with each step on the hard surface.

A ragged unsavoury character followed us for several kilometres. Then he approached, aggressively demanding to know what was in our bags. Kieran's instant reaction was to grab his nunchucks and tell the man to back off because if he didn't he would not be walking away.

Until then I had been feeling uneasy but not unduly concerned. Suddenly, I was scared of what Kieran might do, knowing that an overreaction could escalate the situation with serious consequences. I quickly put my hands on Kieran's nunchucks and, shaking my head and pleading with my eyes, told him to stop. Fortunately they both backed down.

Why was it that men – it was only ever men – had to be confrontational? Yes, I thought, I made the right decision about not going to DR Congo with Kieran.

The ragged man went on ahead and, once out of sight for a while, we both relaxed, our attention returning to our sore feet.

In the years since the trail's inception, the southern half of the route had been tarmacked. Walking enables me to explore places that are hard to reach on two wheels or more. What was the point of suffering on foot when we could just as easily ride?

The decision to abandon the hike was easy. We walked back to Kibuye, then got a passenger ferry up the lake and returned to the guesthouse where our bikes were stored. I searched the map and GPS for alternative tracks to the main road to Kibuye, where we could pick up the southern half of the Congo-Nile trail. After energy-replenishing pizza and Primus beer, and a good night's sleep, we packed our bags and set off.

My excitement level soared as the tarmac faded to unpaved road, becoming smaller and smaller until it was overgrown single track. Oh, how I missed these kind of trails! We took them in our stride. It was hard to believe that nine months ago I'd been tense and unsure riding in the Cederberg and dropping the bike at every other turn on the 4x4 tracks of the Baviaanskloof.

I barely gave this track a second thought as we rode down to streams, crossed over on slippery wooden logs, bumped and jolted up the rocky dirt trails, and followed meandering footpaths. We skirted the hillsides with patches of forest, dark and cool. Cattle grazed on the plateaus of lush green pasture. If the cows had worn clanging bells around their necks, I would have mistaken the scenery as Swiss.

Around another bend on another hill, the less steep lower slopes were terraced, farmed and fruitful; palm fronds fluttered, and tin roofs were clustered like splattered paint on a patchwork canvas of ploughed fields.

A felled tree brought us to a halt. Originally on the upper side of the trail, it now rested at an angle. We pushed the bikes underneath, ducking low. There was no way under the next one. We took it in turns to pass along the outer edge of the path, the vertiginous verge dropping away to our right. First Kieran went, in the saddle, feet on the ground, inching slowly along with careful clutch control, while I held onto the rear rack to keep the bike upright and not let it slip off the edge, and finally to heave the rear end over the log. Then it was my turn.

At times like this, Kieran and I were at our best together. My youth spent playing sports and his twenties employed in the military had made us excellent team players when faced with a physical challenge to overcome. If only we could have approached the hurdles in our relationship the same way, but that required talking and we were better at doing.

With more felled trees and unsure how long the obstacle course would continue, we considered turning back, but then the path opened onto another plateau. At a fork in the trail we checked the GPS to discover that we had gone the wrong way somewhere. The lack of accuracy in the steep forests had made it impossible to determine which of the myriad of trails we were on. Now we weren't on any marked path. We knew the direction to go as the crow flies, but straight line routes don't exist in Rwanda, where every journey overland is at least three times further to navigate the endless hills rising and falling, winding and weaving, zig-zagging and switch-backing.

We picked the right-hand fork and passed a dairy farm, the locals queuing up with plastic containers to purchase milk and cheese from the heart of the country's dairy industry. Fresh milk was consumed in huge volumes in Rwanda.

Eventually we entered a village. We squeezed the bikes down narrow footpaths between hedges and homes, fences and ditches and stopped on the first flat, unoccupied square of ground to check where we were on the GPS. Soon a score of villagers in plastic sandals and rubber boots, holding jerrycans or herding sticks had congregated. One man peered at the GPS screen, then asked if he could help.

'Which way to Kibuye?' I asked.

180

He seemed confused by my question.

'Do you know Kibuye?'

He nodded, but I could tell the question running through his mind: *If you want to go to Kibuye, why have you come this way?*

'We got lost,' I explained.

'Ah! Then you must go that way,' he said, pointing down a path.

We found our way down, out of the hills and through vast tea plantations. My energy and enthusiasm rapidly waned once back on tarmacked, signposted, congested roads. In Kibuye, we checked into the same hotel we'd stayed at before and ate at the same buffet restaurant we'd feasted at during the hike.

The price for a plate of food was fixed, costing more only if you included meat. They offered excellent value for those with insatiable appetites: hikers, exhausted bikers and locals alike. Vats of cooked food lined tables around the dining room. Take whatever you want as long as it fits on your plate. There's no going back for seconds.

There is an art to piling food on a plate. I watched the construction of food towers on numerous lunches, initially in disgust and astonishment, then admiration and envy. I could never eat the quantities some Rwandans did; until now, perhaps.

First, widen the base by fanning lettuce leaves around the edge of the plate. There's no reason not to extend the lettuce over the hand holding the plate. Next pile on a layer of rice to absorb any sauces and juice, then add the full array of carbohydrates: potatoes, pasta and fried plantain. Build up the edges to contain the rest of the food you're about to add: bean stew, beef stew, fried chicken, coleslaw, a mix of vegetables whether spiced, in sauce or fried, and whatever else is on offer that stimulates your tastebuds. Top the creation with a handful of chips. I drew the line at squeezing considerable quantities of ketchup and mayonnaise over the final dish. The results rarely looked tasty, but they rarely lasted long, washed down with a mug of hot, sweet, milky tea.

The second half of the Congo-Nile trail was over in a day of pleasant winding roads. Unfortunately Kieran's front tyre deflated twice in quick succession and shortly after pumping it up a third time, he had a blowout. The inner tube had split at the valve, and there was a thorn and a piece of wire sticking through the paper-thin tyre. We cut up the inner tube to line the inside of the tyre and squeezed the cheap Chinese spare one inside. No sooner had we pumped the tyre back up and set off than my bike started backfiring. We reached Cyangugu at the southern end of Lake Kivu late in the day.

While sipping beer at a restaurant I watched the endless flow of people crossing the bridge across the Ruzizi River. The sister town of Bukavu in DR Congo was visible on the opposite side. I wished I was as free to cross the border.

I'd been circling DR Congo for months, like a moth round a lamp. The memories of my time there flickered in and out of my mind involuntarily. No matter how hard I tried to quell them, they kept reigniting, burning holes in the fragile wings of my relationship with Kieran whenever I let my past emotions cut away at our present connection.

I could not discuss the dilemma and feelings raging within me with Kieran; we could not talk about our own relationship. With no one else to talk to, the idea of my love for Charlie had grown disproportionately in size. Although, love is not finite and knows no boundaries or borders. I could love Kieran whilst retaining my memory of love for Charlie. Besides, the loves were incomparably different, one no more worthy than the other.

I could not describe my love for Kieran, but surely I loved him. However, when we were irritated by one another, rather than talk through the issues, we sulked in silence. My annoyance with him and hatred of myself for feeling that way – about him, about anyone – churned within me, a cauldron of toxic, nauseating feelings. We'd been getting on like 'old times' recently, but the frustration I felt at being tied, my freedom and independent spirit curtailed, was like a stain on our joys that I failed to remove.

———

After a night at the Catholic mission, we rode east through Nyungwe Forest. Once, the country would have been covered by trees. Now only Nyungwe Forest remains. Designated a National Park, it is protected.

A satellite view of the country shows small pockets of green on a vast chequerboard of oranges and browns. For a densely populated country, every inch of ground is used to feed and house everyone. Yet deforestation results in land erosion, the fragile topsoil getting washed off the hills during heavy rainfall, making the land less productive until eventually it will be useless for farming.

The forest covered the hills in a thick protective canopy wreathed in ethereal mist and had an ancient feel, earthy, abundant and prolific.

The air temperature dropped as we ascended in altitude. Damp fog turned to drizzle and then torrential downpour, soaking us despite wearing waterproofs. Places are hard to appreciate through a fogged up visor or squinting through pelting rain. As one of Africa's oldest rainforests, Nyungwe is rich in biodiversity. We decided to forego a prolonged stay up in the clouds, the forecast not conducive to searching for the resident chimpanzees.

Instead, we rode to Butare and checked into a cheap guesthouse to get dry. The next day, in between showers, Kieran cleaned the jets in my bike's carb to improve the stuttering performance. I was tired and glad that he was motivated to work on the bike, although I felt guilty about shirking responsibility. Cleaning the air filter seemed like a token gesture.

Having been single for much of my adult life, I was used to doing everything myself, independently. I never got used to accepting help. When Kieran joked that I only bought him along to fix my bike, I knew it was untrue but feared he believed it. I resented the idea that he thought I was reliant on him.

My bike maintenance and repair knowledge was inferior. I had intended to go on a course before setting off on my travels, but Kieran said he would teach me. Besides, I could always google for advice and watch YouTube for video instructions.

There was little incentive to go out on such a damp grey day. With the bike maintenance complete, we relaxed in our room with Wi-Fi. I was perusing Facebook and noticed that two British ladies had been volunteering at MJ Piki, the women's motorcycle project I'd hoped to visit in Tanzania. Pat and Sheonagh were now exploring Rwanda on borrowed bikes. I clicked on one profile picture and started scrolling, then stopped when I heard a distinctive sound.

My ears have become finely tuned to the sound of motorbike engines ever since I learnt to ride. There were motorbikes at the hotel entrance. I cocked my head to listen more carefully. Once inside the compound and with the engines off, the sound of jovial voices echoed. The voices didn't fit the image in my head of a Rwandan moto-taxi driver. I recognised the pitch and cadence: English-speaking women. Who were they?

Wouldn't it be funny if … I leapt off the bed and walked onto the balcony. As though Facebook had the power to actualise people from their profiles, Pat and Sheonagh had appeared. Sometimes the world is a very small place.

Of the few other bikers we met on our trip, a high proportion were women. While motorcycling is traditionally a male-dominated culture, adventure bike travel seemed more inclusive, and in my view, women were doing the cool stuff.

Pat and Sheonagh were anything but the Dusty Old Bags they called themselves. Vibrant and full of positive energy, I listened to their humorous tales all evening, batting anecdotes back and forth, joking about each other's oddities and idiosyncrasies and winding each other up. I wondered at what point me and Kieran had lost the art of British banter between ourselves. We still laughed but rarely about each other. Our lovable foibles had become unattractive annoyances and attitudes; now the underlying truths behind our sarcasm cut too close to the bone.

Looking back, I see that somewhere along the journey, I fell out of love with Kieran. I'd loved him despite his flaws; yet his imperfections were mounting up into an image I wasn't comfortable with.

I'd compartmentalised our issues into discrete metaphorical boxes, packing them deep in my mind to be dealt with later. Some I'd cleared out as an act of forgiveness.

My need for time alone was in a box that I couldn't throw away and would have to re-open. I'd been hiding it behind a stack of boxes full of great times we'd had together, of laughter and fun and shared experiences. Now I wondered how long it would be before that pile toppled into an unsalvageable heap of rubble?

I understood that Kieran's insecurity and fear of letting me go, in part, stemmed from having been cheated on in a previous relationship. Could he not see that I was not her? Our past sculpts us into who we are today. Kieran was no more able to cut away at his insecurity than I was at my independence.

Whereas I saw my independent streak as a strength in our relationship because my desire to be with him was driven by *want* rather than *need*. With his insecurities, the fact I didn't *need* him meant that he never trusted to let me go. If only he could have seen that despite being free to leave, I always chose to stay.

Ignoring these fundamental issues meant we could still enjoy good times together, but I wondered how long they could last.

Waving goodbye to Pat and Sheonagh, we left Butare behind, winding along the hillsides ever northwards towards Uganda and the equator. Uganda was the one country that allowed motorcycles into its National Parks. We were looking forward to going on safari in search of wildlife.

19.

Motorcycle Safari

Uganda

Rain had turned the orange dirt roads through the Queen Elizabeth National Park slick and slippery. We rode slowly on worn tyres with no grip. The sky was a sheet metal grey, and a concentrated black cloud shed a column of water onto a patch of savannah.

A troupe of baboons lurked in the road. A warthog family raced across and trotted away with their tails erect like radio antennae. We saw buffalo, water buck and impala. Then I spotted movement in the distance, identifiable as a bull elephant through the monocular. Eyes now attuned, we saw more herds as we rode on.

Kieran got two punctures in quick succession, which annoyed him. I remained nonplussed; my good mood at seeing so much wildlife from the saddle overpowered any negativity.

Then he commented, 'I think we should stick to the tarmac from now on and go straight to Nairobi for new tyres. I can't continue with these in this state.'

I'll be damned if we're going to miss half the country, skip the good bits, just to rush direct to Nairobi because you didn't replace your tyres when you had the chance in Rwanda!

I fumed, screaming inside my head and projecting a cold, silent stare that could turn perceptive people to stone or at least cowering wrecks.

He waited without saying another word.

Was he hiding his true feelings too? Were we both masquerading, our relationship nothing more than a thin guise?

I always had trouble defining who Kieran was in relation to me. I never liked labels, but sometimes they are necessary for others to understand a situation without discoursing at length. 'Boyfriend' seemed childish. 'Other half' sounded as though it made me a lesser person, no longer whole, and my independent spirit could never handle that. I had settled on 'partner'; we were a good team when faced with a challenge and enjoyed many adventures together.

Had we, somewhere along the way, become unpartnered? Is this how people split up, slowly, from the inside out? Is the physical separation that marks the end of a relationship simply the last stitch in the fabric to fray?

As usual, I blamed myself. I should have been more forceful in Kigali and insisted he buy new tyres then. Throughout the journey, I'd allowed Kieran to convince me he knew more about the bikes, but getting through Africa on a bike required more than experience of wielding a spanner and screwdriver.

First there was the leaking gasket in Botswana, which he'd known about before the trip; then he complained about the slipping clutch from Lesotho to Angola, and now the tyres. Each time he used the bike as an excuse not to explore more and take the easy road instead. My bike had suffered from sheared starter clutch bolts, a spent rear shock and poor steering from an overly tightened headset, but I'd never let the issues hinder where we went. It made me wonder why he had come to Africa at all. It never occurred to me that he might have done so not to see the continent but to spend time with me.

I don't think he understood how much I loved being on the road and how travelling made me feel. I found it hard to accept that he would never love Africa the way I did. I suppose he loved me as much as I loved Africa. And I guess I infuriated him at times as much as Africa can infuriate anyone.

Remembering we could get tyres sent to us, I tried calling our contact but got no answer.

Keep calm. Just find a solution.

'OK, let's go east on the tarmac to Kampala and buy new tyres there. Then we can loop north to Murchison Falls National Park, which was the main reason we've come to Uganda,' I suggested.

Kieran agreed. I didn't care whether it was because he always agreed or that he realised Kampala was on the direct route to Nairobi; I was still too irritated.

On the main road, speeding trucks overtook anything and slowed for nothing. We dodged them on our small Serows, avoiding people forced to walk in our path because there was no hard shoulder. I don't think Kieran will ever forget being nearly run off the road.

We navigated the chaotic streets of Kampala's urban sprawl, dodging and weaving, stop-starting and racing on. Kieran's irritation at the entire Ugandan population to not follow the Highway Code poured out as expletives and fist shakes with every near miss. Near misses were unavoidable in the melee of traffic.

I rode behind, amused by Kieran's theatricals. The explosion of people and colour, so vibrant and lively amongst apparent disorder and mayhem was like arriving home, flying straight into the cuckoo's nest. It was exhausting yet invigorating. *Yes, this is the Africa I love!*

I had hoped that because Kieran needed tyres, he would have taken the initiative and found out where to buy them. He hadn't. I suggested we try the Yamaha shop. They had none but redirected us to the tyre market, which had tyres but not the size we needed. Someone advised calling people they knew, and by the time I'd made several calls but little progress, my willpower had drained out of me. I couldn't think where to try next.

I wondered whether to suggest that Kieran go ahead to Nairobi while I explored Uganda. But Kieran's ultimatum from Namibia, about ending the relationship if we travelled apart, which I'd put to the back of my mind, resurfaced. I didn't want to have an argument or hurt Kieran, so rather than considering what I wanted or was best for me, I kept quiet.

Then Kieran suggested, 'If we buy and fit new inner tubes, I might be able to limp on if it doesn't rain too much.'

Yes, a positive suggestion! I shoved my thoughts back in their box and hoped the rain would stay away.

We rode towards Murchison Falls National Park in the northwest of the country, stopping for a couple of nights at the Masindi Hotel.

Uganda's oldest hotel was originally built in 1923 by the East Africa Railways and Harbours Company. Masindi was the gateway to a wild and untamed Africa where goods from northern Congo and southern Sudan made their way to Europe by truck, ship and train via Mombasa on the Kenyan coast.

The hotel became a hub for travellers. Famously, Ernest Hemingway recuperated here after being involved in two plane crashes within a week. That put Kieran's repeat punctured tyres into perspective.

Hemingway and his wife had taken a chartered plane from Nairobi on a sight-seeing flight to Murchison Falls. They were flying low when the tail wheel got caught in an abandoned telephone line, forcing the pilot to crash land in a small clearing. They spent the night in the plane visited by elephants. The following day, the crash party headed to the river where they came upon a large launch running wildlife viewing trips upriver. The launch took them to Butiaba, where a rescue plane awaited. Unfortunately on take-off, the undercarriage hit an anthill followed by a thorn bush at the end of the little-used runway and nose-dived. Apparently, Hemingway was the first out and quickly at that. Everyone escaped before the plane caught fire. After that they travelled by car to Masindi and rapidly depleted the gin stocks at the hotel bar, which is now named after Hemingway.

Audrey Hepburn and Humphrey Bogart also stayed at the hotel during filming of *The African Queen*. The 1951 movie, set during World War I, was adapted from C. S. Forester's adventure novel. The story centres around Rose, a prim and proper missionary, and Allnutt, the skipper of the *African Queen*, a steamboat plying a river in southwest Tanzania. Rose persuades Allnutt to use his boat to attack and sink a German gunboat guarding the adjoining lake. Forester's inspiration was the *MV Liemba*, which we'd taken up Lake Tanganyika.

Rooms in the renovated, pink colonnaded colonial-style hotel appeared, and were, out of our budget. We were allowed to camp, though, and spent the money we saved on drinks in the bar.

Whether it was the peaceful garden or the connection with Hemingway, I felt inspired to write. With tables and chairs and our tent pitched under the covered veranda of the garden house, we kept sheltered and dry during the afternoon downpours. I'd look up from the laptop as the drumming on the roof intensified and watch the rain stream down. The palm leaves glistened, and droplets of water trickled to the leaf tips and fell to the ground. The whole garden was bursting with an explosion of vibrant greens and a confusion of colour.

After a couple of days, we set off under leaden skies. The rainy season was upon us. We camped at a lodge on the edge of the National Park on the southern bank of the river, the manicured grounds adorned with beautiful sculptures of wildlife woven from branches: giraffes by the river and hippos behind the bar, herons and a gorilla. The only real animals we saw were vervet monkeys scampering about. We pitched the tent, closed all our bags securely and Kieran prepped his Tool-in-a-Can flamethrower. Fortunately it wasn't needed. News of Kieran's vervet monkey vendetta had not reached this far north.

The next morning we rode east to the top of the falls along orange laterite, sharply sloping at the edges to aid drainage during heavy rains. Occasionally a 4x4 sped past, rangers rushing paying guests around on a whistle-stop tour to see the best places in the park. We commented on the reckless speeds. If an antelope sprang out of the bush unexpectedly, there could be a crash.

Around one corner we came upon a vehicle on its side. The young couple who had rented it were shaken but unhurt. They'd been going too fast around the bend with an adverse camber. A rescue party from a nearby lodge was on its way. There was little we could do, so we rode on cautiously, and I wondered where in the endlessly undulating bush Hemingway's plane had crashed. I had no desire to replicate that part of his trip with my Serow.

The top of Murchison Falls was a scenic but not peaceful place for lunch. The deafening sound of white water thundering down the rocks and biting tsetse flies drove us on.

Later, we took a launch boat trip along the lower reaches of the river. The current was strong and the engine lacked power to get close to the falls. Instead, from a distance, we watched the clouds of spray billowing where the water gushed down the six-metre wide granite cut in the rocks, the narrowest point of the Nile on its 6,650-kilometre journey to the Mediterranean.

During the river journey, we stood at the railings and peered out to the banks. Elephants grazed in the long grasses. Cape buffalo congregated in clearings with cattle egrets pecking at ticks on their legs and other insects disturbed in the undergrowth. Hippos lounged in the shallows, and a baby crocodile lay motionless in the clear water with a cold deadly stare. An arrow formation of cranes flew overhead. Where the riverbanks rose up, I sat back and sipped a cool beer. The sandstone cliffs were pockmarked like a Swiss cheese. Bright yellow, blue and green red-throated bee-eaters with their black banded eyes flew in and out of the holes and perched on fig trees.

River travel was a calm and civilised way to see the wildlife, relaxing as the boat chugged slowly on without having to worry about a thing. What a different experience to the next day when we entered the park on our bikes.

As wildlife is most easily spotted during the first hours of daylight, we packed up in the pre-dawn chill and rode to the river to catch the first boat across, the north side offering the best wildlife viewing opportunities. A line of 4x4s was already waiting. We were allowed to ride to the front and squeezed our bikes onto the ramp, making sure they were in gear and secure on their stands.

We had a printed map of the park but no particular plan. Once across the river, we set off ahead of the 4x4s, picked a track and rode carefully through the sandy parts. When the ground hardened enough to take our eyes off it, we strained to catch flashes of movement in the thick bush or distant savannah.

The sound of the bikes usually scared any animals, but if we stopped in time and killed the engines, we could watch the wildlife peacefully.

Giraffe – cool.

Zebra – there's a few … and more way over there …

Always, though, there was an ever-present unease about whether there might be lions nearby. I wanted to see lions but not too close-up. We joked that we didn't need to out-ride a lion, only out-ride the other person.

A 4x4 caught us up. The dad drove, the mum was in the passenger seat, and the kids had the best view, sitting on a mattress strapped to the roof, clinging to the roof bars. The 4x4 slowed as it passed.

'Have you seen any lions?' the dad asked through the window.

'No,' we replied.

Me and Kieran rode on across open country, each in separate ruts of the 4x4 track, passing a bush here and some scrub there. Kieran was looking left and I was looking right. When I rode up alongside him, he looked across at me, startled.

'H… H…' he stuttered.

Hello? Helen? What are you trying to say?!

His head shot left then back to me. 'H…'

I looked across.

Oh shit! Hyena.

I'd seen hyenas from a distance before. Up close, this spotted one on a dusty mound right beside the trail was huge. Sat on her haunches, she looked beautiful, healthy and terrifying. I thought her thick muscular neck with scruffy tufts of fur was long enough to grab a bite had she wanted. She just swivelled her head and watched us pass, her bear-like ears pointing forward. Only her strong set jaw and drooling mouth gave her a vicious and savage look. I don't know

192

that the hyena was female but assume so based on size, being the larger of the sexes.

We accelerated away, only peering back briefly to check that she hadn't moved. Hyenas are social animals; I was slightly surprised to see only one. *Where are the rest of them?* Hunter as well as scavenger, they are capable of taking down a wildebeest or zebra. A loaded Serow and rider come within the weight range of their typical prey. Yes, hyenas are also cool to see, just not too close-up.

I was still thinking about hyenas and keeping an eye out for other carnivorous mammals when we rounded a bend and saw a small herd of elephants. Kieran was ahead, pointed to them and kept riding. They were a couple of hundred metres away and seemed relaxed, so I stopped but kept the engine running. Most kept grazing; the matriarch and a young bull turned to watch. Keeping my eyes on them, I unzipped my tank bag to get my camera. They started to get agitated, and then the young bull, feisty and eager to prove his worth, with ears fanned out wide and trunk raised high made steps in my direction. I knew he was faking it, but that didn't stop my heart from racing. I fumbled with my camera, because I didn't dare take my eyes off the herd. Then he started running towards me. *Sod the photo!* I shoved the camera deep in the bag, put the bike in gear, opened the throttle and accelerated up the hill, increasing my distance until I caught up with Kieran.

I'd been much closer to elephants in the past, both on foot, bicycle and in 4x4s, but I had never seen such behaviour at that distance. In the 1960s, the park had some 15,000 elephants. Poaching and wars have since decimated the wildlife populations, and elephant numbers have plummeted to 800. Recent regional conflict and instability in and around the park mean that the elephants still see humans as a threat and are easily agitated.

After a tense ride along a slow track through thick bush, we came to the delta where hartebeest, zebra and buffalo congregated in the greener, more open space. We stopped for a bite to eat.

The passenger of a 4x4 called out the window as they drove by, 'Have you seen any lions?'

'No,' we replied.

With a choice of either the Victoria, Albert or Queen's tracks, we took the latter, which turned out to be littered with elephant dung. That shit was so big, we slalomed around the piles, noticing that some was so fresh that not even the flies had landed yet. Then we saw two huge elephants ahead. We waited for them to move, but neither of us was confident to continue without knowing where they'd gone.

The 4x4 with the mattress strapped to the top emerged round the bend, the kids now inside the vehicle.

'You should be careful,' the driver said to us. He seemed shaken. 'The elephants round the corner are really aggressive. We didn't think we'd make it through. The one kept pushing against the vehicle and rocking it.'

Me and Kieran looked at each other. 'Thanks. We'll turn around and take another route.'

The driver's wife leant over. 'We're looking for lions. Have you seen any?'

'No,' we replied.

The Albert track was less eventful, only overrun with giraffes. They always made me smile, the way they ran with gangly legs, lolloping in long strides, and the way they entwined and rubbed their necks with one another, which looked so graceful, supple and flowing, belying the wrestling act of dominance.

Time flew by, and soon we were riding to exit the park before dark, the tsetse flies urging us on with nips and bites. I didn't mind that we hadn't seen any lions. It had been tense enough knowing they were near, somewhere.

We reached a campsite before the rain and ate dinner on the top floor of the large concrete rondavel. The surrounding grass had been burnt to try and stop poaching. A warthog, a regular visitor, trotted over to the watering hole. With extensive views, I could see an elephant on the savannah beyond.

Lightning flashed in the distance, striking the earth with indiscriminate precision. Black clouds edged closer until they blocked the last of the daylight. Another flash and almighty crack made me jump, and the thunder rumbled and grumbled across the sky in rippled echoes.

Then the rain started.

One moment it was dry, the next torrents of water were streaming from the heavens, pounding on the roof and pouring out the gutters. It pummelled everything below, and the thick, rich earthy smell of soaked African soil permeated the air.

We didn't sleep much that night. Our poor tent, as much duct tape as original fly sheet, was no longer waterproof. Months of suffering under the harsh sun had degraded the material until it was so thin that whenever the rain lashed down, water came through in a fine shower. I covered my sleeping bag in my towel and jacket and occasionally wiped the moisture from my face. All signs of the storm evaporated as the sun rose.

We'd had no more tyre trouble, so Kieran was up for exploring the northeast, which I was eager to see. I could give no tangible reason why, except that it's remote. I'm always drawn to places on the map where few people live and even fewer visit. Anywhere dismissed because *there's nothing there* intrigues me. There is always plenty to see if you look close enough.

We arrived at the gates of Kidepo National Park, bordering northern Kenya and South Sudan. A ranger confirmed that camping was not allowed in the park. We'd seen enough wildlife at Murchison Falls and were content to save our money. Going on safari was expensive. Instead, we continued to Nga'Moru Wilderness Camp on the edge of the park. The owner wasn't there but his eighty-year-old father, John, gave us a discount to stay in one of the lodge's safari tents.

I don't know if it was the real bed with a mattress or because the tents never get moved that this night under canvas didn't feel like camping, even though we looked upon the same millions of stars in the sky and slept amongst the same prowling animals as when in our own tent. Perhaps it was the fresh white linen and hot shower. For one night we lived in luxury, in a scene reminiscent of *Out of Africa*, except for our dusty motorbikes, filthy clothes and smelly boots marring the romance.

Sipping coffee the next morning, I saw giraffe and buffalo in the distance and vultures circling in the thermals. The shaded lodge veranda was the perfect lookout for anyone patient enough to wait for the wildlife to come to them rather than rushing around in search of it. Watching the golden plains was like going to the cinema for a big screen show.

The mountains on the horizon marked the South Sudanese border. John mentioned that he'd once been entertained by the army going after raiders from South Sudan, who had come over the border to steal cattle and wives. Cross-border warfare had been going on tit-for-tat for centuries.

We rode deeper into Karamoja, the rural region of northeast Uganda where the Karamajong continue to resist the trappings of the modern world. Although, in Kaabong, people wore rubber tyre sandals rather than going barefoot when wearing their tartan skirts and red and deep green blankets draped over their shoulders.

Turning south, we left the flat, dry dusty plains behind. Again, I wished I were travelling more slowly because soon we were in the populated lush hills of Mount Elgon National Park. Recent rains had transformed the roads into muddy quagmires. Fortunately, they dried enough during a sunny morning to enable progress to the Kenyan border. From there to Nairobi, we had a clear run along increasingly busy roads, except for a series of punctures for Kieran. Now we needed new tyres.

20.
Lamu Island
Kenya

We parked up outside the modern office block. I was perplexed. This wasn't the dirty workshop I'd expected but a dental clinic. No dentist I'd ever been to had offered tyre sales alongside checkups, fillings and teeth whitening.

I double checked the address that my contact in Nairobi had provided, then walked into the immaculately clean reception. There was a poster advertising Botox but nothing related to motorcycles. I explained that, no, I didn't have an appointment but had come to collect tyres – was this the right place? Told to wait outside, I returned to the bikes, wondering what would happen next.

A smartly dressed man came out to greet us. Pranith, presumably a dentist with a side business, told us his man was on his way with our order. He apologised that he must get back to work and returned to the clinic. Ten minutes later, his man turned up and offloaded our tyres. He said to pay inside, pointed at the office block and left.

I handed the cash to the receptionist and received an official dental clinic receipt. Sometimes it's better not to ask questions. We had what we wanted. With two tyres strapped to the back of each bike, we rode back to Jungle Junction where we were staying.

Next we had to sort visas. Ethiopia was the only country on our route besides Angola that officially required getting a visa from our home country. Researching online, I determined that our best chance of getting an Ethiopian visa in Africa was in Nairobi.

There was an unofficial process to circumventing the rules. If I followed the instructions precisely to navigate the nonsensical paper-chase maze that epitomises African bureaucracy, I ought to emerge at the other end with the visas.

First we visited the British Embassy and submitted a written request asking for a letter of introduction to explain that we required an Ethiopian visa but were unable to acquire this in the UK since we had been out of the country so long. Clearing security took longer than getting the letter.

The standard, ready-printed response simply stated that the British Embassy in Ethiopia does not issue letters of introduction. This wasn't quite what I'd hoped for or expected, but we were shooed out with the wave of a hand, indicating that we should take the letter or nothing at all.

At the Ethiopian Embassy, we were told that they only issue visas to Kenyan residents. I handed over the letter of no introduction anyway, not believing that it would make any difference but knowing it was our only chance. The clerk took one glance and told us to go and see the head consul.

I knocked on the door to the head consul's office. There was no reply. I knocked louder. Silence. I nervously pushed the door ajar and peered in. I felt like a naughty schoolgirl sent to the headmaster's office.

'Enter. Sit down,' the woman with braided hair and tattoos on her neck, forehead and arms ordered from behind her desk. She had the persona of a fire-breathing dragon.

A German couple cowered in silence whilst the dragon inspected their paperwork. We took seats at the back of the room, not daring to whisper. I wished I could make myself invisible, blend into the whitewashed walls like a chameleon.

The dragon wouldn't issue a visa to the couple and told them that they could fly into Addis Ababa, where visas were issued on arrival. The couple explained that they were travelling overland in their own vehicle.

'Then you must take return flights to Germany and obtain the visas there,' the dragon insisted. 'Once you have the visas, Ethiopia will welcome you,' she assured them. The overlanders continued to plead their case to no avail, and the dragon became more and more incensed until she ordered them finally to get out. They left subdued. Our turn next.

We moved to the seats in front of her desk and went through the same rigmarole. She was a fearsome opponent. Kieran sat in silence, observing the battle. The dragon spoke with stern authority, one not to be messed with. *I mustn't back down. Don't show that you're intimidated.* I was distracted by her tattoos. I couldn't take my eyes off them, yet I didn't want to be caught staring. *What is their significance? Those ones on the neck must have hurt like hell to get.*

The letter of no introduction proved to be the winning blow. I suspect the wording was irrelevant, the signed and stamped official letter-headed paper the crucial part. She stared at it in her hands for several minutes whilst we waited on tenterhooks.

'You must speak to the ambassador. I am not authorised to issue you visas. Now go.' The tone of her voice exuded acrimony.

We took back our paperwork and fled. Around the side of the embassy building, we found a notice on the ambassador's door. He was out. I called the number provided. A clerk answered and came outside to meet us. He listened to our story, took our passports and the letter, then told us to phone back in the afternoon.

No one answered the phone later that day or the following morning, so I rode back to the embassy to enquire. Identifying an opportunity to go out on my own, I suggested that it was pointless us both wasting time navigating Nairobi whilst there were new tyres that needed fitting.

Free to choose my route and where to stop, and explore if something caught my eye, I felt liberated. I dodged and weaved through traffic, darting here and there, not stopping at obstacles but pre-empting them, slowing slightly, swerving gently, always maintaining momentum and alert to other traffic. I felt a rush keeping up with the *boda-bodas*, following the locals if not the laws. I wished

I had more excuses to get out on my own. The commute was much quicker alone.

The ambassador's clerk scolded me for not coming yesterday afternoon, even though he hadn't told us to, then handed back our passports. The letter of no introduction from the British embassy was sufficient authorisation for the Ethiopian ambassador in Kenya to provide a signed letter authorising the head consul of his embassy to issue us visas. I took this letter to the consular office, completed the visa applications, nervously entered the dragon's den and handed the fearsome tattooed lady the paperwork.

She grudgingly accepted to issue us visas. I sensed her annoyance at having been outmanoeuvred. I'm sure if she ran the embassy, there would be no allowances or exceptions for anyone; in her view, rules were like iron, unbendable and immovable, to be wielded like a sword to slash down anyone who dares to break them.

Once I'd been to the bank to pay the fees, I returned to her office with the receipt. To break the silence, I attempted small talk. She looked up from the passport she was stamping and swiftly mopped up my nerve-induced drivel with a stare. I quickly shut up, lowered my head and, looking into my lap, picked at my nails.

The moment she passed me the passports, I leapt off the chair and out of her office. Only then did I check the visa stamps. *We've done it! Three-month visas for Ethiopia.*

My excitement over the bureaucratic success and anticipation for the next part of the trip was quickly tempered when it dawned on me that the end of the journey was in sight. The visas started counting down from the date of issue, today.

After Ethiopia, we would only be able to get a two-week transit visa for Sudan and a one-month visa for Egypt. My time in Africa was on a countdown. Four and half months did not seem long. We were south of the equator, as close to Cape Town as Cairo and had four countries to travel through. It wasn't long enough to explore them all; I wasn't ready for the journey to end.

Stop worrying about the future. Live for the moment and enjoy today. Four and a half months is several times more than most people get for their annual leave.

———

Lake Turkana in northern Kenya was another sparsely populated area that appealed to me. The route along the eastern shore to Ethiopia was once renowned by overlanders due to the rough terrain and vast distances, some 1,500 kilometres, between fuel supplies. The region is more developed these days, so fuel wouldn't be an issue. The only minor hurdle was the lack of immigration and customs facilities at the border.

With visas allowing us into Ethiopia, we had to make sure we could leave Kenya. The huge waiting room in the immigration department building in Nairobi was crammed with people. I mentally prepared myself for the long wait and was pleasantly surprised. After a short explanation at one counter of what was required, we were sent to another office and provided with exit stamps in our passports valid for two weeks. Then we visited the Kenyan Revenue Authority and got our carnets stamped. Our bikes were not legally in the country any more. I hoped there'd be no checkpoints or problems between here and the border.

Allowed to stay in Kenya for the two weeks and in a bid to slow our progress north, we rode towards the coast. Several years earlier I had visited Zanzibar and loved the vibrant clash of Asia meeting Africa. The resultant cultural fusion was as exotic and varied as the spices grown on the island. It seemed that what Zanzibar was to Tanzania, Lamu was to Kenya. I was interested in visiting the small island only a short boat ride from the mainland but culturally very different with its Muslim heritage.

To get there, we had to survive the Nairobi-Mombasa highway. We'd heard horror stories from expats, who made it sound worse than the main roads in Uganda. Hoping to avoid it as much as possible, I looked on the map and found an alternative route.

I remembered stories from my mum about her time spent volunteer teaching in Kenya with her friend in the seventies. They'd taught at a school not far from Nairobi off the main route to Mombasa.

After a year of teaching there, my mum returned to England and later married my dad. Her friend stayed in East Africa and married a man working for the Red Cross. They had a daughter who, as though destined, later also went into international development.

My destiny seems less clear. It's more like the light reflecting off rippled waves of a lake at sunset, a million sparkling possibilities dancing and flickering but none lasting long enough to reach out and grab.

We left Nairobi and rode to the town of Machakos, turned down a smaller road to Mumbuni and pulled up outside the gates of the Harambee school my mum had once taught at. So, I suppose, in one small part of my journey through life, I have followed her footsteps.

A few wooden stalls selling a colourful array of fresh fruit lined the village road. I could picture my mum in a handmade cotton dress buying a couple of bananas, probably the only fruit available back then. Apart from the tarmac and occasional boda-boda, I doubted the village had changed much in appearance.

Machakos, on the other hand, was nothing like the market town that my mum had described with its single dusty road but colonial-sounding social club on the outskirts with tennis courts, swimming pool and nine-hole golf course. Now multi-storey buildings towered above the petrol station, modern stores selling electronic goods and phones, supermarkets, banks. On the busy main roundabout, there was a sign to the university. Never mind a provincial sports club, there was a full-size stadium.

I expect my mum would have struggled to recognise the town she once knew. Perhaps that's why she had no interest in returning to Kenya; instead, preferring to travel vicariously through me. Sometimes places, people and experiences are best left as memories, perfect and untainted by present reality.

We crossed over the main highway and took the road towards Mount Kilimanjaro. I hoped we might be able to take a small road running east through Tsavo. The sun was going down and we hadn't found a place to wild camp, so we spoke with some smartly dressed men coming out of a church, the only painted building in sight. They were pastors from Nairobi but introduced us to their friends who owned the dusty plot of land. The pastors confirmed that bikes weren't allowed to transit Tsavo National Park. We had no other option but to backtrack and take the highway.

The Serow was like a mosquito compared to the elephantine trucks transporting goods inland from the port. We dodged our way in and out of the hard shoulder where it existed and off the road when it didn't to avoid overtaking trucks heading straight for us. There was nothing enjoyable about the ride, only an ever-present fear for our lives. It was the only road of the trip I didn't like and would never voluntarily ride again.

Fortunately the road up the coast was less chaotic and dangerous. From busy, bustling built-up towns, we rode past luxury properties with palm trees and sandy beaches, then salt works. The large pools of water with crusty edges sparkling white attracted flocks of flamingoes. Where the road continued north but the coastline curved away, we turned towards Mokowe, the village nearest the port for taking boats to Lamu.

We left the bikes at lugubrious lodgings, renting a room at a discount price to store our left luggage and locking the Serows in the narrow courtyard between the two concrete rows of facing rooms. We pulled the musty, dust-stained lace curtains across the small window of the dark and dingy room, padlocked the door and put our trust in the proprietor. The village had that insalubrious air common to many border towns and ports around the world, which beggars and thieves find prime working ground. Though, the guesthouse owner seemed genuine and the police station was down the road.

Boda-bodas raced us to the port just in time to catch the next speedboat. For half an hour we bounced across the rippling deep-blue water, then parallel to the island's shore with boats moored in front of the white buildings, which shone brilliantly in the sun.

There are no vehicles on the island because there are no real roads, the alleyways in the main town too narrow for cars. Instead, people walk and donkeys carry quarried coral building blocks in custom jute panniers slung over their backs.

We stepped onto the main jetty, walked past the shopfronts and restaurants along the waterfront, ignoring calls for 'dhow trip?' from the young men hoping to attract the few tourists onto their boats.

After a series of armed attacks in Mombasa and then one only twenty-five kilometres along the coast from Lamu in 2014, many countries advised against travel here. The decimated tourism industry was slowly picking up again and offered good deals on accommodation.

Navigating the maze of alleyways, we zigzagged through the town until we came to our guesthouse. With buildings so closely packed, living area is increased by adding new floors. Up several flights of stairs, we stepped onto the balcony with views across the rooftops covered with satellite dishes, pots piled waiting to be washed, laundry drying in the refreshing breeze and cats stretched out in the sun.

For the next three days, I woke from a good sleep in a comfortable bed. After a leisurely breakfast cooked by someone else, we explored the town, getting lost and retracing our steps, popping into small souvenir shops and drinking fresh fruit juices on the waterfront.

We wandered around the old fort and peered from the parapet onto the square below, where young men sat with eyes glued to their mobiles and businessmen worked on their laptops. On a large jute mat laid on the floor, old men sat with their sandals removed playing bao. Each mancala board game had several spectators. It reminded me of the Uighur elders in Xinjiang, western China, who spent their days playing chess. Women were noticeably absent from the streets, as is common in Muslim culture.

One morning we walked along the seafront to Shela, a small village with luxury whitewashed villas, continuing along the stone wall until there were no more houses. A tropical paradise of white-golden coral sand beach stretched endlessly ahead. Shimmering turquoise water lapped at our feet, and the sun beat down from the cloudless blue sky. Sweat running down my face didn't bother me because I didn't have a care or concern in the world that we seemed to have left behind. I had no routes to plan, visas to obtain or bike parts to hunt down. There were no annoying hustlers or hectic traffic to avoid. I felt the sand between my toes and the breeze through my hair. *So this is why people go on holiday!*

The next day we took a dhow trip across to neighbouring Manda Island. We climbed out amongst the mangroves to explore Takwa, the ruins of an old Swahili settlement abandoned around the eighteenth century due to local fighting and lack of fresh water. After a couple of hours exploring, we had to rush back to the dhow before the tide went out. We sailed back to Lamu, tacking against the wind so the large slanted sail billowed above us, with the sun setting behind the town.

It would have been easy to stay on Lamu longer. We were relaxed and happy together. I wondered if, by allowing my private battles from the past, of Charlie and the DR Congo, to spill over into the present, I had unwittingly drawn Kieran into a fight that was not of his making. But for now, at least, we seemed to have brokered a peace, with my past and with each other.

After three days of respite, we returned to the main land and collected our bikes from the guesthouse.

The day we had left Nairobi on fully serviced bikes with brand new tyres, my clutch had started slipping. It had behaved impeccably for the entire trip, yet now we'd sorted every noticeable niggle, mine

205

threw a spanner in the works as though it had its own mischievous mind and had been waiting for that moment. I cursed myself for not having foreseen this and felt bad about the irritations I'd felt about Kieran with his worn clutch. However, I had ordered new parts online immediately and arranged for them to be couriered to Nairobi, so the trip would not be unduly impacted

We looped north on our return to the capital. Halted at a checkpoint, the officers wanted to know why we were travelling near Somalia. We had to convince them that we were just tourists going back to Nairobi via Garissa and not militants out to cause trouble in the region. The year before, Al-Shabaab militants had stormed the university in Garissa and taken 700 students hostage. They released Muslims and shot anyone who identified as Christian. The siege lasted fifteen hours with 148 people killed. The region was still in shock and on high alert to further attacks.

The officers suggested it would be safer to take the Mombasa highway. We suggested they'd never travelled that route on a motorbike. They nodded and let us pass.

People who lived on this arid land had it tougher than most. It had rained during the night and there were puddles on the road. Women in *kikoy* and vests collected the water with plastic cups into bottles. They scooped carefully but with urgent speed as though racing to collect as much vital liquid before it evaporated back into the atmosphere.

Aid agency signs on the road highlighted the refugee camps near the Somali border, just as they had near the Burundian border. Established in 1991, the camps currently house (in July 2020 according to UNHCR website) over 200,000 registered refugees and asylum seekers. A lot of the older refugees from the nineties have children and grandchildren born in them. They resemble towns more than temporary shelters and are commercial hubs connecting the two countries. It was hard to imagine so many people in such a hostile landscape.

The road deteriorated until there was less tarmac than giant potholes, which we had to sweep around, weaving from one side of the road to the other and sometimes off the embankment. Once we reached the junction at Garissa, the route back to the capital was direct and fast. Getting the clutch plates cleared through customs, however, was as circuitous and slow as the crater-filled road.

Eventually we got our hands on the parts and fitted them. Now we could continue our journey north to Lake Turkana.

21.

Lake Turkana
Kenya

With the banana plantations, tall green grasses and Mount Kenya behind me, I stood at the edge of the plateau and looked down the long straight road ahead to the open plains of the arid Samburu. Lone acacia trees offered isolated umbrellas of shade.

Nairobi's chaotic traffic that we had navigated the day before and the vivid colours of a land painted by rain were soon a distant memory as we rode down into the desert-like sandy land of subtle shades. In the space of a few kilometres, it was as though everything had been wiped away: the colour, the plants, the noise. I was content to do without all of it.

We stopped at Archer's Post, a lonely settlement that seemed to mark the border into even more inhospitable country. We sat in a lapa within a large compound bordered by wire fencing. A woman my age with a bright kanga wrapped around her waist, brought us ice-cold Coca-Cola, which we savoured straight from the glass bottle. She spoke excellent English and told me she used to live in Copenhagen.

I looked around at the dusty windswept ground, the crumbling concrete building with a tin roof and empty road vanishing to the horizon.

'What brought you *here*?' I asked.

'This is a better life,' she replied simply. 'Europe is too expensive and people there are too busy worrying about money. Here, I have everything I need. I have my friends. I have time.'

I understood before she finished explaining. Her reasons were why I too am drawn to backwater places where the fewer the distractions the more comfortable I feel. I rarely met people with similar ways of thinking and being. I was taken aback that this woman felt the same; many locals I had met in rural Africa sought to escape it.

Soon after Archer's Post, Kieran and I took a track west and wild camped that night, hidden amongst the thorny bushes that consumed this part of the land. The only clear view was towards the sickle moon in the sky. The bush was unusually peaceful and quiet. The only disturbance was at first light when a grey go-away bird cried a harsh call of alarm. I couldn't tell what the warning was for, unless it was the two curious hornbills who investigated our camp whilst we were having breakfast.

The track wound on up through green hills, giant rock formations towering above. Around one corner, an elephant lumbered across the road, reminding me to keep a careful look out. At the top, the wide open plateau was reminiscent of the Mongolian steppe, except for the zebra. Grazing contentedly, they were unperturbed by us, seemingly habituated to human presence, unsurprising since they shared the land with goats from the nearby settlement.

The track became rockier, then descended. We turned north and, after a wonderful days' ride, arrived in sleepy Maralal, the administrative centre of Samburu County. We camped at the Yare Camel Club on the edge of town. The sleepy-eyed camels roamed freely until rounded up at dusk, when they were corralled next to where we'd pitched our tent. Once we'd stocked up on food, we continued north.

The trail weaved across a flat plain towards the horizon of conical hills. I watched a column of rain march slowly across it. The ground would not be revived by a minute's downpour. The harsh land of soft shades, beige and grey to mauve and orange-cream, was a contradiction: merciless and inhospitable yet indescribably beautiful. Fluffy white clouds floated in the brilliant blue sky and cast forbidding shadows like spectral portents.

A metal sign showed an image of silhouetted men with guns pointed at each other and a farmer fleeing with his cattle. In the foreground, wild animals scavenged. It stated, 'War: The banquet of the hyenas. We want peace. Respect Life.'. Unusually, there was no logo indicating a foreign aid organisation. Who had put the sign here? Who was fighting?

Settlements were few and far between, the land unable to sustain much life. The riverbeds were dry. Further on acacias grew tall, offering patches of speckled shade across the trail. Camels sauntered along the sandy track, stopping to nibble the trees, their rough lips untroubled by the thorns.

A boy herding emaciated cattle raced towards us waving an empty plastic water bottle. 'Water!', he shouted. Kieran didn't stop and I followed on. We'd not passed many people, but each one, always boys, had shouted for something. Money. Sweets. Now, water.

I have become toughened over the years to the hardship and suffering I see when travelling, especially through harsh country. It's impossible to help everyone. But there was something desperate and urgent in the boy's shout, and I found myself consumed by guilt long after we'd passed, haunted by the thought that I should have stopped. We didn't have much water to spare, but we did have water.

I should have slammed on the brakes and made a u-turn. Sure, he would return to his village, not die of dehydration, but I know the insufferable craving that thirst induces. The all-consuming ceaseless thoughts of water that plague the mind are far worse than the cracked lips, dry tongue that sticks to the roof of the mouth and lack of saliva to swallow.

I know that if I had been alone, I would have stopped, as I had always done in the past. *I was only following Kieran.* It wasn't fair to use him to justify my inaction. I wished I didn't change my behaviour around him, so not only did I feel guilty but also angry at myself because I didn't stand up for what I believed was the right thing to do.

The nondescript town of Baragoi provided us with chapati and chips for lunch. More importantly, we topped up the fuel tanks, filled the spare bag and a five-litre plastic container, enough to get us to Omorate in Ethiopia.

South Horr was a cool respite, sheltered amongst the trees in the riverbed. Small concrete buildings lined the sandy track, and small domed huts of bent branches were semi-hidden beyond the thorny scrub. Once, they would have been plastered with dried earth. Now they were covered in yellow plastic or the remains of UN-donated tarpaulins. We camped in the dusty courtyard of a guesthouse, lured by signs advertising cold beer. I should have known it was too good to be true. I sipped at the warm beer whilst the owner's daughters plaited my hair, who were fascinated at how smooth it felt compare to theirs.

Further north, the dry rocky landscape was dominated by Mount Kulal until we found ourselves on a wide, graded trail going towards a line of gigantic wind turbines. Africa's largest wind farm connects 365 turbines to the national grid, providing power to around one million homes.

Beyond the rocky sloping terrain and over a rise, we stopped, confronted by the bright waters of Lake Turkana. A manyatta of domed huts was nestled by the shore and a few men tugged and dragged nets from their wooden boat anchored in the shallows. The rich turquoise water was so striking, as though all colour had been drained from the surrounding land and concentrated within it. No wonder it was once called the Jade Sea. A westerly wind ripped across the water, blasting hot air into our faces and stealing our voices as we shouted to be heard.

Now the trail was nothing more than faint lighter sandy tracks where 4x4s had crushed and nudged dark volcanic rocks clear of the tyres. Clumps of pale yellow grass clung to the earth, grazed by a few goats. In the distance, Loiyangalani was an oasis of palm trees, domed huts, a few solid structures and a radio mast.

We camped on the manicured lawn of the smart guesthouse and spent the day drinking beer with a couple of young engineers who were taking a break from their work on the wind turbine project. The hot sticky air had cooled and the sky clouded over.

'It feels like it might rain,' I said.

They laughed. 'Sometimes we think it might when the sky becomes grey like this, but it never rains.'

'Seems all it does is rain where I'm from,' Kieran commented dryly.

A few drops of water fell to the ground. A pitter-patter drum roll crescendoed, then ended abruptly. In the ensuing pause, we looked at one another in surprise. Suddenly, more thick droplets of water fell, and soon they were plummeting to earth incessantly, pounding and ricocheting off the ground, water pooling and glistening on the concrete paths and streaming off the grass-roofed huts. We watched in amazed silence, the white noise drowning any chance of conversation.

'That was Loiyangalani's annual rainfall received in the space of an hour. You must be the rain king,' the Kenyan said to Kieran once the rain stopped. 'You should go everywhere there's a drought; you'd be worshipped,' he joked.

North along the eastern shore, the black rocks petered out. Goats grazed on sparse clumps of grassy vegetation. Ear-torn donkeys with tan coats and coffee-coloured mohican manes stood motionless, looking forlorn.

The riding became muscle-aching sweat-streaming tough. Twice I dropped the bike as the front end dug into loose sand. I just picked it up and carried on. The wilderness, the searing dry heat and physical exertion were essential elements to my happiness.

Despite having new tyres, Kieran got bogged down. I always hung back and waited for the inevitable, then with seemingly boundless energy, leapt off my bike and helped push him from behind. Once, he tried bulldozing through sand that was so obviously too deep his Serow got wedged up to the bash plate, back wheel spinning uselessly before he let off the throttle.

A tall, lean man with a necklace of thick beads, his pregnant wife wearing a bright red kanga and their five children stood watching us with perplexed looks as we struggled to push the bike onto firmer ground. Their home, an *engaji* constructed of branches and dried grass into a golden dome, was crowned with a banded wreath of woven sticks. I wondered what these nomadic pastoralists, whose only possession that didn't come from nature was the five-litre plastic water container the man held, thought of us with our motorbikes, gadgets and many belongings.

I remember hearing a saying that when you have too many things, you no longer own those possessions because they own you. The tipping point was somewhere between the Turkana man's water container and our fully loaded bikes. Too often, our possessions weigh us down psychologically as well as physically. Certainly, the times in my life that I have been happiest and felt freest were when I've travelled light and owned the least.

When Kieran got stuck again, I wondered why he never looked ahead, anticipating problems with the aim of avoiding them, rather than attempting to plough through. I didn't get annoyed or frustrated because I was in one of those untroubled carefree moods. The advantage of being female and usually not as strong is that I have had a lifetime of finding alternative ways to overcome physical challenges. Engaging the brain is usually more effective than brute force. I knew it bothered Kieran whenever I caught him up, unaided, having taken a different trail. I wasn't a better rider, but I think I had a better understanding of what my bike was capable of.

As the trail meandered away from the shore, the going got easier, the ground more compact. We looked back and saw silhouetted on the horizon a camel train some two hundred strong, walking towards the lake.

We made camp on an island in the next dried up riverbed, hidden and protected amongst the bush, which provided cool shade from the sun. We'd not seen a soul since we had left the lakeshore an hour or two ago, but no sooner had we put up the tent and were making tea than a tall, dark-skinned man wearing army fatigues and a rifle slung over his shoulder walked barefoot towards us.

My initial concern was soon allayed when he introduced himself as the local askari and said that we would be safe on 'his' river and, if we needed anything, that his base was just down the riverbed.

'There are three of us there. Your neighbours just beyond those bushes upriver are a nice family too. You won't have any trouble,' he assured us. Then he wandered over to the head man, who had emerged on the other side of the track. They talked a while and some of his children came over to see us, but they were soon bored and went to play their own games.

In the dimming light, two sleek-bodied jackals raced past unaware of us, chasing each other, playfully circling and darting between the bushes. Later, some minutes after a gunshot echoed through the still air, two of the children walked back past our tent carrying a goat. How could one dry riverbed in a desert contain so much life? I wondered just how many people we passed each day, unaware of their presence.

A short ride in the morning brought us to the entrance gates of Sibiloi National Park where we registered with the rangers. There were no restrictions on riding motorbikes. I think they figured that if you'd made it this far, you'd be able to take whatever came your way inside the park.

There was little wildlife in the park anyway, an indicator of the inhospitable climate. Larger wildlife like zebra, hartebeest, topi and kudu were the first to decline in drought conditions with scarcity of food. As for the carnivorous mammals, the leopard, cheetah and lion were all now extinct in the park, primarily due to human activity. I did spot one set of tracks, which were probably hyena. Otherwise, I only saw two hares, a couple of the smaller antelope – the dwarf-sized dik-dik and the slender long-necked gerenuk, some Grant's gazelle and a couple of jackals. At the northern end of the park, the carcass of a cow in the middle of one track was surrounded by prints.

Several goats grazed on the minimal scrub. Whenever the lone shepherd, usually a young boy or sometimes a girl, saw our bikes approaching, they fled in outright fear, sprinting barefoot across the uneven terrain, leaving their herds to fend for themselves. Grazing domestic stock within the park boundaries is illegal. Presumably the children thought we were rangers on the lookout for them.

The human-wildlife conflict in the park was ever-present. The surrounding land has suffered from over-grazing and local families struggle to maintain their herds. Who can blame them from encroaching into the park when they can see the relatively lush grassland? They must wonder who would go to such lengths to provide food for wildlife but let their fellow man starve on the periphery. Why is a hippo allowed to eat but their cattle are not?

The inhospitable terrain means few people live in this region, which is ironic since it is known as the 'cradle of mankind'. Although the first paleontological expedition to the Turkana Basin was in 1902, it wasn't until the 1960s that archaeological excavations continued apace, when Richard Leakey stopped on the eastern shores of Lake Turkana. His discovery of several fragments of hominid bones changed our understanding of human evolution.

Koobi Fora Base Camp, the research station, was founded in 1968. Only two researchers were there when we arrived, the other workers away on leave for the holidays. The youngest, Emmanuel, was happy to have visitors on his birthday. They had run out of beer a while ago and weren't expecting a resupply soon, so we celebrated by drinking ice-cold water straight from the fridge, necking litre after litre until we felt refreshed and rehydrated.

Emmanuel brought the five permanent residents out of a cardboard box and placed them in a row on the table in front of us. The skulls stared in silence like an audience awaiting a performance. They had not spoken in well over a million years. The small museum and dusty rooms of uncatalogued finds were full of other hominid bone fragments, pre-historic tools and animal skulls, more of which have been found here than at the rest of the world's fossil sites combined. It's hard to fathom that this area was once home to so much life.

Emmanuel showed us around but said the best facility was the lake, perfect for a refreshing swim at the end of a hot day. We took his advice, hoping he was right about the Nile crocodiles not being a bother but heeding his warning to keep an eye out for hippos. It felt good to be clean and free of dust for a while.

Beyond the northern boundary of the park, we came to Ileret, a mixture of rectangular adobe buildings and traditional *engajis*, although the domed huts here were constructed from corrugated tin sheets, bent and bashed into shape.

We checked in with the police even though we'd been officially stamped out of the country two weeks earlier. Nelson took our passports into the concrete building with solar panels on the roof. We were in no rush to ride out into the sweltering midday heat so popped to the little shop and bought cold Coke and a couple of *shuka*, Maasai cloth, our only souvenirs of the trip. Then we sat under the shade of a tin sheet on steel girders, waiting for Nelson to return, and were relieved when he told us everything was in order and that we could proceed.

We didn't get far. At the edge of the village, a belligerent military man stopped us. The beer in his hand was not his first judging by his slurred speech. He was a sore sight with several days' growth of stubble and half-tucked misbuttoned shirt. He barked orders from his chair, demanding that we join him for beer. He was insistent that we couldn't continue because this wasn't an official border and only vehicles with Kenyan registration plates could pass. I began explaining but when he raised his voice in retaliation, his young and seemingly long-suffering colleague intervened, explaining instead that it wasn't safe for us.

216

'The north of Kenya is very volatile. Just the other day some men were killed by guns. We can't let you travel this road. We are responsible for your safety. You must go to Moyale instead,' he said.

I laughed. I knew this road north was relatively safe for tourists compared to the main Moyale road, where vehicles were often held up, banditry a problem. They would have us detour over five hundred kilometres through dangerous country because they didn't want us to travel a few kilometres north across their area of responsibility.

I pressed him for details of the killings. He said the culprits were cattle raiders near Marsabit, a town hundreds of kilometres away. I think they were off-duty and bored because eventually they let us pass without one mention of a bribe. Further on, we looped past a thin rope barring the trail. A man ran out of the nearby building with army boots unlaced. 'Wait,' he shouted, pulling a white vest over his head. He quickly checked our passports, then let us proceed with assurances that the road was safe.

Where our GPS indicated the boundary between the two countries, we stopped and opened a bottle of Coke we'd bought earlier. A tall man with not an ounce of fat on him approached. He was surprised by how much luggage we had and wondered what we could be carrying. We explained we didn't have a lot, only the things we needed like camping and cooking gear, a few clothes and bike tools, food and water. He seemed amused.

He showed us his traditional wooden headrest. He mimed how he used it as a pillow for sleeping, resting his neck on the bowed edge, then turned it over to reveal the hollowed out cup that he used for drinking from. Along with the herding stick he carried over his shoulder, that was all the equipment he needed.

We gave him the bottle of Coke to finish. He seemed unsure of the gift and waited until we started riding off. I looked back to see him down the drink, then thoughtlessly discard the bottle. We stopped, waited for him to continue his journey, then returned to pick up the plastic. I guess we both have things to learn from each other about waste and excess.

We passed several bomas, and I heard voices inside the thorn bush enclosures, but the only people I saw were women with yellow jerrycans gathered along one of the riverbeds, presumably getting water.

We camped in a small sandy clearing amongst the dry bush. A young goatherd and his father gave a friendly hello and smiled as they passed. They were both so terribly thin it pained me to see them. When three boys passed and mimed that they were hungry, Kieran took pity on them and handed over the last of our biscuits. We could restock later in Omorate.

In Ethiopia the next evening at a Hamer community campsite, we pitched our tent beneath towering mango trees where it was always cool, the sun never penetrating the thick canopy. A small group of young, white English-speakers were also staying. They were volunteering with an organisation who runs capacity-building projects in health and business, training the locals to be less dependent upon an increasingly unsustainable pastoral lifestyle.

A blonde-haired woman told us about the problems and her experiences. She had travelled extensively but seemed settled; I could imagine her still here a decade from now.

She explained that with the ground bare from overgrazing, the Hamer were being forced to find new land for their cattle, goats and sheep to feed on. As I'd seen south of the border in Kenya, the nearby National Parks, which protected the wildlife and contained rich grazing land, were too alluring to ignore.

The year before, a Hamer man had been jailed for ten months for taking his animals to graze in Mayo National Park; yet, a policeman who killed a Hamer man was jailed for only four months. Violence erupted.

The Hamer used to be peaceful. Not even ten years ago, land conflict was not an issue, but a changing climate and overpopulation has taken its toll. They would have to find alternative ways to make a living if they were to survive. The woman was certain that the projects she was volunteering on would help.

One reason I had first quit my engineering job and cycled through Africa years earlier was the idealistic notion of wanting to make a difference and do good in the world. I knew I needed to see the world and its problems before I could identify how to help, but on the trip I became disillusioned by the international development sector, which had initially interested me. I also realised that there are many ways to make a difference.

I'd swapped books with another cyclist when in the Congo. He gave me a Hemingway book I'd not read. One paragraph in particular struck a chord: perhaps I wasn't meant to save the world; there were other people for that. Instead I could continue to travel and try to understand this world we live in and then write about what I knew.

I considered that my role is not one of intervening but observing like a journalist or foreign correspondent; except that, instead of disasters and headline-grabbing news, I could write about regular people going about their daily life. I could show that underneath the cloaks of religion and culture and climate, we are all the same, with the same hopes and dreams and worries and pains. Once we understand that, how could we let harm come to others?

My internal conflict continues because this seems a feeble excuse to justify and give a small meaning to my journeys when really I'm absolving myself of responsibility and passing the buck, leaving other people to take real action.

Of all the trails we rode, this route through northern Kenya into Ethiopia was the most trying, not because of the rough tracks but because of the obvious struggle and hardship local people have to survive. It played on my mind, highlighting the pointlessness of our journey and the selfishness of my personal pursuit for happiness and contentment.

22.
Everything Ethiopia
Ethiopia

Ethiopia has a reputation amongst cycle tourers for its stone-throwing, stick-wielding children who love nothing more than chasing down foreigners as they pedal through villages, attempting to unsaddle them with a rock to the head or a branch through the wheel. On a motorbike though, I figured I had speed on my side as well as armour and a crash helmet for protection. It would take more than a few unruly kids to stop me from exploring Africa's most geographically diverse country and culturally rich heritage, if what I'd read lived up to expectation.

Sara and Philippe were the first cyclists we'd met since southern Africa. Fit and tanned from twelve years touring around the world, they were on their last leg home to Europe. We were staying at the same guesthouse and went out for dinner in town. They recounted their experiences with humour and not a hint of cynicism. I was lifted by their positivity and envious at the rate they devoured their pizzas and ordered another. I missed having a cycle tourer's insatiable appetite and ability to consume anything edible I set eyes upon.

I didn't miss the early starts. The next morning, Sara and Philippe were already pedalling out of Arba Minch as we went in search of breakfast. We didn't leave town until midday and still caught them up in an hour.

We rode on to a roadside wooden shack serving cold Coke and waited for the cyclists to arrive. Our motorbikes parked outside attracted the attention of the passing children, alerting them to the presence of *farangi*. Meaning foreigner, this word was to become a familiar name call and taunt over the coming two months in the country. Then the two cyclists arrived. The small groups of children walking home from school transformed into a screaming horde, racing the bicycles like a swarm of bees to a honey pot.

Sara and Philippe had a relaxed attitude towards the attention they garnered. They laughed and smiled and took photos, then sat on stools beside us. To not get wound up or riled, especially when tired, required saint-like patience. The children gathered around, pressing closely against the flimsy shack walls, bright eyes peering through the cracks, little hands reaching inside to wave and touch. Beaming, wide-smiling faces and excited shouts and screams echoed inside as a kind of mass hysteria began to take hold.

The cafe owner grabbed a stick and beat back the crowd, a temporary reprieve since the chaos only attracted more children. Then the owner's wife, who had been tending fish on the grill, took up the cause. She stood up assertively and retied the colourful wrap around her waist as though preparing for battle. With a bucket in her one arm, she scooped water with her free hand and threw it at the nearest children.

When the children grew accustomed to the showers, another deterrent was required. Not to be defeated, the woman put down the bucket and picked up a handful of stones. This was my first-hand encounter with Ethiopia's unofficial national sport of rock throwing, one of the few games, it turns out, I find more enjoyable and entertaining as a spectator than as a participant and target.

It started with theatrics: the threat of action. The woman drawing back her arm in preparation was enough to send the children scarpering. When they returned, she shot well-aimed small pebbles at the ground close to their bare feet. Most leapt back lightning-quick, but a persistent hardy few were undeterred and now competed to see who could get closest to the shack without being hit.

Onlookers cheered from a safe distance; a few hid round the side of the cafe and pestered us from behind. The noise made conversation impossible. Traffic could not pass the congested street.

The number of participants in the game multiplied; increasingly large stones were hurled with mounting aggression. It was time to leave before the game turned to all out war.

The last thing I saw was the woman taking a running aim at three boys. The tallest one picked up a huge rock almost the size of his head and hurled it. The lady turned and fled, and the rock bounced and hit her calf, a look of horror on her face switching to livid anger in a flash. She turned and, furiously grabbing rocks and lobbing them on the go in rapid succession, chased the boys, who fled to the bush like vervet monkeys.

A little smile washed over my face beneath my helmet as we rode away knowing that the lady would have the last say. Justice would be served.

As the afternoon wore on, it became clear that wild camping out of sight wouldn't be easy. Either houses lined the roads or the land was productive and being used for agriculture. We rode to the next small town hoping for accommodation and were directed through the busy street to a small wooden building between rows of concrete block shops. Around the side in the narrow space, old men sat at low rickety wooden tables and hand-built chairs. It had a salubrious feel and my immediate reaction was to walk away, but the owner insisted on showing me the rooms that lined the alley.

The small room was dimly lit by a single light bulb hanging from the ceiling. The only furniture was a rickety double bed, but the sheet looked pristine white, clean and smooth. Based on my experiences of central African accommodation, I suspected this place also served as a brothel and wondered what the old man with wrinkled face and rotting teeth who had raised his glass to me with a smile had been thinking.

With daylight fading fast, we were running out of options, so I changed my outlook. Brothels had been good places to sleep for a night in the past, the owner was friendly, and the old men seemed harmless enough. Had I been alone, I would have joined them at one of the tables, asked for a beer, written my journal and been certain that no one would bother me because they would be like elders protecting the young once we had exchanged a few words of common courtesy and curiosity. Adding another person to the equation somehow changed my perspective. With our own company, we'd be left to ourselves and without any interaction I'd feel less comfortable, so we'd retreat to the room, isolating ourselves from the world. That wasn't why I travelled.

I returned to the street and into a horde of people.

'What's going on?' I shouted, pushing my way through the mass of bodies, amused at the attention we'd garnered, thinking this must be what it was like all the time for the cyclists.

I found Kieran at the centre, helmeted up and on edge, eyes darting to the hundred hands caressing our bags and bikes. I started to describe the accommodation and realised I hadn't asked where we could safely store the bikes. They clearly wouldn't remain untouched if left on the street.

Kieran interrupted, 'We need to get out of here,' and he began manoeuvring his bike around. There was a touch of fear in his voice that made me switch my outlook from amusement at the game to cynical risk assessor seeing danger at every turn. I judged that we weren't in danger, although I know how quickly situations can deteriorate for no apparent reason. Alone I would have turned to the bar-cum-brothel as sanctuary. Kieran's escape was to hit the road. I followed.

Now we had to look afresh for a place to stay but with even less time until darkness descended. Out of town, we rode towards a small river snaking across a wide rocky plain of dried rivulets.

'Let's ask at this house if it's OK to pass by and camp beyond their compound near the river,' I said. If we had assurances from some locals that we would be safe and not disturbed, I'd feel happier and sleep better considering the open view.

The family were at the back of their house. A young woman with a red shawl draped over her hair greeted me while an elderly woman remained hunched on a step. I began explaining our predicament, but the slim man who was lying on a blanket on the ground interrupted me.

'You must stay here. Here it is safe,' he spoke calmly and clearly, carefully choosing his words. 'I am sorry I do not get up. I have a bad leg.'

Mohammed had had a hip operation six days earlier and was recuperating. 'It is painful but better on the floor,' he commented, looking distinctly uncomfortable as he tried to shift position. 'Please join us.'

Soon we were seated on plastic chairs and telling stories, translated by Mohammed for his family of six children to hear as the stars appeared in the sky. Under cover of darkness, we pitched our tent behind the building, out of sight of the main road, and went to bed, grateful for the kindness shown and feeling fortunate at how the day had ended.

We packed up and rode on in the chill of early morning in search of breakfast. The hills were gently lit by the pale yellow sun whose warmth barely reached us through the mist. Through town, smoke from stoves lingered in the heavy air, horses with carts trotted past and children's calls of 'You, you!' and 'Money, money, money!' pierced our ears. Kids shouting for money was already a daily feature of Ethiopian travel. It amused me, the accents making the word barely decipherable. How long until the words grated and irritated?

For now, Ethiopia offered more enjoyment than exasperation, and pleasure could be found at every roadside corner concentrated in caffeine-rich coffee. Coffee was not only a drink but an entire sensory experience that I never tired of.

Coffee beans were roasted over charcoal, then ground while the water heated. The espresso-strength coffee, once ready, was poured from the narrow-spouted pot into small coffee cups. Grass laid over the floor, incense burning and freshly cut herbs all added to the earthy aroma. This wasn't an espresso shot to gulp quickly before rushing off but a ceremony to savour. These roadside cafes were like safe havens, where everyone sharing coffee was a friend united and the world beyond paused until we were ready to rejoin it with renewed energy.

The caffeine boost helped get us to Dodola, the main town in Bale National Park, which being a tourist destination meant inflated prices for faranjis, bartering for any product bought or accommodation sought, and keeping constant watch of crafty men with quick hands. I was out of practice and soon tired, but by the end of the day, we'd arranged a guide to take us on a four-day hike through the hills and had bought food supplies. Our bikes and luggage could be kept at the hotel, a secure place given it was largely occupied by the military.

The government had recently declared a state of emergency due to ongoing violence by the majority Oromo and Amhara ethnic groups against the Tigrayan-led government. After a year of protests, road blocks and attacks on businesses with state links across the Oromio region, the military had been brought in to enforce security. Restrictions on freedom of speech, including internet access, had been imposed. We'd seen burned out skeletons of buses and cars beside the road, a visual reminder of the underlying tension we felt in town.

Salim, our guide, was as easy to talk to about life and the politics of his country as he was to walk alongside in silence. Usually we preferred to walk without a guide, but Salim proved invaluable as an interpreter for all we saw and acted as a buffer to the children's shouts of 'You, you! Farangi! Money, money!'

It felt good be on foot. We walked across open rolling country along wide dirt paths. Villagers lead laden donkeys between golden stubble fields, the teff, Ethiopia's staple grain, recently harvested. In the hills of Afromontane forest I breathed in the fresh mountain air. Amongst the lush green rises and valleys, we wandered past homesteads of adobe homes amongst juniper woods with clothes drying along rustic fencing and horses grazing unfettered. At night we slept in basic huts with wood burners that kept us warm and dry in the evening when it poured.

We arrived in one village on market day. Everyone who lived within a day's walk appeared to be going. Men on horseback herded pack animals and loose horses to be sold, some shepherded cattle and sheep, and plenty more walked empty-handed while children bounded down the steep paths unhindered. With such a melee of people and produce, no one cared about two tourists in the mix, and we were free to pass through without being pestered.

Dodola seemed like a different place on our return. We were not the naive tourists of a few days earlier, no longer uncertain about prices or customs. With an armoury of Amharic at our disposal, the town had transformed from daunting to endearing. Even the children seemed to have accepted us and didn't bother to beg.

Exploring the area on motorbikes, we found dirt tracks to the top of a valley. Oh, it always felt good to ride off-road, bumping and bouncing along narrow trails. With so many paths pounded over the centuries by wandering donkeys, livestock and people passing from one rural home to another, it was inevitable we'd sometimes take one that veered away from where we wanted to go and have to backtrack.

Later we made our way slowly across the Sanetti Plateau, an open high plain of scrub, silvery as though covered in a wintry frost, with pools of water, mirror images of the reflected blue sky. My Serow stuttered in the thin air as we rode past giant lobelia cacti up to Ethiopia's second highest peak at 4,377 metres.

I scanned the land all day hoping to spot an Ethiopian wolf. Once widespread throughout the highlands, its range is now restricted to here and the Simien Mountains.

I was giving up hope of seeing one when, in a shallow depression, I spotted movement. Slamming to a halt, I grabbed my camera and quickly put on the telephoto lens. I didn't have binoculars, but this worked as well. Through the viewfinder, I saw one with a rusty orange coat, white throat and four matching white 'socks', more fox-like in colour than wolf.

It looked straight at me, and I feared it would run off, but Kieran had stopped up ahead, so I rode on slowly and killed the engine once beside him. The wolf waited a few moments, decided we weren't a threat and trotted on, nose to ground. It paused and sniffed, then crouched, waiting with poise and patience, the moments passing … and suddenly it leapt, all four feet in the air. Its pounce missed the prey, probably a giant mole rat, which constitutes the wolf's primary diet, so it circled and jumped again.

I'll never tire of watching wildlife in their natural environment, but the wildlife doesn't always comply, so when the wolf wandered behind a rise, we rode on, back to our campsite for another freezing night in our inadequate sleeping bags. We woke to a frozen tent and a family of warthogs snuffling through the long grass.

———

To reach the capital, Addis Ababa, we took dirt roads for a couple of days through the Wabe Shebelle gorge directly north. The only traffic was thin short-horned cattle being herded by tall lithe men in matching turquoise blue loose-fitting shirts. One carried a kettle, another a calf; the man with the broadest smile carried a rifle slung over his shoulder and wore an ornate knife tucked into the wrap around his waist.

The trail rejoined tarmac all too soon. Approaching the Awash River, we had to navigate a traffic jam of trucks. Lorries lined the roadsides, others tried to squeeze through. We nipped between them until brought to a halt. The new bridge, opened the year before, would apparently enable all the trucks that ply this trade route from Djibouti port to Addis Ababa to safely cross the river. The backlog at the customs building suggested otherwise.

Crossing the bridge was not allowed by motorcycle. It was illegal, apparently, for security reasons. The security reasons were that it was illegal. This Catch-22 conversation with the security officer was going nowhere, like most of the trucks.

'How are we to get to Addis Ababa then?' I asked, trying a pragmatic approach.

'Go back the way you came.'

'That isn't an option. We didn't come from Addis.' We didn't have enough fuel to go back the way we'd come. The only alternative route was an even longer detour.

I demanded to speak to whoever was in charge, but the conversation was the same, logic caught in an impermeable barrier.

A voice filtered through from behind. 'Excuse me madam.'

'What?' I shouted in frustration, turning to the man and removing his hand from my shoulder.

'Excuse me madam. Maybe I can help. I can give you a lift.'

'But we have motorbikes.'

'Yes, yes. We put the bikes in my truck. Come, I show you.'

I was still tense and my immediate reaction was not to trust this fat man, but we had no other obvious options. We agreed to the help, knowing it would cost us. Within minutes, a group of men had gathered to lift our bikes into the back of this man's pick-up. We scrambled in and wedged ourselves amongst our bags with the fat man and off we went, his driver speeding across the bridge, wind whistling.

I took my camera out to photograph us and the bikes. 'No photos, no photos!' the fat man exclaimed.

'Oh, sorry, I wasn't thinking,' I replied quickly. Photographing critical infrastructure was illegal in many African countries and a sure way to get arrested. Even just having a camera out could get you into trouble.

'There,' he commented as I shoved the camera away, 'there's a good girl.'

And he patted me on the arm like a dog who'd obeyed a command.

Kieran saw the burning fury in my eyes and laughed. 'Oh, he shouldn't have said that!'

'The condescending twat!' I spat under my breath and erupted in laughter too, the tension in me floating away. This was the Africa I loved, after all.

With the bikes quickly unloaded on the far side by using an embankment as a ramp, we pre-empted the fight over the cost by thanking the obtuse obese man, who had nonetheless helped us out greatly, and handed him a one hundred birr note.

'What is this?' he said and handed it back.

I had not expected him to refuse any money. Had I misjudged him? Was he a genuinely honest, altruistic person?

'Please, take it,' Kieran said. 'We're very grateful.'

'This is a joke!' he exclaimed. 'And you owe me five hundred birr to clean my trousers. See, they are dirty from the bikes.' *Ah, there we are. That's more like it.*

'Your trousers were already dirty!' I exclaimed. 'Take the one hundred.'

Tempers were rising. The fat man tried to see how much cash we had in the purse, and even Kieran toughened his stance and spoke up. The driver interrupted. 'Take the hundred birr,' he said to the man, then turned to us and spoke quietly, 'Please give him fifteen birr, which is the cost of cleaning his trousers.' I got the impression this wasn't the first altercation his driver had mediated in.

That evening at the Buffet d'Aouache Hotel, once a station servicing the Djibouti railway and one of the country's oldest hotels, we sat on the leafy veranda sipping beer amid whitewashed colonial architecture and laughed about the bridge crossing and other challenges and irritations that Ethiopia provided in abundance. Having a common adversary seemed to strengthen our bond and united us, our relationship strong, as it once had seemed. The urge for solitude, to travel and experience Africa alone, that had coursed through me for most of the year, seemed to be pacified.

We arrived in Addis Ababa in time to celebrate Christmas on the 25th December. Genna, the Ethiopian Christmas, is two weeks later. We splashed out on a modern, clean hotel room and gorged on a delectable array of foreign foods from Italian pizzas to Indian curries.

Ethiopian cuisine in the more rural areas was limited, typically *injera* and *shiro*. Whilst *shiro wot*, a pureed chickpea stew, was perfectly palatable, the same could not be said for the staple carbohydrate served alongside it. Injera, made from fermented teff dough and served like a floppy pancake, had the taste, smell and texture of a dirty damp dish cloth. I managed without.

I did love the standard breakfast of *ful*, a spicy bean dish. Otherwise, we lived on readily available avocados, tomatoes and nutrient-poor white bread. When the avocados dried up, we added a touch more salt. I would not survive long as a vegan – the pounds, for once, were dropping off me.

The majority of the world operates according to the Gregorian calendar, which was adopted in 1582. Ethiopia, however, stuck with the Julian calendar, which runs seven years and eight months behind. It consists of thirteen months, twelve of which are thirty days while the last month makes up any remaining days to match the solar cycle. What's more, Ethiopian time is split into two 12-hour cycles beginning at six o'clock in the morning (according to European time) and again in the evening. Except, its not always clear which dates and times are being used. Fortunately, with the way we travelled, days and months were largely irrelevant, our plans dictated by the seasons and red tape. Red tape – onward visas for Sudan and Egypt – was our main reason for coming to the capital.

The road north of Addis Ababa did not go smoothly. During an oil change, I noticed two broken spokes on the rear wheel of my bike. That night the bottle of meths we were carrying for cooking on our Trangia stove exploded, spilling the contents. To our surprise, we found genuine Yamaha replacement spokes in the next small town, albeit ones that we had to bend with mole grips to fit. We stayed at a hotel there as we'd run out of daylight, reluctantly fleeced with *farangi* prices, and when I woke in the morning, I stepped out of bed and straight into a pool of water. The entire room had flooded, soaking our bags on the floor.

Despite these minor setbacks, we made it to Lalibela and spent a couple of relaxing days wandering through the famous rock-hewn churches along with hundreds of other pilgrims, mostly elderly people in traditional Tigrayan white robes carrying long staffs. But our bike troubles continued. First another broken spoke. Then, the morning we were due to explore the Danakil Depression, we discovered one of the tyres had deflated overnight. After a mad dash through town from one petrol station to another interspersed with visits to various cash machines, we eventually managed to find fuel to fill the tanks and money to fill our pockets.

At around one hundred metres below sea level, the Danakil Depression is one of the lowest places on earth, as well as one of the hottest. Two years earlier I had been cycling through Siberia, one of the coldest places on earth. The contrast between the two and how people live in these inhospitable places intrigued me.

Because of political and security reasons, we had to join a tour into the Danakil. For four days we were 'escorted' by ten 4x4s and had the luxury of riding without all our kit, which was transported for us.

We descended from the highland plateau until the wind blew hot like a hairdryer, and I wondered if travelling here by motorcycle wasn't such a good idea. Momentarily envious of everyone else in the air-conditioned 4x4s, I remembered the great thing about motorcycle travel is the direct exposure to the climate and terrain. The feeling of vulnerability and being connected to nature is impossible to experience from the confines of a vehicle.

During a lunch break, while our guide made payments to the local officials to ensure our safe passage, some young boys took the liberty while our backs were turned to liberate the bar bag on my bike of its contents. They were spotted and chased by older boys, spurred on by the angry shouts of the cafe owner. Our belongings were eventually returned, the kids caught and cautioned with a swipe to their heads. Kieran was relieved, concerned that he might not have survived the coming four-day inferno without the sun cream.

We rode across the salt flats glistening white in the sun, the thin film of surface water splashing over the vehicles. We stopped to watch camel trains transporting salt tablets to inland towns. Later we watched local Afar extracting the salt in six kilogram blocks from the saline crust of Lake Karum as has been done for millennia. While us tourists sipped continually from our water bottles and reapplied sun cream, the Afar men with heads wrapped in cloth to protect from the sun worked tirelessly without a break. They carved, cut, chopped and carried the blocks to load onto weary camels, who sat with heads lowered, long eyelashes protecting their eyes and rope lines tied around their lower lips waiting for the long trek to town.

Fifteen kilometres from the Eritrean border, the Dallol hot springs bubbled like a cauldron, and we stepped carefully beside the bright green, yellow and orange toxic sulphur pools. When the wind changed direction, I breathed through my neck scarf to filter the noxious fumes.

That night we slept under the stars on thin mattresses placed atop rickety wooden frames, enjoying the cool hours of darkness before the sun rose on another day. The route to Erta Ale was hard riding. The 4x4s made light work of the powdery dirt and sand, kicking up thick clouds that made it impossible to see through on our bikes. We struggled to keep up until we reached the edge of a rocky ascent at the base of the volcano. Then the bikes were in their element, and we had to keep waiting for the 4x4s as they lurched awkwardly over the jagged rocks.

We pulled into camp as the sun was setting, the highlight for the day still ahead of us. The three-hour walk up Erta Ale was a less appealing prospect after a hard day's ride than for those who'd been confined to the leisurely (and arguably boring) back seat of a 4x4. As midnight approached, we finally took the last careful steps over the solidified lava crust and peered into the volcano's core.

Fiery molten lava bubbled in the cauldron, pockets erupting in bursts of flaming orange bright against the black night. It boiled and popped and lava shots sprayed skywards, sometimes falling on the far side, streaking the walls and sliding back into the pot like boiling treacle. There seemed little reason why the lava couldn't erupt over us.

Retreating to a safe camp, we rolled out our mattresses to sleep for a few hours under the stars before making the descent in the cool hours before sunrise. After breakfast we began the return journey. I was physically exhausted riding the sandy terrain again, relief washing over me when we returned to the main tarmac road. We expected a smooth, easy ride back to town.

Kieran's bike had other plans.

The engine cut out and refused to restart. Changing the spark plug got the bike running, but a few kilometres further on the engine cut out again. Nothing Kieran did could coax it into action. The 4x4s had to return for people to catch flights, so we said we'd make our own way back. Using a piece of twine tied to the foot peg of my bike, we towed Kieran's bike 150 kilometres through the mountains.

The problem was contaminated fuel. The container with the replacement fuel our guide had provided must have had remnant diesel in it. Back in town, Kieran emptied the tank, cleaned the carburettor and replaced the washed out spark plug. With clean fuel, the bike started first time. We replaced another broken spoke on my bike, then took both straight to a river where our tour guide gave them a thorough clean to wash off the salt until they sparkled like new.

The dramatic dry canyon-land of Tigray was a biker's delight, the road sweeping through golden valleys amongst towering red sandstone formations and flat-topped high plateaus. We continued into the Simien Mountains, stopping at the National Park office to hire the obligatory armed scout, who nervously rode pillion on Kieran's bike for a day. Then, after visiting Gondar's castles we headed towards the border.

Weeks of incessant taunting calls of 'faranji!', demands for money, inflated tourist prices and racing to avoid the occasional hand-thrown rock missiles (only one hit Kieran on the helmet) had taken their toll. Our patience dwindled to an all-time low when navigating a demonstration in one town, I narrowly avoided a branch being jammed through my front wheel. One of the last sights before we reached the border post was of a child running into a field ahead of us, dropping his shorts and taking a shit. It was time to leave.

I'd found Ethiopia fascinating, both historically and geographically, but never felt any real connection to anyone, the cultures too confusing for me to fully comprehend. How, I wondered, would Sudan compare? Just as Ethiopia's notoriety for rock-throwing children preceded it, so did the Sudanese reputation for kindness and hospitality. I couldn't wait to see if the next country would also live up to expectation.

23.

Nubia
Sudan & Egypt

Everything that had started to irritate us in Ethiopia soon faded into memory. When we stopped for lunch across the border in Sudan, there was no shouting or chanting or demanding; no hands with unstoppable urges to touch our bags, fiddle with brake levers, pull on throttle cables, yank at fuel lines, flick switches or press buttons. Instead, children stood quietly and looked at the bikes for a moment, then went on their way, leaving us to enjoy a plate of ful and cup of tea in peace.

When time came to stop for the night, finding a place to stealth camp was easy because Sudan meant space. Our first night, camping around the base of a rocky hill flanking the road, we were undisturbed despite goats wandering past at sunset and hearing the call to prayer from the nearby village. And it was wonderful to be warm again, the freezing restless nights up in the Ethiopian highlands forgotten. *I think I'm going to like Sudan.*

With only three days to officially register our presence in the country, which could only be done in Khartoum, we headed directly to the capital, where the White Nile and Blue Nile converge. We'd last seen the White Nile in northwest Uganda over three months previously, whereas we'd camped at Lake Tana, the source of the Blue Nile, on our last night in Ethiopia.

Despite the fertile land provided by the nurturing Nile and pockets of green within the city, Khartoum was largely a dust bowl, the polluted sand-laden soupy air rasping my throat as we navigated the ordered grid of congested streets. In between red tape paper chases to the airport to register and then the office of tourism to obtain a photography permit, we visited the National Museum and dined out.

Khartoum was a culinary haven after our limited Ethiopian diet. We feasted on shawarma and salads, falafel and fizzy drinks, and found a patisserie selling a delectable array of sweet pastries. I devoured the box full of desserts in one sitting, then returned the next day to replenish supplies, which disappeared just a quickly. We needed to leave Khartoum before I caused a food shortage.

We rode north past the Coptic church, the shops selling tyres, clothes and electronics, and the stalls of fresh fruit and colourful veg until only the dark tarmac remained, running into a land faded to dusty grey with a strong crosswind to fight. After a few hours we turned off the main road onto a sandy track, seemingly going nowhere, the desert open and inviting.

I'd suggested we go and see the remains of an ancient city that was marked on the tourist map. I imagined crumbled ruins, vague outlines of walls visible in the sand and a few exposed remnant rocks. It would be a chance to leave the asphalt, which runs smoothly the length of our route through Sudan, and to maximise the use of our two-week transit visa, delaying the inevitable end of this African journey.

After spending the night camped near a dry wadi, nestled by scrubby bush for shelter from the wind that occasionally whipped up the sand, we continued along the trail to Naqa, which was deserted except for a single caretaker who took our entry fee.

It was hard to imagine a thriving population two thousand years ago when Naqa was a major centre of the Kushite Kingdom. Thirty kilometres – a day's donkey or camel ride – from the Nile, it would have served as a trading station en route east to the coast.

We walked towards the Amun Temple along a wide avenue of twelve sculpted rams, their faces weathered, although the spiral patterns carved into their bodies resembling wool remained intact. The Lion Temple stood largely complete, towering reliefs of a king and queen on the huge sandstone block pylon and various Egyptian gods carved into the other walls.

As a child I had been fascinated by the ancient Egyptians, learning about the pharaohs and pyramids and excavation of Tutankhamun's tomb. I imagined I would one day be an archaeologist, digging in the desert, discovering items of unimaginable wealth and international interest. But I had never known until now that equally advanced, competing kingdoms with intertwined cultural connections had existed far south through Nubia in present-day Sudan.

I wandered the site marvelling that such structures stood defiant so long after the people had left. As the sun rose and the shadows shortened, and sweat beaded on my forehead and soaked into my shirt, we took to the bikes and rode to the Meroitic site Musawarat es-Sufra. Entering the Great Enclosure, we walked along old walkways and ramps between what would have been courtyards and other buildings to see the three temples.

Having arrived over sweeping sandy trails with no signs and only the GPS location to guide us, and with no other tourists, it felt like we were the first foreigners to stumble upon these isolated and deserted sites, although they were first excavated over a hundred years ago.

Explorers, treasure hunters and archaeologists of the past never had to negotiate entry fees. As with Zambia, there was a dual pricing structure. One guide we met agreed that the foreigners' fees were unreasonable and phoned ahead to each of the sites we intended to visit. After that, we paid the local price. It was just one of many acts of kindness shown to us in Sudan, whether bought coffee on the street or invited for lunch to a family home when we stopped to ask directions.

Meroe, further north and visible from the tarmac, didn't evoke the same feelings, especially when greeted by a tout and asked if we wanted a camel ride. These Nubian pyramids have distinct steep sides. Sadly, most of their peaks were demolished by an Italian treasure hunter in the 1830s. Despite that, with unique abutted temple structures, their prominence and grandeur is no less diminished.

Nubian pyramids were partially modelled on the ancient Egyptian style and mostly constructed some thousand years after the first Egyptian pyramids were built. Though, today there are twice as many Nubian pyramids still standing as there are Egyptian ones.

The guides lingering at the entrance gate said there was a good area to camp in the dunes behind the site, and we would be safe and undisturbed, which hardly needed saying. That evening, we traced insect tracks across the sand, then sat and watched the golden sun float towards the hazy horizon and the rippled shadows in the dunes deepen like wavelets.

We had more beautiful nights camping while crossing the stony Bayuda Desert. We had been following the course of the Nile, but here the road struck directly northwest while the river looped north and then back on itself.

When we'd ridden far enough each day, we'd turn off the tarmac and ride until we found an ideal spot, perhaps hidden behind a hilly rise or beside an exposed rock that offered a viewing platform and shelter to make a small fire. We'd run out of camping gas for my stove in East Africa and now couldn't find meths for Kieran's Trangia burner. Wood was sparse, so we stopped throughout the day whenever we spotted a few twigs or scrap wood and rode with bundles tied to the rear racks.

I loved the simplicity of cooking over a fire, of sitting on a hilltop and watching the sun set over the vast desert spread out below and lying on my back to watch the stars sparkling overhead. Even Kieran seemed content; the desert was winning him over.

Those evenings seemed timeless, yet all too soon another day dawned and we would return to the tarmac and occasional traffic to continue riding north.

Just as I had wished I could slow down our progress across the Kalahari and had become enlivened in the Namib Desert in the south, so the Sahara evoked equally strong emotions that had me at once full of energy and also entirely at peace.

The desert is full of contradiction for me; I feel I could live there and never leave, yet it is a harsh inhospitable place. And while time seems to stand still there; it is never long enough. I love the infinite sandy expanse that kisses the low horizon and imagine that our ancestors once looked upon the same image. But I know, not only that the Sahara was once a thriving fertile land, but that even the sands I see today are continually shifting, the dunes' march an unstoppable tide. Perhaps it's their impermanence and untameable spirit that appeals.

My burning desire for freedom cannot be held back either; I realised that now. It is the essence of who I am. Try to grasp and hold me back, and I will slip through your fingers like grains of sand to be carried away on the wind. Not even love can overcome this driving force within me.

The road rejoined the Nile at Dongola where the river resumes its journey northwards. The contrast between the vast arid desert and the narrow lush plain fertilised by the Nile is stark. Water provides life, but here the desert gives gold.

We passed people scouring the ground with metal detectors. They search with the same desperate hope I'd seen of people panning for diamonds in DR Congo. One night when wild camping north of Kerma, the distant hum of generators and rumble of heavy machinery of larger mining operations penetrated the darkness.

Sudan is Africa's third largest gold producer with more than two million artisanal miners responsible for producing eighty per cent of the gold. In the ancient world, the Kushite Kingdom was the largest producer of gold. Tools and grinding stones for crushing ore to obtain gold flakes dating back to 2000 BC have been discovered in this region.

We rested a couple of nights in the sleepy village of Abri, the guesthouse a clean whitewashed compound decorated with locally crafted pots and lanterns. As his only visitors, the friendly owner took us for a drive in his vintage 1946 Morris Minor, shining black with a red taxi sign on the roof. Whilst we saw several old beehive shaped tombs on our ride, the tomb he showed us was a much larger step pyramid shape, more like the tombs at Saqqara we later saw in Egypt. It had been in the same family for 700 years.

Fascinated by every historical site I'd seen in Sudan, I wondered what more Egypt could offer.

Whereas crossing between the countries once required taking the once weekly two-to-three day journey by barge between Wadi Halfa and Aswan across Lake Nasser, now there is a road and regular short ferry crossing to Abu Simbel. The only time-consuming part is navigating Egyptian immigration and customs.

We contacted a recommended fixer, who explained and directed us through the process. He suggested I get our passports stamped while Kieran waited with the bikes. The immigration hall was crammed full of men waiting their turn. With passport in hand, I waltzed through the crowd and found the women-only queue at the far end with only two Sudanese ladies in it. Clearing customs was painless and before long we had our paperwork stamped and Egyptian plates for our bikes.

On our first evening in Egypt, we watched a Sound and Light show at Abu Simbel. The open air event told the history of the Temple of Rameses through images projected directly onto the rock and temple. Rameses II was one of the great pharaohs and this imposing temple fronted by not one but four 20-metre high statues of himself is perhaps his grandest monument. If one thing became clear on the ride through Egypt, it was that the pharaohs had an unwavering belief in both the afterlife and their own importance.

Inside the temple, I marvelled at more statues of a deified (and clearly egotistical) Rameses and exquisite carvings on the walls depicting him and his queen making offerings to the gods.

What impressed me was that the temple was originally sited on the west bank of the Nile, but the threat of flooding from the construction of the Aswan dam in the 1960s instigated a huge relocation effort. The entire temple was cut into blocks between three and twenty tonnes each and reassembled like a giant 3D jigsaw on higher ground.

At Aswan, behind the dam, guides waited by gleaming white pleasure boats hoping to take the few tourists over to a small island where several smaller temples were also relocated prior to the dam's construction.

There wasn't the aggressive hard sell as I'd expected; instead guides and touts and souvenir sellers treated us warmly, more akin to the friendly hospitality I've seen throughout the Muslim world. The tourism industry had been decimated following the 2011 revolution and visitor numbers were just starting to increase again. It was as though those in the industry had accepted a lack of work and income and, rather than competing, had joined forces in mutual assistance, simply pleased to see any foreigners.

Further downstream at Luxor, I stared up in amazement amongst the tall carved columns of the Great Hypostyle Hall and obelisks at the Karnak Temple complex and explored the Luxor Temple as the sun went down and cast long shadows. These sights were only surpassed when we crossed the Nile and visited the Valley of the Kings, where over sixty tombs were cut into the rocks for successive generations of pharaohs.

Despite damage from treasure hunters in the past, flooding and more recently mass tourism, the interiors of the tombs were the most impressive man-made sights I had seen on the continent. Every inch of wall, ceiling, column and sarcophagus was covered in intricate carvings and colourful paintings of pharaohs and gods and creatures, food and drink, and scenes of daily life with offerings for rewards in the afterlife.

I'm not usually impressed by shows of grandeur and self-importance, finding that the quietest and humblest people often have the most interesting things to say, but I couldn't help but marvel in wonder at the lasting legacy of the ancient Egyptian pharaohs. What's more, every day new discoveries are being made; the entire country is an archaeology site. We rode past a behemoth statue lying horizontal below the level of the land that was being slowly excavated amid the bustle of city life, traffic roaring past; not a single person paused to look closer at such a common sight.

I was glad we'd travelled north visiting the ancients sites of increasing magnificence. Had we been to Luxor first, I might have quickly lost interest in the temples and pyramids in Sudan.

If only Luxor had been the destination of our journey, our trip ending on a highlight that somehow epitomised the wonders of Africa and all that I loved about it. Life, however, rarely gives us perfect endings and the last days in Egypt were a let-down.

Picked up by the police when leaving the city, we were escorted slowly through the busy streets of the endless villages and towns along the banks of the Nile for three days with sirens blazing and horns blasting, passed like a baton from one detail to the next without stopping from breakfast to sunset. Suddenly we were given thorough searches at historic sites, dictated where to eat and sleep, and we weren't allowed to communicate with local people.

Eventually, though, on entering Cairo, to our relief the police just as quickly abandoned us and we were free to ride alone to Alexandria on the coast where our bikes were then shipped to Greece. Our guesthouse appeared run down but when I opened the shutters in our dimly lit room, a cool sea breeze wafted through, and I looked out onto the brilliant blue waters of the Mediterranean and smiled.

Epilogue

On the third day of being hostage to Egyptian security on our ride to Cairo, my frustration had got the better of me. We risked missing the boat bound for Europe that our bikes were booked onto. I'd spent hours researching shipping options and weeks of emailing back and forth with agents to arrange safe transport and smooth clearance through customs. I wasn't going to let that effort go to waste.

I'd smiled and shown willing and suggested options, then pleaded and begged to be allowed to proceed alone or to take the fast main desert road. My pleas were to no avail.

It was well into the afternoon and I hadn't eaten since an early breakfast. I got frustrated at Kieran's indifference and inaction and took my hungry anger out on him, hating myself for the outburst.

'Sorry, but I just need to eat,' I exclaimed and broke down in tears, the tiredness having taken its toll.

To my surprise, Kieran took the lead. He set out the rules by which we'd be escorted from now on, starting with a meal. My hunger appeased, we joked about the situation, but my annoyance at him lingered. I hated having these negative feelings towards him.

Why did it take me to reach breaking point before he showed initiative, took responsibility or backed me up? I'd hoped our issues were behind us, we'd been good for weeks, but I realised that neither of us had fundamentally changed. It's often said that Africa changes a person, but I think Africa only solidified our existing characteristics.

As we approached the end of our journey in Africa, we talked about what came next and discussed practicalities like earning money and living together. Yet when I dreamed of new adventures, the image was of me undertaking physical challenges in remote corners of the world, testing my endurance and mental determination, alone.

Back in England, I began work immediately and Kieran returned home to visit family. For the first time in almost two years we were apart for more than a day and I felt myself unfurl, spreading to fill the

243

space around me. I needed to stop ignoring the essence of who I was and acknowledge my true self. I wanted to be free like a butterfly.

When I didn't reply to his many messages throughout the days because I was working, he implied I was ignoring him. *Please allow me some time to myself.* And when he returned to live with me in my camper van, he carried on as though nothing had changed. I could not return to my cocoon this time, could not deny myself the solitude I had yearned.

As he encroached on my newfound space, I exploded.

I can't do this anymore!

And suddenly it was over between us.

I hated seeing Kieran so upset and that I was the one causing him pain. I wish there had been some other way. But after he'd gone and I'd finished crying, I was overwhelmed with relief. I knew then that I'd done the right thing, no matter how much I'd miss him and all the adventures and good times, of jokes and laughter, we'd had together.

Perhaps we were doomed from the start, independence and insecurity incompatible traits for two people trying to forge a relationship. It took the journey across Africa to realise that my desires for freedom and solitude are a part of my true nature and not even love, in any of its forms, can cage them.

———

Over the years I have ridden the waves of contentment and happiness, exulting in the highs and fearing the troughs of despair and crashes of depression. I now read the warning signs like the weather forecast, sensing a storm approaching, and I do all I can to steer around it rather than batten the hatches, lash down the sails and confront the tempestuous seas because I know how long it takes to rebuild a strong hull from the wreckage.

And that is why it took so long to write this story. For whilst my love of Africa has never wavered, I've been consumed with doubt about other aspects of my life. I have wanted to tell you about the Africa I love, but for too long those memories had been marred by conflicting emotions. I have painstakingly wiped away the grey stains of hate and anger I felt towards myself, for hurting Kieran and for denying my own needs, until once again I see Africa in all her brightness and colour, and I feel her wild spirit within me.

Acknowledgements

Thank you to Clare, Lucy, Will and Mum for reading the manuscript and providing valuable feedback, and also to the We Love Memoirs Facebook group. Thank you also to my other good friends whose unwavering support over the years has given me courage to persevere with this book, especially when I have doubted myself. I could never mention everyone here, but a special shout-out goes to Phil and Angie, Si and Sarah, Gareth and Maria, Lizzie, the ACHQ crew and those who know The Fortress.

Leave a Review

I would appreciate it if you would rate and review this book on Amazon. It is with your feedback that I can become a better writer. If you enjoyed it, please tell your friends and family about it, even spread the word on social media.

I am always interested to hear from you. Tell me what you thought of my books or just write and say 'Hello'. If you are inspired to go on your own adventure, feel free to ask me questions about it. I could not have begun any of my journeys without the help and knowledge of those more experienced than me. I hope that now, in turn, I may be able to help others.

If you'd like to read more about my other adventures, past and present, or get in touch, see my website:

www.HelensTakeOn.com

You can also find me on Facebook and Instagram:

www.facebook.com/helenstakeon

www.instagram.com/helenstakeon

More Books by the Author

Desert Snow - One Girl's Take On Africa

This is the story of one girl, one bike and 1,000 beers in Africa. By daring to follow a dream and not letting fear prevail, Helen cycled across the Sahara, Sahel and tropics of West Africa, paddled down the Niger River in a pirogue, hitch-hiked to Timbuktu and spent three months traversing the Congo, which she thought she may never leave...

A lot can change in 2 years, cycling 25,000km from England to Cape Town. So can nothing. Helen takes you with her on the journey through every high and low of her memories and misadventures. She describes a continent brimming with diversity that is both a world away from what she knows and yet not so different at all.

A Siberian Winter's Tale - Cycling to the Edge of Insanity and the End of the World

A gripping adventure travel book about Helen's most challenging journey by bicycle.

In the depth of winter, she spent three months cycling solo across one of the most remote, coldest inhabited regions of the planet - Siberia.

In temperatures down to -50°C, she battled against the cold, and overcame her fear of wolves and of falling through the ice of a frozen lake. Yet, alone in a hibernating land with little to stimulate the senses, the biggest challenges were with her mind.

Helen portrays her struggles with solitude in this sparsely populated region whilst weaving a story brimming with characters she met on her journey along the Road of Bones.

Iceland Serow Saga - Big Adventures on a Small Motorbike

Searching for solitude in the wilderness, Helen Lloyd went to Iceland via the Faroe Islands for the summer of 2018. She found freedom and adventure riding her old Yamaha Serow motorbike, tackling the rough trails and deep river crossings for which Iceland is renowned.

The Land of Ice and Fire is more than crevasse-ridden glaciers and lava-spewing volcanoes. Despite killer sheep, cold winds and driving rain, Iceland's steaming hot pools, strong coffee and generous people melt snow and warm hearts.

With illuminating descriptions, Helen Lloyd weaves the history and traditions of the country and the colourful characters from the sagas into her own riveting story, which she tells with typical humour and humility.

A must-read for anyone interested in Iceland or motorcycle travel.

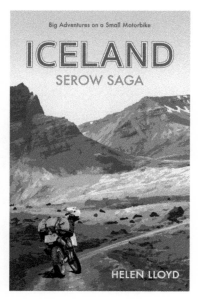

Milton Keynes UK
Ingram Content Group UK Ltd.
UKHW041821060923
428148UK00004B/210